How Silent Were the Churches?

Canadian Protestantism and the Jewish Plight during the Nazi Era

How Silent Were the Churches?
Canadian Protestantism and the Jewish Plight during the Nazi Era

Alan Davies and Marilyn F. Nefsky

Wilfrid Laurier University Press

This book has been published with the help of a grant from the Humanities and Social Sciences Federation of Canada, using funds provided by the Social Sciences and Humanities Research Council of Canada.

Canadian Cataloguing in Publication Data

Davies, Alan T.
　How silent were the churches? : Canadian protestantism and the Jewish plight during the Nazi era

Includes bibliographical references and index.
ISBN 0-88920-288-5 (bound)

1. Christianity and antisemitism. 2. Holocaust, Jewish (1939-1945). 3. Protestant churches – Canada – History – 20th century. 4. Antisemitism – Canada. I. Nefsky, Marilyn Flecher, 1948- II. Title

BM535.D38 1997　　　261.8'34892404　　　C97-932330-4

Copyright © 1997
WILFRID LAURIER UNIVERSITY PRESS
Waterloo, Ontario, Canada　N2L 3C5

Cover design by Leslie Macredie, using an illustration by Sandra Woolfrey

Printed in Canada

To
Ernest Edwin Best
1919 – 1994
Teacher, ethicist, friend,
in
affectionate memory

I send a message of good cheer to the Jewish people in this and other lands. None has suffered more cruelly than the Jew of the unspeakable evils wrought on bodies and spirits of men by Hitler and his vile regime. The Jew bore the brunt of the Nazis' first onslaught upon the citadels of freedom and human dignity. He has borne and continues to bear a burden that might have seemed beyond endurance. He has not allowed it to break his spirit. He has never lost the will to resist. Assuredly, in the day of victory, the Jew's suffering and his part in the present struggle will not be forgotten. Once again, at an appointed time, he will see vindicated those principles of righteousness which it was the glory of his fathers to proclaim to the world. Once again it will be shown that though the mills of God grind slowly, they grind exceedingly well.

Winston S. Churchill, as reported
in the *Montreal Daily Herald*,
January 7, 1942

Table of Contents

Introduction

IN THEIR EXPOSÉ OF THE NATIVISM and antisemitism that lurked behind the refusal of the King cabinet and its bureaucratic servants to open the gates of Canada to Hitler's Jewish victims, Irving Abella and Harold Troper accuse the Canadian churches of silence. "Although some organizations and high-placed members of religious groups, such as the Anglican and United Churches, actively campaigned on behalf of Jewish refugees, most Canadians seemed indifferent to the suffering of German Jews and hostile to their admission to Canada."[1] This judgment from *None Is Too Many* is later amplified: "As long as the churches remained silent—which they did—the government could dismiss the [Canadian National Committee on Refugees and Victims of Political Persecution] members as well meaning but impractical idealists to be patronized but not taken seriously."[2] Are Abella and Troper correct, or does their observation require modification, even serious modification? Were the churches really silent? Or did they address the afflictions of the Jews of Europe? The matter is important, not only for the sake of the historical record, but also as a test of the integrity of Christian Canada and its social conscience. In this study, a work of collaboration on the part of a Jew and a Christian, the Protestant churches of Canada are probed. Outside of Roman Catholic Quebec, Protestantism was the dominant force in shaping the moral ethos of the nation. For this reason, it stands on trial. Roman Catholicism in Canada also stands on trial, but someone else must examine its annals.

Any trial demands a careful investigation of the relevant evidence. Consequently, we have delved into as many extant sources as we could locate, including official documents, sermons (insofar as they survive)—the pulpit has always been an important focal point in Protestant Christianity—and, most of all, church journals, since the voice of the churches found collective expression through their official and semi-official public organs. At once, certain difficulties present themselves. For one thing, official documents, particularly diocesan letters and synodical, presbyterial and conference resolutions, although obviously central to

---

Notes to the Introduction are on p. 137.

our study, are not easy to weigh; should they be accepted at face value, or should they be dismissed, as William E. Nawyn has said, as "gratuitous and emotional protests" of a kind that churches love to engage in when their sensibilities are aroused?[3] Making the right noises is a good device for doing nothing because words are cheap and actions are expensive. Whether the spoken and written statements of the mainstream Protestant churches of Canada deserve such a negative appraisal is a matter of opinion; our view emerges in the text.

For another thing, church journals do not always speak unequivocally for the churches, even when they are denominational. Editors are editors and cherish their independence; rarely are they slavish agents of their employers, who may or may not wish to keep them on a short leash. In some churches, notably the United Church, a deliberate hands-off policy was adopted toward *The New Outlook* and its successor *The United Church Observer,* allowing its editorial staff a large measure of freedom. In other churches, notably the Jarvis Street Baptist Church, which had become a de facto denomination of its own, the matter was different. *The Gospel Witness* was the virtual mouthpiece of its central figure, T.T. Shields. Moreover, church journals vary greatly in character. The Mennonite press, especially *Die Mennonitische Rundschau* and *Der Bote,* allowed a wide range of discourse into its pages, including some quite extreme claims, but their authors spoke more for themselves than for anyone else, at least in a communal sense. Sometimes also, incidental factors played a role. In the case of *The Canadian Churchman,* the main publication of the Church of England in Canada, staff infighting during the Nazi era interfered with its reportage on various matters, raising doubts about the degree to which it should be regarded as a reliable reflection of its sponsoring communion.[4] Hence, facile equations between the churches and their newspapers must be avoided; nevertheless, the latter were unique forums for debate and Christian opinion, and their editorials, articles, columns, letters and book reviews cast indispensable light on the mood of Protestant society in Canada in the thirties and forties. Without such a rich vein to mine, this book could not have been written.

Simply assembling an assortment of contemporary utterances on the Jews and their plight, however, would be little more than an exercise in what R.G. Collingwood described as "scissors and paste" history,[5] or history that is not really history at all but only a juggling of texts and testimonies, without some attempt to place what the churches said (and did not say) in a larger frame. True history, according to Collingwood, concerns itself with the inside as well as the outside of events. In this book, we are very much concerned with the inside of events, which means the Canadian Protestant mentality in the thirties and forties. Protestant Christianity is highly varied, and its diversity cannot be ignored when assessing the responses of the Canadian denominations to a crisis of this nature. For the sake of convenience, the Church of England in Canada has been included on the Protestant roster, although many Anglicans do not regard themselves as Protestants, and would not accept such a classification. Quite apart from the peculiarities of Anglicanism, enough distinctiveness is found among the major Protestant churches to warrant their separate and special treatment. Only in the case of the smaller evangelical and fundamentalist groups has this rule been forsaken, since their theologies seem to merge in most decisive respects. There were, of course, points of similarity in all of the Christian traditions vis-à-vis the Jewish people and their religion, but classical anti-Judaism, the common legacy of historical Christendom, was more diluted in some receptacles of faith than in others. Moreover, certain extra-religious forces, for example, ethnicity, helped to determine the pro- or anti-Jewish reflexes of particular Protestants and their constituencies in Nazi times. United Church members, Anglicans, Presbyterians, Baptists, Lutherans, Mennonites and Quakers more or less conformed to their types, allowing for personal exceptions and, because human beings are human beings, the element of surprise.

If the churches differed in significant ways, colouring their attitudes and responses to events in Europe, they did not differ in their captivity to the modern age and its problems. None escaped the ravages of the Great Depression and its demoralizing effects on the Canadian soul. The ravages were spiritual as well as material, touching the psyche as well as the flesh, and leaving a gaping hole in the nation's self-esteem. Dark moods arose— disillusionment, isolationism, xenophobia, nativism, racism and especially antisemitism—that, in turn, bred certain dangerous temptations, notably a flirtation with radical new political and social forms and their manifestations across the ocean. These temptations, which were felt across the religious spectrum, disturbed and divided Protestant Canada as much as they disturbed and divided Canadian society at large; it was disquieting to read anti-democratic and pro-fascist or pro-communist sentiments in the church press or elsewhere—one's loyalties were outraged. Most Protestants, like most Canadians, rejected the radical options, but the battle against the false prophets was a real battle, and antisemitism, one of the most potent weapons in their hands, was no stranger to Canada's shores. It was also no stranger to Canada's churches, Catholic and Protestant, French and English, conservative and liberal, as it made its invidious contribution to the distemper of the times. Even when the Jews became the objects of Christian sympathy, its malevolent power remained.

Antisemitism, therefore, is the setting of our subject and its leitmotiv. The alleged silence of the churches was presumably an antisemitic silence, although Abella and Troper do not say so. While the refugee crisis on the eve of the Second World War and its continuation during the war years is the central focus of our investigation, its germination in the Aryan laws of the Third Reich and its consummation in the Holocaust also belong to our backdrop. How silent were the Protestant churches of Canada in the early stages of Hitler's persecutions? How silent were they when reports of mass murder were released by the World Jewish Congress in the middle of the war? If silence is the bone of contention, the twelve years of the Nazi empire should be canvassed. Although our concern is with Canadian Protestantism and its several vehicles of communication, especially its denominational journals, other voices in Canadian society also made themselves heard. These cannot be explored in this book, but the reader should be aware of their presence. It seems, for example, that the secular press in Canada, especially in the prairie provinces, made Canadians aware of morbid changes in the German state well before the end of the thirties.[6] If this was the case, and if the churches remained mute or largely mute in their face, one must ask why. If they spoke, the nature of their speech and its burden must be scrutinized.

We have attempted this task. Whether our endeavours have been successful is not for us to judge. Following a description of the era as well as the churches, the text unfolds as a series of denominational profiles in which the theologies and other characteristics of the various church bodies are related to their action or inaction during the fatal years. A few key figures receive special attention. If anyone wonders why so much time is spent on French Canada in the first chapter when English Canada is the main subject of the remainder of the text, the answer lies in the peculiar point-counterpoint of Canadian history and the fact that neither Canada can be understood without reference to the other. As our study reveals, Anglo Protestants were often trenchant critics of Catholic Quebec, a fact not without bearing on what they said and did about the Jews. If the reader also wonders why some churches have been omitted, the answer is that Protestantism has too many offspring. To a certain extent, size has been our rule of thumb, resulting in the omission of some of the smaller Protestant denominations, for example, the Standard Church and other holiness groups; still, for special reasons, the numerically insignificant Salvation Army and the even more numerically insignificant Society of

Friends have been included. We cannot claim to have located every scrap
of relevant evidence and do not pretend to have pronounced the final verdict. What follows is in no sense an apologia and should not be read as
such. Nor, on the other hand, is it a condemnation, but rather an exercise
in understanding. The interpretations are ours alone, and any mistakes are
ours alone as well.

We wish to add a personal word. A profound concern with the evil
fruits of antisemitism and its tragic relationship to historical Christianity
determines the perspective of our study and its larger motivation. Both of
us have taught in this area, and have participated in conferences on the
Holocaust in North America and Europe. Both of us feel an obligation to
do as much as we can in our small corners to make certain that the past is
not repeated, and that the current purveyors of old poisons, especially the
new breed of Holocaust deniers, do not prevail. Both of us wish to clar-
ify the historical record for its own sake, and for the sake of the churches
themselves, and their integrity. By the churches, we mean the active membership of the various denominations, both clergy and laity—what is
sometimes called the community or communities of faith as represented
by official church publications; conference, synod and presbyterial resolutions; sermons, church journals and occasionally newspaper articles. We
do not mean "Christian Canada" as an undifferentiated whole, nor is this
a sociological study of the attitudes and actions of individual church members. Indeed, as we point out in the concluding chapter, Christianity and
Christendom should not be confused with each other. In one sense, they
are synonymous, but in another sense they are antithetical. Much depends
on this distinction, and on the fact that the churches as churches did not
command and could not have commanded an unrestricted influence even
over their own following, quite apart from the rest of the nation. They
were not powerless, but their power was limited. The precise definition of
their political effectiveness in the context of the times is a question that
we do not settle, although our thoughts on the matter, for what they are
worth, have not been omitted. However, the scope of our study stops
short of a full investigation of the social role of religious institutions in a
modern democratic society; we leave this to others. Instead of pursuing
this line of thought in a theoretical mode, we have preferred to paint a
sequence of portraits, full of light and shadows—an exercise in impressionism. They tell their own story, and the reader can infer the rest.

Many persons have helped us, too many to be named. However, it is
impossible not to mention John Webster Grant and Alan Hayes, church
historians who saved us from several pitfalls, as well as Walter Freitag,

John Moir, the late Rabbi Harry Joshua Stern, Magdalene Redekop, William Klassen, Lawrence Klippenstein, Lydia Pedersen (who helped with the German), Moira Hutchinson, David Hoeniger, together with the archivists of the United Church of Canada, Toronto, the Anglican Church of Canada, Toronto, the Pentecostal Assemblies of Canada, Mississauga, the Salvation Army Heritage Centre, Toronto, the Mennonite Heritage Centre, Winnipeg, the Canadian Baptist Archives, McMaster University, Hamilton, the Baptist Historical Collection, Acadia University, Wolfville, the Quaker Archives, Newmarket, as well as the librarians at Knox College, Toronto, Conrad Grebel College, Waterloo, Wilfrid Laurier University, Waterloo, the Lutheran Theological Seminary, Saskatoon, the Canadian Jewish Congress, Montreal, the National Archives of Canada, Ottawa, and the officials of the Jarvis Street Baptist Church, Toronto. Only once were we refused admission to an archival collection: Knox Presbyterian Church, Toronto. Our thanks to all of the above, and special thanks to June Hewitt of Victoria College, a tireless, patient and amazingly competent amanuensis.

We are also grateful to the Social Sciences and Humanities Research Council of Canada for a generous research grant that made our research possible, and to Victoria College, Toronto, for covering the costs of an expedition to Ottawa and the National Archives of Canada.

A final note: experimental earlier versions of some of the material have been published as follows:

"The United Church and the Jewish Plight during the Nazi Era 1933-1945." *Canadian Jewish Historical Society Journal*, 8, 2 (Fall 1984): 55-71.

"The Church of England in Canada and the Jewish Plight during the Nazi Era." *Canadian Jewish Historical Society Journal*, 10, 1 (Fall 1988): 1-19.

"How Silent Was the United Church?" *Touchstone*, 3, 3 (October 1985): 5-10.

"The Cry that Silence Heaves." In *Remembering for the Future*, Theme 1, pp.429-446. Oxford: Pergamon Press, 1988.

Alan Davies
Marilyn F. Nefsky

I

The Setting

CANADA DURING THE DECADE OF THE THIRTIES was a nation in travail. The Great Depression had descended, and the social order was threatened with catastrophe. Because of the havoc wrought by the Great War of 1914-1918, the economic system was in a ramshackle condition—a house of cards waiting to fall—but its collapse, induced by the failure of the Kredit Anstalt in Vienna, came as a surprise nonetheless. All segments of society and all regions of the country were affected, but the prairie provinces, which suffered the added affliction of a terrible drought, were affected profoundly. Southern Alberta and Saskatchewan were left in a state of devastation. Yet, as John Herd Thompson and Allen Seager point out, a glut of wheat in the world rather than a scarcity was responsible for most of the misery, since it made the farmer's crop virtually worthless on the market.[1] A resource-dominated economy, Canada could no longer export its agricultural, mining, forestry and fishing products owing to a sudden drop in international demand and the rise of tariff walls across the seas. This misfortune, in turn, weakened the manufacturing industries by weakening consumer demand at home, and a tragic spiral was soon set in motion. Instead of rising to the occasion, the successive governments of the day, headed by prime ministers William Lyon Mackenzie King and Richard Bedford Bennett, proved incapable of even understanding the true dimensions of the crisis, and the nation drifted toward the shoals. Only the advent of another and more alarming apparition in the form of a new world war produced a change of direction, but at a frightful cost. Many ordinary Canadians, particularly those whose livelihoods were imperilled, sank into a state of fear, which in turn produced a complex of other irrational and dangerous moods.

One widespread feeling was that of disillusionment, both with existing institutions and accepted values. This is one of the primary symptoms of what a great twentieth-century thinker, the Protestant theologian Paul

Notes to this chapter are on pp. 137-141.

1

Tillich, has graphically described as the breakdown that accompanies an end of an era.[2] At the end of an era—in this case the end of the world of the Enlightenment and its facile assumptions about inevitable progress—acute anxiety arises, and society feels itself caught between the past, with its "horror of being trapped," and the future, with its sensation of falling "without a place to fall upon."[3] Canada was in this situation, if less severely than the war-ravaged European nations. The Great Depression, according to the historian Donald Creighton, was a disaster visited on all of the orders at once: economic, social, economic, political and constitutional.[4] Familiar organs were simply not working, and their disintegration was fraught with peril. Already in Europe totalitarianism was in the air, breaking "the continuity of Occidental history,"[5] and no one could claim with confidence that Canada was immune to anti-democratic maladies. The fact that an alien intrusion such as the reborn American Ku Klux Klan was able to kindle intermittent brushfires in Ontario and the western provinces, especially Saskatchewan, furnished proof enough of Canadian vulnerability.[6] Ominously, in Quebec, the Parti National Social Chrétien, organized in 1934 under the leadership of Adrien Arcand as a compound of German and Italian fascism, was promising to save the nation from a "bankrupt" democracy. Extremist rumblings could be heard also in English Canada as a host of "petty fascisms" sprang up almost from coast to coast.[7] At the other end of the political spectrum, the Communist Party of Canada, and the affiliated Workers' Unity League, were busy preparing for the forthcoming revolution—a revolution that, in the words of the Communist leader Tim Buck, would "make the late War look like a chicken fight"![8] With such rhetoric, and with incidents such as the election of a "Red" town council in Blairmore, Alberta, in 1933, an apprehension of violent insurrection began to stir on Canadian soil.[9] This apprehension was never really justified, but its existence was no minor sign of a troubled time.

Another widespread frame of mind was that of isolationism, a more potent sentiment, to be sure, in the American republic with its historic distrust of European politics, but also present in the Dominion of Canada despite its imperial connections. If Europe "is going to insist on destroying itself," wrote Thomas A. Crerar, minister of Resources, to J.W. Dafoe, editor of the Winnipeg *Free Press*, in 1937, "it is no part of our mission to destroy ourselves in attempting to preserve it."[10] Isolationist feelings were especially pronounced in French Canada, with its special antipathy to British interests and its bitter memories of the conscription crisis of 1917. Anti-imperialism also existed in English Canada, especially on the political left, and the burgeoning muscles of an incipient nationalism contributed to the distrust. Canada had problems enough of its own. Why should Canadians involve themselves in foreign troubles? They are not "worth the bones of a Toronto grenadier."[11] Outside of French Canada, however, these negative emotions were countered by an old imperial patriotism, particularly on the part of the veterans of the Great War and their families. For this reason, isolationism, although not an insignificant force during the unhappy thirties, never acquired the political muscle of its American counterpart. Still, it was influential enough to render much of the populace indifferent both to European affairs and to the plight of those caught in the coming maelstrom. Canada, which had welcomed refugees in the past, abruptly closed its doors to refugees, particularly Jewish refugees, in Nazi times.[12]

Another predilection was that of xenophobia, with its companions nativism, racism and antisemitism. Nativism, or the assertion of the rights of the so-called "native" over immigrants and aliens, took the form of Anglo Saxonism in English Canada and French nationalism in Quebec. Both communal ideologies had old histories. The vague "race" myth of Anglo Saxondom flourished in nineteenth-century Britain, and found many apostles in both the United States and Canada. Men such as Robert Knox (the "British Gobineau"),[13] Charles Dilke, Herbert Spencer and John Fiske glorified the Saxon racial genius and its supposed superior capacity for political democracy, while depreciating the talents and mental abilities of other peoples.[14] Since evolutionary theory and Social Darwinism were conscripted to support these claims, it was easy to claim scientific and philosophical validation for Anglo Saxon (i.e., British-American) hegemony in the great age of empire, and to associate the "Pax Anglo Americana" with the onward march of human progress and betterment. Canada was part of this ethos. English Canadian society was suffused with Anglo Saxon enthusiasm and thus with its racial overtones, as a fashionable contemporary interest in eugenics and biological politics— a Canadian "master race"—reveals.[15]

French Canadian nationalism, promoted by the priest-historian Lionel Groulx, the newspaper *Le Devoir,* the journal *L'Action nationale,* and the organization *Jeune-Canada,* was coloured by antisemitic elements imported from France, i.e., from anti-Dreyfusard political and religious circles that distinguished the "true" France—*un pays réel*—from an inauthentic and merely legal France.[16] Groulx, in particular, the Fichte[17] of Quebec nationalism, devoted himself to elaborating the myth of the French Catholic nation in North America, and to the reeducation of his compatriots accordingly.[18] A larger need to survive—*la survivance*—

embedded in the Quebec psyche since the eighteenth-century conquest, was a constant driving force. The ultramontane Catholicism of the province provided the medium for its public expression.

During the social stress of the thirties, these ethnocentric notions and their assorted mythologies were promulgated with a greater xenophobic intensity. At the end of an era, when familiar things are threatened with destruction, and when evil acquires menacing proportions in the public imagination, it is tempting for society—any society—to demonize its enemies.[19] Mere nativism, in certain quarters, transformed itself into virulent racism and antisemitism. The positive aspects of the Canadian "race" myths—the Anglo Saxon sense of noblesse oblige and the Quebec sense of moral responsibility as the agent of Christian civilization—were overwhelmed by their negative and potentially malevolent aspects: the rejection and denigration of foreign-born Canadians, particularly Asians and European Jews. In the case of the former, an anti-Asian nativism in British Columbia (and elsewhere) with nineteenth-century roots acquired a new intensity as war shadows loomed across the Pacific Ocean, enabling the government of the day to intern the indigenous Japanese Canadian population in 1942 with relative impunity.[20] Not only was this policy motivated by the most naked of racist precepts, but also the actual step-by-step process—uprooting, confinement, dispossession of property and deportation to vague destinations "in the east"—paralleled to an uncomfortable degree the Nazi treatment of the European Jews, except, of course, for sheer physical brutality and the Final Solution itself.[21]

In the case of the Jews, an antisemitism with old roots in Canadian society manifested itself in the fringe politics of the era and in the anti-refugee policies of the same Canadian government during the pre-Holocaust and Holocaust years.[22] It also manifested itself on occasion in the Christian churches of Canada. This shadow from the nation's past lies in the background of our investigation, and cannot be ignored if Canadian behaviour during the Nazi era is to be seen in its proper light. Canada is not Germany, and Canadian history does not resemble German history, but the ties of Christendom and modernity unite the religious and intellectual strands of their cultures at a basic level, even if Britain and France rather than Germany were the colonizers of North America. Antisemitism, moreover, was not a German invention, although the term itself, from the German *Antisemitismus*, was in fact a coinage of the Second German Reich. It existed in Britain and France as well, especially in the latter, and was imported from these mother countries to their daughter land. Many of its motifs were the same in both worlds.

Usually associated with the nineteenth-century political pamphleteer Wilhelm Marr, the compound "antisemitism" possessed a pseudo-scientific ring and a vagueness of meaning that made it useful to those Germans who wished to dignify their antipathy toward Jews and Jewish emancipation in the German empire by employing the then fashionable language of "race."[23] As children of their age, they wore the new label of antisemite as a badge of pride. Although its problematic character has long been recognized, the word has remained, for better or worse, as a collective designation for all sorts and degrees of anti-Jewish hostility, ancient, mediaeval and modern. To the extent that Jew-hatred is indeed a single entity, the use of a single term is meaningful; to the extent that what is called antisemitism is highly variable, the use of a single term is a source of confusion. Religious or Christian anti-Judaism is clearly not identical with racist antisemitism, yet a common ideological thread seems to join them. Both modes of disliking and marginalizing Jews are found in Canadian history. Religious anti-Judaism was pronounced during the colonial era when the role of the churches, both Catholic and Protestant, French and English, in shaping the nation was direct and powerful. The same religious anti-Judaism combined with the newer secular currents to form a potent brew during the Confederation era, leaving an imprint on the subsequent social patterns—patterns that help explain the conflicts and contradictions of the time of troubles that we have chosen as the focus of this study.

Antisemitism in Canada

There were few Jews in colonial Canada.[24] Jewish immigrants were simply not admitted to New France—nor, for that matter, were Protestants, although some Huguenot merchants managed to settle in eighteenth-century Quebec despite this prohibition.[25] The situation changed, however, following the British conquest of 1759, setting the stage for future anti-Jewish incidents, of which the celebrated Hart affair of 1808 was the first. Ezekiel Hart, a Jewish settler elected to the Legislative Assembly as the member for Trois Rivières, was refused his seat on "Christian" grounds, having taken his oath of allegiance on the Hebrew Bible in the Jewish fashion rather than on the New Testament.[26] When, following a second election, he agreed to take his oath on the New Testament, he was rejected again by the Assembly, for reasons not entirely clear. Despite this fact, the Hart affair certainly contained an antisemitic component, as a jest on the part of some wag comparing the choice of a Jew as a legislator to the choice of a horse as a Roman consul by the mad emperor Caligula is ample proof.[27]

Catholic catechetical writings throughout the eighteenth and nineteenth centuries consistently cast the Jews and Judaism in a mediaeval Christian mould, i.e., as a deicide people under a self-inflicted curse destined to suffer dispersion until the end of time.[28] The "wandering Jew" of mediaeval folklore was actually—so it was claimed—seen in Kamouraska, Quebec.[29] Because of the deeply conservative character of Quebec Catholicism, and because of its historical and emotional links with the vanished old regime in France, the nineteenth-century church was susceptible to the peculiar blend of anti-revolutionary and antisemitic rhetoric found in the books and sermons of disgruntled French aristocrats and clerics that regularly crossed the Atlantic Ocean. To these malcontents, the Jews, along with the Freemasons, and sometimes the Protestants, were the true authors of the French Revolution of 1789, in league with the devil. This made them once again conspirators against Christendom as they had been during the late Middle Ages. Such a charge, already in circulation in the mid-nineteenth century, acquired almost hysterical proportions toward the end of the Dreyfus affair, when the *Action Française,* the cradle of French fascism, was born. Quebec being Quebec, it is scarcely surprising that the diatribes of Edouard Drumont, Maurice Barrès and Charles Maurras received a sympathetic hearing in the new world as well as in the old, especially in the writings of their ardent local disciple, Abbé Groulx.[30] Thus Quebec antisemitism "in its modern guise" was an 1880s import from France.[31]

Its arrival coincided with a surge in Jewish immigration, caused by pogroms in a Russian empire stumbling toward revolution. The fact that the newcomers tended to congregate in cities, especially in Montreal, the site of Canada's largest Jewish community at the turn of the century, was disturbing to both English and French Canadians, since it seemed to upset the social equilibrium. English Canada, no less than French Canada, was infected with anti-Jewish feelings, although civil if not political rights for Jews had been recognized in Britain since the mid-eighteenth century. Much of Anglo Canadian anti-Judaism took the form of classical economic and social imagery—the thieving Fagin-like figure of western folklore immortalized by Charles Dickens—together with certain Protestant religious fixations not unlike their Catholic counterparts.[32] The Anglo Saxon "race" myth grew increasingly stronger throughout the nineteenth century, creating at best a condescension and at worst a profound and ill-natured suspicion in the English Canadian soul whenever racial and religious aliens entered its purview.

Moreover, English Canada produced at least one extremely eminent nineteenth-century antisemite: the celebrated anti-imperialist, pro-American apostle of liberalism, Professor Goldwin Smith of Toronto, revered as the "sage of the Grange."[33] Smith's antisemitism, which was surprisingly virulent—he detested Benjamin Disraeli as an ersatz Englishman and actively solicited the latest antisemitic materials from Europe through a London agent[34]—was not extrinsic to his liberalism, but its obverse side. The Jewish refusal to cast aside Talmudic laws and customs, as well as time-honoured religious and national aspirations, and to assimilate into what Smith regarded as modern universal civilization, scandalized him. In reality, of course, the modern universal civilization of the professor's imagination was simply an idealized and universalized Anglo Saxon tribalism, but no Anglo Saxon panegyrist of the time, whether British, American or Canadian, ever noticed this fact. During the Dreyfus scandal in France, the same set of assumptions prevented the English community in Canada from discerning the real measure of antisemitism at the heart of the affair. Anglo Canadian journalists only noticed how inferior French Catholic society was to English Protestant society, concluding that such a travesty of justice could never have occurred on Anglo Saxon soil.[35] In this conclusion, they were almost certainly wrong.

Anglo Saxon condescension did nothing to smooth the difficult path of English and French relations in Canada, or to assist the integration of east European Jews into their new country. In Quebec, almost as a matter of necessity, the latter became embroiled in English-French frictions, which never seemed to lack fresh stimuli. The Anglo Boer War, for example, divided the two Canadas, since English Canadians identified strongly with Britain (even if Goldwin Smith was an exception) and French Canadians with the Boers in their struggle against British imperialism. Caught in the middle, Canadian Jewry felt sympathy for both sides, but turned increasingly against the Boers as Quebec nationalists such as Henri Bourassa gave their anti-British harangues an anti-Jewish twist, claiming that the war was being waged on behalf of Jewish interests in Capetown.[36] The fact that many older Canadian Jewish families had British roots themselves, and thus nurtured a degree of British patriotism, did not endear them to Bourassa and his fellow nationalists.

Not only did Jewish immigrants, both early and late, generally choose English over French Canada for a host of reasons, including political and economic ascendancy and a higher degree of religious toleration, but also they managed to threaten French Canadian values at a deeper, more visceral level. A rural and homogeneous community, strongly attached to the soil and the life of the village, Quebec was not comfortable with religious, cultural and racial aliens of any description. Their presence undermined the treasured ideals of its own self-contained and clerically dominated world. Commercialism, in particular, at once secular, anti-clerical and suffused with a dangerous individualism, was regarded with disfavour, as well as other features associated with urban middle-class existence. Anglo Protestant merchants were bad enough, but at least they were fellow Christians; Anglo Jews such as the Harts were worse, but at least they were few in number and otherwise indistinguishable from the rest of the English community. Yiddish-speaking Jewish immigrants from eastern Europe fitted every conceivable anti-Jewish and antisemitic stereotype, and stirred such atavistic emotions that sermons were preached against them.[37] Indeed, such was the anti-Jewish climate in fin de siècle Quebec that the great French Jewish actress Sarah Bernhardt was once forced to flee an angry mob during a visit, following the publication of a fabricated interview in which she was reported as having described the French Canadians as "priest-ridden Iroquois."[38]

If the influx of east European Jews prior to the turn of the century altered the social climate in French Canada unfavourably, the effect was similar in English Canada, especially in Toronto. Anglo Canadian Jewry had achieved a measure of public recognition during the nineteenth century, and even Goldwin Smith had attended the dedication of the new Holy Blossom Temple on Bond Street in 1897, along with the mayor of Toronto and several members of Parliament.[39] After 1900, however, the mood changed, largely because of the visible differences in class and culture introduced by the foreign arrivals—in 1916 Toronto alone had six hundred Jewish rag peddlers[40]—and because of the "Red scare" associated with the Bolshevik revolution in Russia, the land from which most of the new immigrants had fled. Did these ex-Russian Jews represent a seditious radicalism that could only bode ill for the peace and order of the Canadian nation? Antisemitism, on the rise in Europe, was on the rise in Canada as well, as the relatively secure and stable world of the nineteenth century found itself shattered by world war and political revolution, and new Promethean forces were unleashed.

As a spinoff of the xenophobia that swept the North American continent in the early twenties, a spate of savage books against religious, racial and ethnic aliens was generated. Especially notorious was Madison Grant's *The Passing of the Great Race* and the auto magnate Henry Ford's *The International Jew,* a work that made antisemitism a mass idea for the first time in the United States and Canada. This was the golden age of the

Ku Klux Klan and its black and Jewish lynchings. No blacks or Jews were lynched in Canada, but the spirit of the Klan, as well as the Klan itself, crossed the border and invaded the dominion of the north. It was in a Klannish spirit that, on September 22, 1924, the Toronto *Telegram* saw fit to warn its readers that the Jewish invasion "puts a worm next [to] the kernel of every fair city where they get a hold.... They [the Jews] engage in the wars of no country, but flit from one to another under passports changed with chameleon swiftness, following up the wind the smell of lucre.... They remain cosmopolitan while war drains the blood of the solid citizens of a nation."[41] In this way, the poor beleagued "native" Canadians were encouraged to think of themselves as under seige.

In western Canada, where Jewish immigrants had also settled following the great exodus from eastern Europe, usually though not exclusively in the cities, antisemitic currents began to gather strength as well. Following the Winnipeg general strike of 1919, a Red scare that had more to do with Anglo Saxons than with Jews, an anti-immigrant backlash in the city inspired newspaper advertisements calling for the deportation of undesirable aliens, including a number of prominent Jewish Canadians.[42] In 1921, a new rural populist party, the United Farmers of Alberta, won a stunning electoral victory in that province, bringing to power an anti-elitist, anti-big business, anti-big bank and, potentially at least, anti-Jewish protest movement with its true intellectual origins in the American mid-west. According to one social historian, the latter included a dualistic (good versus evil) mindset and a conspiratorial view of history, both important elements in modern antisemitism.[43] However, this disorder did not erupt in Alberta politics until the next decade, when the Social Credit Party replaced the United Farmers in another landslide election in the midst of the Great Depression. As the entire nation plunged into the misery of the thirties, all the anti-Jewish and antisemitic threads in its history began to gather into a large and alarming ball.

Quebec antisemitism was not confined to Arcand's blue-shirted fascists, even if they certainly represented its most visible and virulent expression. It permeated every section of society, including the Church (not only Abbé Groulx), the intelligentsia, the press and the political arena. It was also present in Anglo Quebec, notably in the Montreal establishment that controlled McGill University, despite the fact that Jewish immigrants usually anglicized themselves as soon as possible, adopting the English community and its values.[44] In English Quebec, however, its tone was different, since it was not intermingled with Roman Catholicism and French nationalism, but rather Anglo Saxon nativism with its "gentlemen's agreements" and its quotas on aliens. No more than French Montreal was English Montreal eager to admit a flood of Ashkenazi Yiddish-speaking Jewish strangers into its neighbourhoods and institutions.

A French institution, l'Hôpital Notre-Dame, provided the occasion for what some regard as the high-water mark of the antisemitic agitation of the era. In 1934, a Jewish intern, Samuel Rabinovitch, fluent in French and the highest-ranking medical graduate of his year from the University of Montreal, was forced to resign from the hospital roster after a scant three days following a protest strike of gentile interns against his presence.[45] The incident scarcely attained the status of a national cause célèbre, but it sent powerful reverberations throughout the province, mostly anti-Rabinovitch, and it stirred ancient fears in the Jewish community. As so often before in history, a seemingly small spark ignited a potentially dangerous conflagration. Fear, of course, prompted the strike: a fear that Jews might usurp French Canadian places in the medical world, as well as in the other professions. The delicate equilibrium between English and French Quebec, and its vulnerability to any form of social tension, was an underlying factor. Were the new Jewish professionals and businessmen the vanguard of Anglo power?

If the Rabinovitch affair was the most scandalous public manifestation of Quebec antisemitism in the early thirties, the Christie Pits riot in Toronto (August 1933) was probably its Ontario equivalent.[46] This episode, a fight instigated by an Anglo gang at a baseball game between Jewish and non-Jewish teams at Willowvale Park in the west end of the city, produced similar reverberations of alarm among local Jews because of its violence and its Nazi overtones (e.g., the flaunting of swastikas). The fact that neither the police nor the courts took the offenders seriously did not help. However, no real fascist threat arose in its wake, even if the anti-Jewish mood in the province did not abate as the decade wore on. Rather, it intensified, fuelled by local Nazi propaganda on the part of some resident Germans and German Canadian organizations such as the *Deutscher Bund*,[47] as well as the German government itself, at least until German militarism in Europe rendered pro-German and pro-fascist sentiments uncongenial to most Canadians. The object of these efforts was to prevent German immigrants from melting into the Anglo Saxon ethos of their adopted nation by cultivating their Teutonic essence: "blood [is] stronger than citizenship papers."[48] From across the American border floated the mellifluous tones of Canadian-born Charles E. Coughlin, the charismatic radio priest of the Depression era who inveighed against both international capitalism (the "modern Shylocks") and international communism, holding the Jews responsible for these contradictory evils.[49] A demagogue and a populist, Coughlin helped to feed the mood of alienation that allowed the Social Credit Party to sweep Alberta in 1935 on a so-called "Christian" platform that, of necessity, had anti-Jewish overtones. The new premier, William ("Bible Bill") Aberhart, actually paid both Coughlin and Henry Ford the compliment of personal visits only three weeks after his dramatic electoral victory.[50]

Despite this obeisance, however, and despite his own fundamentalist convictions—it is difficult for Christian fundamentalism not to be tainted with theological anti-Judaism—Aberhart did not encourage antisemitism in Alberta politics. Instead, the antisemitic "Douglasite"[51] wing of the party was relegated to the margins, eventually to be expunged altogether by Aberhart's successor Ernest Manning in a final showdown.[52] Nevertheless, for a brief moment, the possibility of political antisemitism loomed in English Canada. The antisemitic Social Credit members elected to the federal House of Commons during the same era, especially Norman Jaques, M.P. for Wetaskiwin, and John Blackmore, M.P. for Lethbridge, remained a disturbing presence in Canadian politics for many years. Their speeches against Jews and the mysterious recesses of Jewish power—Jaques, like Major Douglas himself, was hypnotized by *The Protocols of the Elders of Zion*—were delivered in the highest Parliament of the land, recorded in its public record (Hansard), and reported on occasion by the press.

On many counts, therefore, the 1930s constituted a dangerous decade, at home as well as abroad. The gathering storm in Europe cast its clouds over Canada as well, even if its full fury did not smite the North American landscape. Yet, had Hitler's armies ever invaded Canadian soil, and had a Canadian Quisling or Pétain ever ruled in Ottawa, and had antisemitic measures ever been imposed in an occupied or Nazi-dominated puppet state, such measures almost certainly would have been accepted by some Canadians with equanimity, if not with enthusiasm. For Canada did not lack its antisemites, and its culture and history were not free of antisemitism.

Antisemitism in Europe

The real drama occurred in Europe, and it is to the European setting that we must turn next. Hitler's Third Reich did not arise in a stable and healthy social order, but in a Germany already saturated with xenophobic, nationalistic, racial and anti-Jewish images and ideas. It arose in a society truly at the end of an era, having witnessed the fall of a proud imperial system that claimed for itself the legacy of the Carolingians, the great emperors of the west, after a humiliating defeat in a war that the confident Germans had expected to win. Such a great nation could not have been overcome by fair means; it must have been stabbed in the back. When the French suffered a similar catastrophe in 1870—the unexpected rout of Napoleon III at the Battle of Sedan—Judeophobia, reinforced by racial ideas, enjoyed a sudden resurgence in Paris, setting the stage for the later Dreyfus affair. Defeated nations sink into dangerous moods. Post-war, post-imperial Germany became susceptible to tales of conspiracy featuring, once again, Europe's oldest scapegoats. Nor did the crippling burden of punitive reparations and the rapid onslaught of mass unemployment and social unrest help to relieve the ills of the day. Nor was the new Weimar Republic popular; many Germans regarded it as an illegitimate and decadent state foisted on a vanquished nation by vindictive "pagan" enemies, as the Allied powers were perceived by German Christian nationalists. Germany, in short, was poised for a collective neurosis, and antisemitism, which had entered German politics with the election of Otto Bockel (1887) and Hermann Ahlwardt (1892) to the old pre-war Reichstag, was its predestined form.

The reason why the Jews found themselves blamed for Germany's ills is not difficult to discern; the soil of German culture had been fertilized too long with anti-Jewish myths of one kind or another for the noxious seeds of antisemitism not to blossom and bear fruit. Even some of the greatest modern German intellectuals and artists saw German history as a type of passion play in which the Jews were cast in their old patristic role as the agents of crucifixion, except that the German nation was now their anointed victim; hence the redemption of Germany was contingent on an anti-Jewish national revolution.[53] To be sure, other explanations abound for the Third Reich and its aberrations. Perhaps, as the political philosopher Hannah Arendt argued, the true roots of antisemitism lie less in old myths than in the peculiar social, economic and political configurations of a century that conspired to place the Jews in the storm centre of events.[54] Perhaps, as the Jewish historian Arthur Hertzberg argued, the true roots lie less in the Christian Middle Ages than in pre-Christian antiquity, its anti-Jewish conceits rediscovered and mediated to the modern age by adulators such as Voltaire.[55] Perhaps, but the historical continuum of the Christian ages cannot be ignored, a continuum studded with nefarious themes and fantasies: deicide, malediction, degeneracy, carnality and diabolism, together with the defamation of the Talmud and an obsession with the Jews as the foes of Christendom.[56] Religious myths, moreover, are easily converted into secular myths, and it is easy to detect their metamorphosis.

What was the modern Semite, as defined in the Aryan myth, the great "race" myth of the white modern Europeans,[57] but the ghost of the carnal Jew of Christian theology?

Christian anti-Judaism was by no means the sole fountainhead of Jew-hatred in the modern world; other forces, in many cases antithetical to Christianity, made their terrible contribution. The Age of Faith was succeeded by the Age of Reason, and the Enlightenment found its own "rational" grounds for disliking the Jews, adding its legacy to the Christian legacy in stirring the passions of those elements in Europe that resisted Jewish emancipation.[58] A secular "high moral" antisemitism that rejected Judaism for a priori reasons was one of its special fruits.[59] Nevertheless, the dominant religion of western civilization played the part of midwife, and this fact cannot be diluted or denied. Germany, in addition, was, with Switzerland, the true seat of the Protestant Reformation, and, to the chagrin of modern Protestants, Martin Luther, its greatest figure, has been compared to Adolf Hitler because of the savage character of his anti-Jewish tracts, especially *The Jews and Their Lies* (1543), a writing that seemed to anticipate the Nazi era.[60] Canadian Protestantism, the subject of this study, is inextricably linked to Luther's spiritual revolution, and cannot break this link without disavowing its own raison d'être.

The rise of European antisemitism is too vast a tale to be told in these pages; even its German chapter is too vast. There are many available works on the subject in any case.[61] Instead, certain milestones on the road to Auschwitz, as well as Auschwitz itself, must command our attention, since Christian opinion in Canada was formed mostly in response to the publicity that Canadians received in the national and international press. Our study will revolve around: (1) the Aryan Laws of the Third Reich, together with the boycotts and acts of brutality that attended their implementation (1933-35); (2) the *Kristallnacht* pogrom (1938); (3) the mounting refugee crisis triggered by Hitler's territorial violations (1939); and finally (4) the Holocaust itself (1942-45). While all are familiar, each requires a brief synopsis in order to set the stage for our discussion of the Canadian churches and their responses.

(1) The Aryan Laws: Adolf Hitler, an "infantile," "monomaniacal" and "mediumistic" personality who rose from "the gutter to be the master of Europe,"[62] was an antisemite from his early youth, and the political order that he foisted on Germany was antisemitic at its core. Saturated with racial obsessions derived from an earlier generation of "race" thinkers, his new Reich introduced the Aryan paragraph on April 7, 1933, with its legislation to "reform" the German civil service. These measures, designed to

exclude non-Aryans (i.e., Jews) from public office, were soon extended into the professions and other areas. The German Protestant churches, which contained a powerful "German Christian" faction devoted to what they called "positive Christianity" and "heroic piety" in the so-called "German spirit of Luther,"[63] were subjected to tremendous internal and external pressure to conform. Aryan and non-Aryan pastors and congregations, the German Christians maintained, belong apart. Non-Aryan meant of Jewish extraction.

Some eminent theologians fell into line. Should not the visible church correspond to the *völkisch* (racial) divisions of the world?[64] Luther himself had distinguished between the private and the public realms of the Christian life; consequently, men such as Paul Althaus and Werner Elert saw nothing wrong in arguing that the spiritual unity of Christian believers—all are one in Christ Jesus—was fully consonant with their temporal and historical segregation. Their argument ran as follows. Since the laws of biology were fashioned by the Creator, and since, according to these laws, Jews and Germans constitute discrete "races," and since the different "races" are not intended by nature and nature's God to mingle or interbreed, they also ought not to worship or work together. Otherwise God's Word would be dishonoured. With these sophisms, nationalistic Lutherans embraced the racial legislation of an antisemitic state. Challenging, as it did, the basic principles of Christianity itself, the issue quickly attracted the attention of the Christian world outside of Germany, placing the regime in a bad odour. Antisemitism in the evangelical churches and antisemitism in German society—questions about the one led to questions about the other—drew the fire of foreign criticism.

(2) *Kristallnacht:* The night of the broken glass, which was not a single night but several days and nights of violence against Jews and Jewish properties (November 9-12, 1938), has been described as the last old-fashioned pogrom in Germany, meaning the last public explosion of a rabble on a rampage.[65] It drew angry outcries from abroad, embarrassing the Nazis. Thereafter, the regime decreed, matters were to be handled differently, with a premium on secrecy and careful planning along more "rational" lines. Not Goebbels, the instigator of the pogrom, but Himmler, the master executioner, became the presiding genius of the next phase; from now on "the Jews were going to be dealt with in a 'legal' fashion ... hasty action was precluded."[66] This meant replacing the clumsy and counterproductive (in terms of adverse publicity) methods reminiscent of the mob mentality of the past with the calculated approach to problem-solving that informed the bureaucratic spirit of the present. For *Kristallnacht*

did not sit well with international opinion; it was widely reported in the non-German press, including the church press, and changed an earlier perception in the United States that Hitler's antisemitism was unrelated to his other policies, including German foreign policy.[67] Germany suffered considerable damage in the eyes of the world, and this damage had economic implications. The propaganda minister, as his fellow Nazis swiftly realized, had overplayed his hand, and the mistake cost him his dreams of greater power.

(3) The refugee crisis: Persecution, as it always does, produced a flood of refugees, and the rising tide created an international problem that the governments of the day could not ignore. Large numbers of Jews sought sanctuary in the democratic nations of the west: a west that had received the victims of earlier pogroms in the Russian Empire. No less than 138,000 Jews had entered Canada between 1900 and 1921.[68] In the 1930s, however, the mood in both Canada and the United States, not to mention other possible host countries, was less congenial; refugees—at least Jewish refugees—were not welcome. Evian, a conference organized in July 1938, by the American president Franklin D. Roosevelt to resolve the crisis, was a failure, partly because it was designed to deal with the politics of the problem rather than the problem itself, and partly because it could not have succeeded in any event, since no participating government was prepared to alter its immigration laws. A "dismal series of speeches" was its only true result.[69] The world, as two American authors, Richard Rubenstein and John Roth, have declared, seemed to be divided into two camps: "one that wanted to be rid of Jews and one that would not accept them."[70] This observation is confirmed by the peculiar fate of the St. Louis, that modern flying Dutchman which, like its legendary counterpart, was forced to sail the seven seas in search of haven. Spurned by Latin American, American and Canadian ports, its Jewish passengers were returned to Europe and the spider's web, where some of them perished. This incident, which was widely reported in the American and Canadian media of the day (although not always sympathetically[71]), epitomized the Jewish plight, and still haunts the memory. Antisemitism in Germany launched the St. Louis, and antisemitism in other nations, including Canada, charted its strange and tragic course.

(4) The Holocaust or, as some prefer, the Shoah:[72] It was on August 1, 1942, that Gerhart Riegner of the World Jewish Congress, at his listening post in Bern, Switzerland, learned from a highly placed German industrialist of the true nature of the Nazi "Final Solution" (Endlösung) to the Jewish problem (Judenfrage), and its rapidly accelerating implementation.[73] His

attempts to relay the particular information to the Allied governments, and the delays that he encountered until the message was finally heard and received in November, are now familiar.[74] Riegner was assisted fortuitously by Hitler's Sports Palace speech on September 30 in which the German dictator affirmed his earlier prophesy in the *Reichstag,* uttered on January 30, 1939, that the Jewish "race" would not survive another war.[75] That a premeditated intention to destroy rather than merely persecute lay behind his words was too fantastic a notion for the outside world to embrace in 1939. In any case, the "artist-politician," whatever his thoughts, had not finalized his plans at this point, and three years were to pass before the Wannsee Conference turned the thought of extermination into a carefully orchestrated reality. Not until Riegner's revelations, which were released by Stephen Wise in the United States on behalf of the World Jewish Congress, confirming death camp rumours already in circulation, did the true significance of the Führer's speech begin to unfold. When it did, however, belief and disbelief contended with each other. Were the reports true, or were they simply more anti-German propaganda, akin to the false atrocity tales of the savagery of the Hun during the First World War? No one could be certain, not for lack of information—according to Robert W. Ross, virtually no detail of the Final Solution had not been mentioned in the American Protestant press by 1943, except the total number of extermination centres and their more refined cruelties[76]—but for more complex reasons. For one thing, an aura of suspicion attended purely Jewish sources in gentile eyes; for another, the tales seemed too terrible to be true, and therefore must be either false or greatly exaggerated.[77] The alleged silence of the Canadian Protestant churches must be addressed in this setting.

II

The Churches

IN THE MAIN, CANADIAN PROTESTANTISM can be described as an extension of English Canada, since the Protestant presence in French Canada (Francophone society, not only in Quebec) has always been negligible. English Canada, moreover, owes its historic origins to colonists from the British Isles, although many Americans, themselves the descendants of British colonists, and many non-British peoples have poured into the country in modern times, bringing in their train a score of cultures and religions that can scarcely be described as "English" except in the bare sense that English has become the language of their adoption. While not all Canadian Protestants are of British stock—most Lutherans and Mennonites, for example, are of continental extraction—and while not all of the Protestant churches of Canada are tributaries of the English and Scottish Reformations, the major denominations—the United Church, the Anglican Church, the Presbyterian Church, the various Baptist and other evangelical churches, including the Pentecostal Assemblies and the Salvation Army—are largely British or American in origin.

During the pre-World War II era, when Canada was a land of small towns rather than large cities, and when the imperial connection was highly esteemed, the Anglo Saxon character of much of Canadian Protestantism was far more pronounced than in the post-war era, and of far greater import. This was still the age of "Anglo conformity," a social mould that can be and has been interpreted in different ways. At its worst, it implied the rule of Anglo Saxon tribalism and the suppression of non-Anglo Saxon minorities.[1] At its best, it represented the spirit and principles of Anglo Saxon political democracy, with its generous notions of toleration and fair play. The Protestant churches contained both instincts, as well as certain religious convictions forged in the crucible of faith and the struggles of history, notably freedom of conscience and worship, including the right of dissent. While they saw Canada as essentially a

Notes to this chapter are on pp. 141-144.

Christian country, they were not prepared to deny its non-Christian citizens the full measure of civil equality. Jews, in other words, were allowed to be Jews, even if they were sometimes the target of Christian missions, and expected to "adjust" to the Christian ethos of the nation.[2]

In spite of their common British roots and shared Anglo Saxon values, the major Protestant denominations of Canada, like their American counterparts (also of British origin), were far from identical, either theologically or in polity and religious practice. They differed not only among themselves but within themselves, having both conservative and liberal, fundamentalist and modern, pietistic and non-pietistic, and, in the case of the Anglicans, high church and low church wings. In addition, the Baptists, Lutherans and Mennonites lacked denominational unity. Of these various dichotomies, the liberal-conservative split was the most pertinent to the Jewish crisis during the Nazi era: so, at least, William E. Nawyn discovered in his study of the American Churches:

> Liberals had been deeply affected by the Social Gospel with its roots in the conviction that the kingdom of God could be and should be actualized upon this earth. Society, not only the individual, was to be redeemed. The immanence of God was stressed and consequently He was perceived as a dynamic force within the social process. Christians were to work hand in hand with God to create, in this world, a society based on love and brotherhood.... Men and women holding these positions did not always engage in social activism, or necessarily adopt more "liberal" attitudes toward social issues. Yet most supported a more active role for the church ... in social and ethical affairs outside of the immediate "spiritual" concerns of the church.[3]

If liberal Protestants of an earlier day stressed the this-worldly character of the kingdom of God and "horizontal" relationships with their fellow humans, conservative Protestants tended to emphasize the other-worldly dimensions of the kingdom of God and vertical relationships with the heavenly King. To the latter, personal faith and evangelism rather than social reform mattered the most; the world and its problems were dealt with best by populating the world with saved individuals. This meant that social and political questions were deemed to lie for the most part beyond the proper bounds of the church, which ought not to "engage in politics" in a direct and overt manner. However, generalizations do not always hold, and actions do not always reflect their progenitors, or at least the ideologies professed by their progenitors. Because liberal Protestants were preoccupied with "a society based on love and brotherhood," they were more inclined (in theory at least) to be critical of social disorders such as antisemitism, as well as sympathetic to its victims. They were also less likely to endorse the theological anti-Judaism of Christian tradition. Yet, as the famous case of J.S. Woodsworth, that "bearded, ethereal idealist in Canadian politics,"[4] reveals, even their greatest figures had feet of clay. In his youth at any rate, the saintly father of Canadian socialism was deeply infected by Anglo Saxon nativism.[5] So were some other great Canadian liberals. On the other hand, as will be illustrated later, the conservative pietists in various churches who had their hearts set on Jewish conversions not infrequently became the leading advocates of rescue and opponents of antisemitism. Nawyn, incidentally, found that being involved in Jewish evangelism had a similar effect on American evangelical Protestantism.[6] Moreover, even conservatives with vertical notions of religion were not necessarily devoid of a social conscience or indifferent to the effects of evil in human affairs. Nor were they necessarily apolitical.

The United Church

The United Church of Canada, the largest of the Protestant denominations—in 1941, it embraced 2,204,875 members and adherents[7]—was formed in 1925 as a union of Methodists, Presbyterians and Congregationalists. From the beginning, the new church became the "liberal" church par excellence: a reputation that, for good or ill, the denomination still retains. Its inception, in the words of one chronicler, represented "a triumph of the social gospel."[8] A movement with German, British and American intellectual bloodlines, social Christianity had established itself on Canadian soil early in the century, where the Methodists in particular had embraced it with the "zeal of devotees of a new evangel."[9] However, by the time church union was consummated, the social gospel was becoming a waning force, largely because of the calamity of the Great War and its aftermath of disillusionment. Bright glowing dreams about the "Christianization" of the social order became difficult to sustain when the world was falling apart during the Great Depression. Yet the United Church never fully lost its faith; its theological vision always incorporated a "social passion," which meant a passionate concern with human issues in the body politic. Methodism was more than individualism; John Wesley's doctrine of Christian perfection implied the perfecting of society as well as the perfecting of the individual, as his great tract against slavery in the eighteenth century British Empire bears witness.[10] Presbyterianism, an English and Scottish variant of Calvinism, had always concerned itself with the vision of a holy commonwealth, and Congregationalism, with its foundations in English independency, had always concerned itself with matters of personal conscience. The mingling of these strains in the United Church produced an ethical predisposition against social evils of every description, including the special evil of antisemitism.

Liberalism, however, has its blind spots, one of which is the assumption that all liberally minded persons share the same basic values and principles, regardless of particular affiliations and religious and ethnic loyalties. The Christianization of the social order was an ambiguous concept at best, especially if one did not happen to be Christian. In late nineteenth-century Germany, for example, the liberal Jewish community regarded the liberal Protestant view of society with the same distrust with which it regarded the conservative clerical view; both contained the dangers of spiritual "totalitarianism."[11] In the United States, Walter Rauschenbusch, the greatest theologian of the social gospel, naively expected his "Jewish fellow citizens" to recognize in Jesus "a prophecy of the future glory of humanity, the type of Man as he is to be."[12] In Canada, Richard Roberts, a theological liberal and one of the United Church's great preachers, echoed the same spiritual triumphalism in a paean addressed to the Jewish soul:

> For consider the case of the Jews. Here was a nation endowed with a peculiar genius for religion, and if there is a Divine Providence in the ordering of the world, we should say that this people was ordained to bring to mankind the knowledge of God. First among the nations they learned the towering truth of the One God of all the earth ... their abiding historical distinction lies ... in that great succession of inspired giants who laid the foundations of the religion of the Western World, Abraham, Moses, Isaiah, Jeremiah, St. Paul and many another; and supremely ... that out of the loins of Jewry came Jesus of Nazareth, who is still the hope of the world.[13]

The glory of Judaism, if one accepts this line of reasoning, resides ultimately in the fact that it gave birth to the still more glorious religion of Christianity! Roberts intended no affront; in fact, his words were designed to win Christian sympathy for the Jews in the rapidly changing Germany of 1933. But he was a creature of his age, and a mind formed in the classical liberal mould invariably universalizes its own convictions and assumptions. In all probability, most members of the United Church thought in similar terms. Few at the time, liberal or otherwise, would have noticed the subtle denial of any other abiding historical distinction on the part of the Jewish people and their religious propensities.

The Church of England in Canada

The Church of England in Canada, as the Anglican Church of Canada was formerly known, numbered 1,751,188 members and adherents in 1941.[14] Anglicanism was closely intertwined with the early history of the nation, supplying a natural religious home for English immigrants and providing a powerful bond with Britain in every conceivable respect. Staffed in no small measure by English and English-trained clergy, the Canadian branch institution bore, not without reason, the popular appellation of the "English Church."[15] Loyalist, traditionalist, paternalistic (because of its episcopal system), with early dreams—soon frustrated—of political establishment,[16] the Church of England in Canada was not a likely breeding ground of liberal or controversial ideas, in spite of certain radical strains in its British counterpart, notably the Christian socialism of Frederick Denison Maurice and Charles Kingsley in the nineteenth century. "Of the larger denominations, the Anglicans found the greatest difficulty in fielding the social gospel, the Methodists the least, and somewhere between them lay the Presbyterians."[17] One reason for this difficulty lay in the Catholic-Evangelical, or high and low church, tension in Anglicanism. While British Anglo Catholicism possessed its own tradition of social radicalism, this strand in English Christianity had only a minor impact on its Canadian offspring.[18] Evangelicalism leaned in a pietistic and therefore individualistic direction. Yet, such was the prestige of the English archbishops during the thirties and forties, especially William Temple, archbishop of Canterbury, and Cyril Garbett, archbishop of York, as well as other eminent Anglicans in Britain, that their utterances on the great moral questions of the day carried considerable weight among Canadian Anglicans. Temple was not an ordinary figure: an original philosophical theologian, he has been described as one of the "four great doctors" of the post-Reformation Anglican communion, along with Richard Hooker, Joseph Butler and Maurice.[19]

Since Anglican pedagogues, both catholic and evangelical, drank deeply from the well of tradition—even modernist Anglicans usually paid the classics their due—ancient Christian misconceptions about Jews and Judaism were rife in Anglican religious literature, and usually taken for granted. Few Christians of the time, Anglican or non-Anglican, discerned a causal connection between this hoary polemical material and the fate of the Jews in both mediaeval Christendom and the post-Christian modern world.[20] Not only did most Anglicans not find fault with the old *adversus Judaeos* strain in their ecclesiastical heritage, but many also evinced a peculiar zeal for

Jewish evangelization. Thus the Church of England in Canada maintained active Jewish missions in Montreal and Toronto, staffing them with ordained converts whose progress reports were filed carefully in diocesan records and journals. Needless to say, most Jews did not regard these missions with favour, their suspicions of such Christian attention being more than justified by recollections of the Middle Ages and its infamous "vale of tears." They also resented the spiritual premises adopted by the missionaries. "Christianity," according to one of the latter, "must be presented as the crown and completion of Judaism ... [for] any special privileges and blessings promised to them [the Jews] were inherited by the New Israel, the Church of Christ, when the Old Israel rejected Him."[21] Yet these proselytizing activities were generally accompanied by high motivations, including a pronounced concern for Jewish bodies as well as Jewish souls. Christian supremacists and usually scriptural literalists as well, the Anglican evangelists nevertheless listened sympathetically to ugly tales from the lips of Jewish immigrants about the trials and tribulations of their friends and families across the ocean. As a result, they developed a genuine dislike of antisemites and antisemitism, both in Canada and Europe, while serving to keep their church informed as to the true state of affairs in Nazi realms. This was especially true of a few priests of Jewish origin.[22]

The Presbyterian Church

The Presbyterian Church in Canada emerged after the union of Methodists, unionist Presbyterians and Congregationalists in 1925 (the United Church) as a continuing body—one might almost say, a rump—of anti-unionist Presbyterians for whom the principles and doctrines of Calvinism remained of paramount value. In 1941 it tallied 829,147 members and adherents.[23] As the schism was bitter, and its final act dramatic,[24] the new-old church was left in a state of confusion and disarray that persisted for many years. Continuing Presbyterianism lost many of its most able leaders, preachers and teachers to the United Church, especially the theological liberals and heralds of the social gospel most likely to address public issues.[25] Moreover, fundamentalist currents, largely American in origin, had started to appear, attracted by the anti-unionist campaign, which maintained the ideal of a pure Calvinist faith resistant to modern humanism in its myriad forms.[26] Defensive and preoccupied with its own survival, the post-union Presbyterian church in Canada was not in a strong position to contend with extraneous challenges, especially the terrifying spectres of economic collapse, totalitarianism in its fascist and communist forms, and, by the end of the thirties, an impending world war, not to mention the rise of antisemitism and the troubles of the European Jews.

On the other hand, the Calvinist tradition itself included a strong theology of the social order, without which Calvinism would not be Calvinism, and even a truncated Canadian Presbyterianism was attentive to more than its own institutional progress. Moreover, historic Calvinism was not saddled with as strong a heritage of either religious anti-Judaism or social antisemitism as some other ecclesiastical traditions. John Calvin himself never regarded the Jews and their religion with Martin Luther's ferocious hostility: in fact, in his later sermons, the Geneva reformer actually linked the suffering of Protestants and the suffering of Jews in a "hidden community of fate."[27] His thought was also coloured by Hebrew accents—commandment, law, election, covenant, the holy commonwealth—and, unlike Luther, he did not cling to mediaeval anti-Jewish stigmas such as usury, a major source of historic animosity. It is probably no coincidence that countries with Calvinist cultures—Switzerland, the Netherlands, Scotland, England (in part) and the United States (in part)—have not been notorious for mistreating their Jewish populations. At the same time, the doctrinally conservative and sometimes fundamentalist Calvinists of the Presbyterian Church in Canada found ample room for the same anti-Jewish assumptions as most of the rest of Christendom. Yet the Jewish religious "genius" did not pass unnoticed,[28] nor the righteous qualities of the religion of Jesus, which, after all, was not Christianity but Judaism.[29]

Like the Anglicans, the Presbyterians had a special interest in Jewish missions. In the eyes of the Presbyterian evangelicals, infidelity, atheism and materialism were rife in the Jewish immigrant community: a result of the "fall of the ghetto" and the disastrous effects of the "neo-pagan conditions of modern life" on traditional customs and beliefs.[30] Judaism was in extremis; consequently, Christians had a solemn duty to lead the lost children of Israel to the waters of baptism. The evangelization of the Jews was not seen in any sense as an anti-Jewish activity; instead, the missionaries saw their enterprise as the logical extension of their empathy. Antisemitism was perceived both as an evil in itself and as a stumbling-block to conversion. Moreover, an "element of romance" was added to the life of the church through the "high worth" of its Jewish converts.[31] Despite the dark clouds lining the political horizons, and the threat to the anticipated religious harvest, their optimism remained undiminished, at least until war actually commenced. One Presbyterian in particular, the Jewish convert Morris Zeidman,[32] was among the first Canadian Christians to grasp the true enormity of the Jewish plight.

Baptists and Evangelicals

The various Baptist churches in Canada comprised 483,592 members and adherents in 1941.[33] Largely the spiritual descendants of British Independents and Separatists of the seventeenth century rather than the continental Anabaptists,[34] they never became a single entity, either institutionally or theologically. Believer's baptism, usually by immersion, was their only real point of convergence, although certain other ideas, notably a congregational polity and a belief in the separation of church and state, have been Baptist principles since the sixteenth-century Reformation. Evangelicalism, a powerful strain in Protestantism that emphasizes the primacy of faith,[35] permeated all of the churches, but especially the Baptists, as well as various cognate groups of a conservative bent. Quite unabashedly, the fundamentalist evangelicals, Baptist and non-Baptist, joined with the continuing Presbyterians in a profound distaste for the liberal United Church as "a sort of Canadian antichrist."[36] The same sentiment was shared by the Pentecostalists, a holiness movement with turn-of-the-century origins that constituted itself as the Pentecostal Assemblies of Canada in 1919. Its special trademark consisted of the gift of tongues, otherwise known as the "latter rain." Since the various "Bible" churches of Canada were relatively small in the 1930s and 1940s—the Pentecostalists numbered 37,646 and the Salvation Army 33,598 members and adherents in 1941[37]—and since a dislike of modernism was almost universal in their ranks, it is convenient to classify them with the largely similar anti-modernist Baptists. Still, by no means were all Baptists fundamentalists; many in varying degrees were liberals, and the manifesto of the social gospel at least reached their ears, even if it failed to win many hearts.[38] After all, Walter Rauschenbusch himself had been a Baptist, albeit an American Baptist.

The great schism between the liberal and fundamentalist Baptists in Canada occurred in 1926, when, after several years of turmoil, the Baptist Convention of Ontario and Quebec decided to expel the controversial T.T. Shields, minister of the Jarvis Street Baptist Church in Toronto, the largest congregation in the Convention, and leader of the fundamentalist faction. This "infamous expulsion," in the words of a sympathetic Baptist historian,[39] was inspired by the preacher's crusade against "modernism," or modern German critical scholarship, especially in the theological faculty at McMaster University. Its consequence was the formation of dissident Baptist organizations, allowing Jarvis Street to become a kind of cathedral church of fundamentalism in eastern Canada, and Shields its arch-champion. The liberal Baptists did not possess a preacher equal to their formidable bête-noire, but they possessed a brilliant man-of-letters in the person of Watson Kirkconnell.[40] Not unlike the United Church, this segment of the Baptist communion dealt somewhat ambiguously with Jewish subjects, praising the Jews for their "religious genius" on the one hand, and describing Jesus as a Jew who had transcended Judaism on the other with his "universal mind and heart." "The Christian of any nation never thinks of Him as a Jew. Jesus belongs to all nations and to all ages. He is the world's centre."[41] This religious magniloquence did not prevent prominent Baptists from joining other Protestants (and Catholics) as well as governmental officials in a public service in 1936 in celebration of the eightieth anniversary of the Holy Blossom congregation in Toronto during the tenure of Rabbi Maurice Eisendrath. The timing was significant. Such a service, boasted *The Canadian Baptist,* could not have taken place in Europe where the Jews were being "harried from pillar to post," but in Canada British "religious and civil liberty" comprised the order of the day.[42] In fact, the entire occasion was a tribute both to the British traditions of the nation and to the Jews themselves, to whom, in the editor's opinion, the world owed an incalculable and unrepayable debt. This scenario was recreated two years later, when Holy Blossom dedicated its new temple, and the governor general of Canada, Lord Tweedsmuir, delivered an address surrounded by Baptist and United Church clergymen as well as Jewish and other dignitaries.[43]

Lutherans, Mennonites and Quakers

There were 401,153 Lutherans in Canada in 1941, divided into nine separate synods, or church bodies.[44] As the descendants in many cases of British soldiers (the king of Great Britain was also the king of Hanover until the accession of Queen Victoria) and United Empire Loyalists of German stock, the Lutherans were scarcely new arrivals in Canada, although their numbers were not large, and they were late to organize themselves. Long nurtured by mother churches in the United States, the scattered Canadian congregations, mostly in the maritimes, south central Ontario, and the prairies, were also divided by language and national origin, with Norwegians, Danes, Swedes, Finns, Icelanders and Slovaks as well as Germans in visible number. Canadian Lutheranism, therefore, was neither autonomous nor united, but a branch of American Lutheranism during the 1930s.[45] A single unified Lutheran church in Canada still does not exist.[46] Because of this fragmentation, the Canadian Lutherans were immediately affected by the doctrinal disputes and other winds of controversy that blew across the border from the midwestern capitals of this highly confessional form of Protestant Christianity. Although the Lutheran churches emerged largely unscathed by the fundamentalist controversy, certain synods, notably the Missouri Synod, allowed fundamentalism to colour their statements of faith.[47] Significantly, the Missouri Synod also engaged in Jewish prose-lytism, as did Lutheran pietists in other synods.[48] Topics that absorbed the American Lutheran theologians of the day—the nature of "true Lutheranism" and its denominational implications, the merits of repristina-tion (or orthodox) theology and a proper definition of the authority of scripture—affected Canadian Lutherans as well.[49] The latter also listened to Walter A. Maier's immensely popular radio sermons on "The Lutheran Hour." Maier, incidentally, spoke favourably of Hitler's patriotic revival in 1933, and for a time discounted tales of Jewish suffering in Germany.[50]

Martin Luther himself, as we have seen, was an antisemite of excep-tional ferocity, even for the sixteenth century.[51] While, as the Jewish his-torian Uriel Tal has declared, a straight line cannot be drawn from Luther to Hitler without distorting historical truth,[52] the reformer also cannot be absolved of all blame for the events of the twentieth century. One impor-tant modern German Lutheran theologian, Emanuel Hirsch, became an ardent Nazi;[53] others, as we have also seen, flirted with National Socialism and its racial laws. Even in North America Luther's anti-Judaism cast a shadow. Not only his tirades, but also his theology itself, with its radical gospel/law dualism and its social and political conservativism, encouraged Lutherans to regard Jews (and Judaism) in preconceived and essentially negative terms. This tendency was not softened by the social gospel, since there was little sympathy for its liberal accents among indigenous Lutheran theologians.[54] In addition, the fact that a substantial part of the Canadian Lutheran community was of German extraction coloured pop-ular perceptions of the old country and its new political system. The American (German) Lutheran press adopted an apologetic stance toward Germany in the pre-World War II era,[55] and the American influence was never weak in Canada. However, the powerful British imperial loyalties of the Canadian Lutherans settled the patriotic question.

Also largely of German as well as Swiss and Dutch stock, and also in many cases the descendants of United Empire Loyalists, although, because of their pacifist convictions, not of British soldiers, Mennonite settlers have been in Canada at least since the American Revolution, set-tling north of Lake Erie in what is now south central Ontario.[56] In 1941 their descendants, augmented by other arrivals (including the more communal Hutterites), numbered 111,380 members and adherents.[57] During the late nineteenth century, as a result of a change in tsarist policies of special toleration and privilege, many Mennonite subjects of the Russian empire, to which they had migrated in the reign of Catherine the Great, departed for North America. A certain number, later known as the "Kanadier," selected Canada rather than the United States as their new home, making it a second centre of this non-conformist type of Christianity, with its spiritual and historical roots in the left wing of the Reformation. Between 1923 and 1930, still another wave of Mennonite exiles from the new Russian empire of the "Red tsars" Lenin and Stalin, driven out by persecution, arrived in Canada, settling for the most part in the west.[58] These were the "Russländer." Interspersed between these strata was the remarkable array of Mennonite churches, comprising, according to Frank H. Epp, no less than eighteen congregational families, each with its own peculiar personality and each part of a "mosaic as richly patterned as the quilts designed by Mennonite women or the fields laid out by Mennonite men."[59] For this reason, the highly decentralized Mennonites have never been able to speak in a single denominational voice.

Drawing their inspiration as well as their name from Menno Simons, the sixteenth-century Anabaptist apostle of non-violence, the Mennonites, like the Quakers, are distinguished by their dedication to a peace ethic and its attendant repudiation of the armies, military machines and sometimes even the police forces of the world.[60] Such an ethic is certain to collide sooner or later with the host nations, especially when the trumpets of war are sounded, as happened in 1914. Of varied but often German extraction as well as pacifist conviction, the Canadian Mennonites found themselves doubly unpopular during this jingoistic era, drawing the fire of the mainstream Anglo Saxon churches.[61] Numerically small, divided into different bodies, sectarian in worldview but with varying degrees of accommodation to society, they were not initially part of the religious mainstream in Canada, preferring to have as little to do as possible with the other churches and with the state.[62] Not surprisingly, such aloofness bred misunderstanding and irritation in the minds of other Canadians. Historically, their own vale of tears—the persecuted and stateless Anabaptists of the sixteenth century have been styled the "Protestant Jews"—predisposed them to commiserate with their Jewish fellow sufferers. Yet Balthasar Hubmaier of Reformation fame, who died at the stake himself, was virulently anti-Jewish,[63] and an undetermined number of Mennonites of the Nazi era, like an undetermined number of Lutherans, were pro-German for cultural and linguistic reasons, even in the face of the terror in Europe.[64] Some, as we shall see, adopted *völkisch* and Nazi ideas, including antisemitism. The anti-semitic fundamentalist preacher Gerald B. Winrod of Wichita, Kansas, often spoke in Mennonite churches in the United States, attracting considerable support in the American Mennonite community.[65] Because of close links across the border, his influence must have been felt in Canada as well. Some of his articles on Nazi Germany were translated and published in the Canadian Mennonite German press.[66]

The Quakers (or Society of Friends) were too few in number to be listed separately in the 1941 Census of Canada, consisting of less than one thousand members at that time. Like the Lutherans and Mennonites, they arrived early in Canada, both before and after the American Revolution, as a result of military and political disruption, as well as a larger westward migration.[67] Their English descent and gratitude for past favours in Pennsylvania inclined them to support the British crown, whereas their pacifist convictions alienated them from the revolutionary call to arms; hence, they made natural loyalists, although loyalism was only one element in their desertion of the new republic. Settling for the most part in Upper Canada, the Quakers acquired new roots in the largely rural society of the early nineteenth century, but failed to flourish numerically, especially after the great schism in 1828 between the "Orthodox" (or doctrinal) and "Hicksite" (or anti-doctrinal) factions.[68] Subsequent divisions caused further fragmentation.

Quakerism itself, a mystical form of seventeenth-century Protestantism with Stoic and renaissance antecedents, employed its doctrine of the "inner light," or the divine spark lodged in the individual soul, to stress the dignity and nobility of human beings.[69] This emphasis produced a universalist, and, by extension, an internationalist worldview: the opposite of an enclosed sectarianism. "Friends assumed that God's Spirit worked through Turks, Chinese, or American Indians, as well as through the Englishmen who knew that the Spirit's proper name was Christ."[70] Through Jews also, one presumes, although the seventeenth-century Quaker Margaret Fell, the author of two friendly tracts regarding the Jews of Amsterdam and their chief rabbi Manasseh ben-Israel, still found it necessary to upbraid the latter for "legalism."[71] Far more liberal than most Lutherans and Mennonites, and far less wedded to traditional theological formulations, the Quakers were not predisposed to either anti-Judaism or antisemitism.

Because of their tireless moral activism, notably in the form of peace issues and relief activities, their social influence has always been disproportionate to their size. Unlike certain other Canadian pacifists, who were converted to the cause of war once war had begun (both in 1914 and 1939) the Quakers, like most of the Mennonites, remained steadfast in their pacifism throughout the war years. This does not mean that Quaker pacifism is identical to Mennonite pacifism; in contrast to the "separational" Mennonites, who prefer a strategy of withdrawal rather than engagement with the power structures of the world, the "integrational" Quakers prefer the path of direct action.[72] As active rather than reactive pacifists, they believe in social reform and alternative forms of public service, provided the latter do not promote militarism either directly or indirectly. At least one prominent Quaker, G. Raymond Booth, a transplanted American, was deeply involved in the cause of Jewish refugees during the Nazi era.[73]

III

The United Church

NEITHER THEOLOGICAL ANTI-JUDAISM nor its offspring, modern anti-semitism, were strangers in the so-called "Canadian antichrist"—the United Church of Canada. This is not difficult to understand. A denomination composed of variant strains was certain to contain anti-liberal as well as liberal elements, with dissonant results in more than one area of intellectual and social concern. The following lines from the 1927[1] church yearbook reveal the crude and unreconstructed character of a segment of contemporary opinion. Their author is not identified.

> Whenever the Jew has settled in any part of the world he has created new problems, political, social, economic and religious.... The power these people wield among the nations is out of all proportion to their numbers. They have attained positions in finance, commerce, industry, science, philosophy, law, politics, statecraft and in the press, enabling them to mold thought and public opinion and to influence the life and destiny of nations.... In Montreal there are 76,000 Jews, in Toronto 60,000, in Winnipeg 16,000, and in all of Canada, 160,000.... No democratic nation can survive unless its roots sink deep into the soil of moral religious truth. It is the task of the Church to teach these things unto the people and especially unto their children.[2]

This, of course, is antisemitism, and nothing but antisemitism; nor is it the only antisemitic item ever to appear in a United Church publication.[3] To read this passage is to hear again the ring of half-forgotten voices belonging to an older, more tribalistic Canada, whether Anglo Saxon Protestant or French Catholic, as well as to encounter the ghost of Goldwin Smith, the sage of the Grange. The moral religious truth that the church is enjoined to teach is not elaborated, but can easily be surmised. What was the Jew, according to the author of the above, but the enemy of the gospel as well as the subverter of the social order. In allowing this paragraph to be printed in an annual report for public consumption, the Solons of the newly established United Church proved themselves less than wise.

Notes to this chapter are on pp. 144-151.

Were they merely inattentive or insensitive or were they also antisemitic? Sensitivity on Jewish and other minority matters was a rare commodity anywhere in 1927.

The fascist temptation

During the early 1930s, occasional pro-fascist sentiments insinuated themselves into the pages of *The New Outlook,* the official organ of the denomination. In itself, this occurrence was not anomalous. So widespread was the loss of faith in the democratic social order during the Great Depression that anti-democratic tremors were certain to reverberate in the churches as well as elsewhere in Canadian society. Because of its British traditions, and also because of its social gospel affinities, the United Church was strongly committed to western democratic ideals. Still, among the rank and file, and even among some of the clergy, the attractions of other political and economic models on both the left (communism) and the right (fascism) made themselves felt. The number drawn to fascism was no doubt small—the dominant temptation was in the opposite direction—but, at least in the beginning, it was no less possible to idealize Italy and Germany than to idealize Soviet Russia, if one saw only what one wanted to see. Mussolini was not without United Church admirers, at least before the Italian invasion of "Christian" Ethiopia, for having restored order and discipline to his country. Hitler also had his claque.[4]

The case of Harold Hendershot, a young minister with postgraduate aspirations, provides an edifying illustration. An ardent Germanophile in love with German scholarship, Hendershot was also much impressed during a German sojourn by German "idealism," especially among university students, in the first summer of the Third Reich (1933). "Two years ago while I was studying in Marburg University in Germany the very finest of the student body were the most indignant against the Jews."[5] While not approving of current persecutions—his article was prompted by the bad press Hitler was receiving at the time in the west—he regarded the Nazi anti-Jewish measures as both natural and intelligible.

> Our own Canadian hearts burn with indignation when we hear of Jewish atrocities in Germany—yet the fact stands that when the heat of released passions will have subsided the Jews in Germany will be seen to be happy compared with the lot of the Chinese in our own land.
>
> ... A reasonable German would argue with us that the Jews had unfairly pushed themselves to too great prominence during a period of dislocation and unrest, and the present situation is a rather natural reaction.

... The galling irritation of the whole situation to the Germans was not merely the *de-facto* situation of Jewish supremacy, but the knowledge that the Jews had climbed to the seats of the mighty since 1914.... To the average German the logic was clear: "While our brave sons were away shedding their life's blood for home and loved ones, these selfish unpatriotic Jews seized control." If we place ourselves in the position of the young German—educated—seeking a position and finding none, and finding unpatriotic Jews—war profiteers—in control, it can scarcely be wondered that he would readily be disposed to make the Jew a scapegoat for his own misfortunes. *For be it remembered that every deposed Jew means a job for a good Nordic German.*[6]

These words betray more than their author intended, even in 1933 when some allowance can be made for naïveté. Hendershot was scarcely representative of United Church opinion, and his infatuation with the Germanic scheme of things drew a swift rebuttal in the next issue from Claris Silcox, the soon-to-be-appointed secretary of the Christian Social Service Council of Canada.[7] The fact, however, that such conceits were possible reveals much about the tenor of the times. Fascism, with its cult of the leader, had a seductive appeal, even in Canada, and even in a liberal Christian communion. Another United Church minister with pro-Nazi feelings was Frank Hoffman, an ethnic missionary in Saskatchewan who eulogized "real democracy" in the brave new world across the Atlantic: "Blue shirts, black shirts and shirts of other colours, bandoleers on their shoulders, marched side by side in the working battalions going to the fields. The rich man's son marches beside the poor man's son."[8] The joyful egalitarianism of this chimera certainly made its impact, especially during the Great Depression. That Hendershot and Hoffman were not solitary in their admiration is demonstrated by various letters published throughout the decade. One, written in 1938 by a Nova Scotia minister, still chills the imagination:

A lot is being written these days about Fascism in Canada and the danger it may hold for democracy. One wonders if democracy is not its own greatest danger, and whether a period of Fascism would be all bad.... The whole system of government and the social order needs revamping....

A strong and unselfish man or group of men, having real vision of a country's well-being, given powers to correct mistakes and set up an order adapted to modern needs, could effect changes in the social and economic set-up easily and quickly. If one dictator could give a broken and dismayed people a soul, could not another keep a hopeless weary one in possession of theirs? Blood purges and regimentation of life appear abhorrent. But one must always die for the nation, and more of orderly discipline would be a real blessing.[9]

While such Draconian convictions were infrequent in the United Church, they were frequent enough to worry the editorial staff and the church leadership, and to provoke regular denunciations. "It is quite the fashion nowadays to criticize and find fault with democracy.... But it may be the part of wisdom ... to consider what we have to put in its place if we should decide to get rid of it. The more closely we look into the substitutes ... which are being tried, the less we are convinced that they are really an improvement."[10] Justifiably, the church was alarmed at the vindication of blood purges for the sake of the nation. Exactly who did the writer think should be purged in Canada?

Other defenders of democracy such as King Gordon, professor of Christian ethics at the United Theological College, Montreal, warned Canadians that the seeds of fascism existed in Canada itself—an observation that was certainly true, especially in Quebec.[11] Another United College professor, R.B.Y. Scott, a distinguished biblical scholar, composed a trenchant condemnation of Quebec's "Blueshirts," who, however, worried him less than the anti-democratic proclivities of the powerful Roman Catholic hierarchy headed by Cardinal Villeneuve, the real fascist menace in the province.[12] Still other democrats warned of the spiritual as well as the political dangers posed by any flirtation with fascism.[13] During the actual war years, when, for patriotic reasons, fascist and antisemitic ideas were no longer in vogue, the denunciations intensified and multiplied. "The Fascist state is founded on contempt for the living person ... and Germany has followed this contempt to its logical conclusion by doing away with free elections, free exchange of ideas, representative government, responsible government as well as trade unions, free co-operatives, free professional associations, etc.... Fascism is the death of democracy."[14]

Persecution in Germany

Hendershot's attempt to defend the German point of view regarding the Jews (and, incidentally, the Danzig Corridor) placed an old question in a new light. Are anti-minority measures merely a natural defensive reaction on the part of an anxious majority afraid of losing its own rights, or do they have deeper and darker roots? At the beginning, *The New Outlook* could not refrain from finding the "deep distrust and hatred" toward the Jews in Germany somewhat "understandable."[15] Indeed, this notion never entirely disappeared.[16] However, Silcox, in his reply to Hendershot, reminded the youthful enthusiast for things German that antisemitism was not only of "*post bellum* vintage"; Houston S. Chamberlain's 1899 best-selling racial classic *The Foundations of the Nineteenth Century* as well as other anti-Jewish writings had tilted public opinion against the Jews well before the war years.[17]

Insofar as one can judge, United Church opinion, by and large, agreed with Silcox. Antisemitism, especially racial antisemitism, was deplored from time to time in the pulpit as well as in the press by some of the more eminent preachers of the denomination, including Richard Roberts, E. Crossley Hunter, G. Stanley Russell, Peter Bryce and Ernest Marshall Howse.[18] Ministers with lower profiles also raised their voices. Nelson Chappell of Westminster United Church, Saskatoon, Saskatchewan, worried about the growth of antisemitism on the home front as well as abroad in a letter to the Saskatoon *Phoenix* (October 31, 1938): "What are we going to do to stop this movement? If we are truly Christians, we must not avoid this challenge."[19] In his autobiography, Rabbi Reuben Slonim of Toronto describes his friendship with Gordon Domm, the affable minister of Bathurst Street United Church who once invited Slonim to preach on this touchy topic to his congregation during the war years.[20] Like Chappell, Domm took seriously the menace of antisemitism in Canada.[21] To allow a Jew to lecture Christians from a Christian pulpit on the roots of this malady in New Testament misrepresentations of Pharisees and Sadducees required no small degree of personal courage in the pre-critical 1940s.[22] Few Christians of the day were prepared for the notion that their religion had sown the seeds of historic animosity long before the harvest was garnered by the antisemites of the twentieth century.

As we have seen,[23] Jewish persecution during the Nazi era was marked by certain milestones, notably the Aryan Laws (1933-35), *Kristallnacht* (1938), the refugee crisis (1939 on), and the Holocaust itself (1942 on). The United Church pulpit and press reacted with growing alarm to each successive outrage, producing a fairly steady stream of castigation. In the case of the Aryan Laws, the entire issue of "race" rose to the fore, since the controversy kindled by the Nazi racial legislation within the state-related German Protestant churches drew international attention. The contest, as Silcox put the matter, was between a pro-Nazi party that believed that the church should be the "soul" of the nation and an anti-Nazi party that believed that the church should be the "conscience" of the nation.[24] Thereby arose the famous German "church struggle" (*Kirchenkampf*) associated with the names of Karl Barth, Martin Niemöller and Dietrich Bonhöffer.[25] Canadian Protestants of all persuasions followed the battle closely, as the future of Christianity itself was at stake. In this struggle, the cause of ecclesiastical integrity overshadowed the predicament of the Jews, but the persecution of Christian and other dissenters, along with the construction of concentration camps, created an antipathy among religious liberals in Canada to the new regime and its "Nordic racialism."[26] While not every United Church member was a liberal, and while the Nordic racialists were not without United Church sympathizers—one contributor to *The New Outlook* declared that the "anti-materialism" and "sacrificial idealism" of the German Christians deserved greater sympathy than the "new synagogism" of their opponents[27]—the Nazi program did not sit well with the majority in the United Church of Canada.

> The great land where Protestantism was born is casting Christ out of her faith....
>
>   The Nazi Government cares for only two things—the unity of the nation and the supremacy of the national ideal....
>
>   If religion conflicts with race, religion must go. Already more than thirty pastors ... have been banished or interned in concentration camps under conditions which have been described as appalling....
>
>   The Nazis have turned the Jews out of the country. They are now realizing that Jesus was born a Jew. They have said openly that Germany is "contaminated" by the Judaism in Christianity....[28]

With growing perspicacity, neo-paganism and antisemitism, the attack on Christians and the attack on Jews were seen as companion evils. Awareness of one stimulated an awareness of the other, even if the plight of the German church, faced with a political ultimatum, stirred the greater initial concern.

By the mid-thirties the two forms of oppression merited the same general condemnation. The church struggle had become an international scandal, and the anti-Jewish policies of the Nazi state had reached a "pitch of brutality and injustice" that the world should tolerate no longer.[29] When Mussolini began to imitate Hitler in 1937, relief was expressed that thus far he had not embarked on a direct purge of the Italian Jews.[30] Careful note was taken of the escalation of the German anti-Jewish campaign and the "aimless cruelty" in which its authors seemed to delight.[31] Wholesale arrests, new discriminatory laws, Jew-hunts in cafés and theatres, etc., were reported, together with the mounting violence that accompanied these acts. Its official press was not the only organ of the United Church to notice and deplore the worsening situation. In September 1938, approximately two months prior to *Kristallnacht*, the General Council adopted the following resolution:

> We, the Eighth General Council of the United Church of Canada ... extend to all our Jewish fellow-countrymen sincere New Year's Greetings on the observance of the immemorial feast of Rosh Hashana.

Our fathers suffered for religious freedom and we would be disloyal to their sacred memory if we did not seek in word and in deed to sympathize with those who today are threatened in many countries with the loss of their civic rights.... We have learned with deep sorrow and mortification of the sufferings inflicted upon the Jewish people by many nations which profess to believe in Him who was the Light of the Gentiles and the true glory of His people, Israel, as well as on many Christians.... In your sufferings, we suffer; and in any earnest and considered efforts to effect the appeasement of the lot of those who, for conscience's sake, or because of the [sic] racial origin are enduring political persecution, we pledge our active and devoted co-operation. May the New Year bring to you some mitigation of the grievous anxiety which you are called upon to bear and may our mutual confidence be in Him who alone can comfort his people and in whose will is our peace.[32]

Germany, for some reason, was not named, although Germany was obviously the offending nation nonpareil. Perhaps its framers did not wish to exclude Canada; already, the members of the Sub-Executive of the General Council had deplored antisemitic agitation in their own land.[33] One suspects that the reference to Jesus as the "true glory of His people, Israel" diminished the resolution in Jewish eyes, but Christian sensitivities were less refined in 1938 than in subsequent years. Its intent was sincere.

Kristallnacht, the last old-fashioned pogrom, left most of Canada in a state of severe shock. *The New Outlook* decried the "primitive savagery and totalitarian state methods" that had driven the German nation to "new depths of infamy."[34] When the Canadian Jewish Congress and civic officials from coast to coast organized a score of non-sectarian public rallies in towns and cities across the nation to protest the Nazi actions, prominent United Church figures joined other Protestant, Catholic and Jewish leaders on the platform. Thousands attended, and the King government found itself on the receiving end of a series of strongly worded and thoroughly unwelcome pro-Jewish, pro-refugee resolutions.[35] That something was terribly wrong was evident both in the event itself, and in its shameless justification by Goebbels as an expression of the "healthy instincts" of a "young Germany."[36] Now the future was indeed ominous both for Jews and the world. Deborah Lipstadt's observation that *Kristallnacht* changed more generous earlier perceptions of the Nazi regime in the United States seems to have been true of Canada as well, at least in the eyes of the astute.[37] "We may be facing the 'mood and method of violent revolution,' and the horror of the onslaught on the Jews may be dwarfed by its significance as an indication of the new powers and purposes of the Third

Reich."[38] Christians could also expect to suffer, and, indee
ing already, as the deepening German church struggle, th'
stant scrutiny, was ample proof.

The refugee crisis

The Jewish refugee crisis, which arose swiftly on the heels of persecution, saw calls for Christian action in the middle of the decade, mostly prompted by the International Missionary Council (IMC) and its Committee on the Christian Approach to the Jews.[39] When James G. McDonald, the League of Nations' High Commissioner for Refugees, announced his resignation in order to draw attention to the German situation (January 15, 1936), an ad hoc group of Canadian ecclesiastics, organized by Silcox, responded with a manifesto declaring that further silence on the part of the churches was impossible. Neither sympathy for Germany's problems nor a fear of international complications nor a fear of stirring antisemitism in Canada nor doubts concerning the truth of allegations against Hitler could justify bridled tongues. Among the thirty-one signatories favouring the admission of a "reasonable number of selected refugees"[40] were United Church notables, Anglicans, Presbyterians, Baptists and Quakers. A reasonable number was scarcely a cry for out-and-out rescue, the word "selected" was ambiguous and the reluctance to specify Jews was a concession to the political fears that, then as now, dictated public policy in Canada, but the moral imperative was clear: "as a Christian people, it is ours to see that those whom the spirit of anti-Christ has bruised, whether they be Aryans or non-Aryans, are healed by the compassionate spirit of Him, in whom 'there is neither Jew nor Gentile, Greek nor Barbarian, bond nor free.'"[41] Sympathetic Christians were willing to lobby Ottawa in the interest of Hitler's victims, although exactly how non-Aryans were to be healed by the spirit of Christ was not explained; no doubt some of the liberal Protestants, if not all, still thought in terms of conversion.

Only the Quakers, according to Conrad Hoffman of the IMC, were engaged in practical assistance to the besieged Jews of Europe.[42] *The New Outlook* deemed this general lack of action unacceptable. Other Canadian Christians should take a "realistic look" at their own discipleship and do likewise.[43] As European Christians were also in flight from Nazi oppression, the refugee problem was a Christian as well as a Jewish problem and should be recognized as such.[44] The Evian Conference, although unsuccessful—one delegate described it as a "modern wailing wall"[45]—revealed the scope of the crisis, as well as its urgency; a disinterested response in aid of both Jewish and Christian refugees was required on the part of the churches.[46] Both the *Anschluss*, or forced unification of Austria with the German Reich in March 1938, and Hitler's seizure of Czechoslovakia almost exactly a year later, had created a mass of new Jewish hostages, shifting the balance. It was shortly before the Czech débacle that the following editorial was published:

> A Hangman's lot is not a happy one. No one envies the public executioner, but circumstances have placed us all in a position where merely our indifference will pronounce the doom of at least a million men and women. The refugee problem has been placed on our doorsteps and we can neither minimize it nor ignore it. The periodic outbursts of anti-Semitism in Germany are not accidental; they are part of a deliberate policy, and it is interesting to note that the Schwarze Korps[47] ... has announced that Germany is faced with "the hard necessity of exterminating the Jewish underworld by those methods which we always use in dealing with criminals, namely, fire and sword." "The result," it adds, "would be the final end of Jewry, its total destruction."
>
> ... it is certain that both the immediate task of rescuing refugees, and the ultimate problem of settling them are matters in which "governments will be called upon to take more than an academically benevolent part." As Lord Castle Stewart has pointed out in a letter to the (London) *Times*, "It is a duty before God and their peoples that the English-speaking governments should act and act quickly."
>
> There are ... no clear promises of such prompt action, and there is every sign that the Canadian government, if it acts at all, will act with discreditable hesitation.... It is true that the House has just received a petition, signed by over a hundred thousand members of the chief French-Canadian patriotic society, protesting against all immigration, and, more especially against the admission of Jews. If, however, our government is to be intimidated by the narrowest forms of nationalist parochialism, it should forgo the luxury of associating with the other civilized nations in such statements as that issued by the Evian Conference ... if we do not translate our professions into practice a very horrible chapter will be written in the history of human hypocrisy.... To keep out others, when our own house is largely empty, is to be "guilty of a political immoralism as grave in its implications as the crude immoralism of the Nazis."
>
> ... We might expect the Churches of Canada to be courageous and humane, but on this subject there has been (officially at least) a disconcerting silence.... We are the largest Protestant denomination in this country, and we pride ourselves on being a progressive Church, with a sensitive social conscience.... Where the Church leads so haltingly, is it surprising that the government stumbles?[48]

The prescience of the editorialist, as well as the force of his appeal, remains undiminished over fifty years later. Like the augurs of old, he seemed to sense the shape of things to come. Paradoxically, his words both confirm the charge that the churches were silent or largely silent, and refute it. Other United Church voices of the day also spoke in favour of rescue.

Nineteen thirty-nine was the year of the royal visit. In January, Silcox urged Canadians to welcome King George VI and Queen Elizabeth to Canada by demonstrating to their sovereign and his consort that the "spirit of British fair-play" was "still alive in this Dominion by our answer to the challenge of the refugees."[49] In April, Ernest Marshall Howse preached two sermons on the refugee situation in his large Winnipeg church (Westminster) based on the Matthaean text (25:40): "Inasmuch as ye have done it unto one of the least of these my brethren, ye have done it unto me." The sermons were broadcast on the radio, and later published for local distribution.[50] Both referred explicitly, though not exclusively, to the Jews, and both called for the relaxation of the rigid immigration laws hindering their sanctuary in Canada. The refugees, Howse declared, particularly the Jewish refugees, far from swamping the country with undesirable types, would prove to be "refined gold from a very fierce crucible."[51] How many other United Church sermons called for succour with similar arguments can never be known.

The first signs of official as opposed to sermonic and journalistic concern from the United Church were emitted in 1937, when the Board of Evangelism and Social Service followed the thirty-one ecumenical church representatives in urging the government to provide a haven for at least a "reasonable number of selected refugees from certain countries in Europe."[52] Once again, Silcox played the part of helmsman. Once again, the language was hedged in order not to stir public alarm. Once again, the selected refugees would not be Jewish only, though Jews were to be included. A year later, the same board endorsed the activities of the newly constituted Canadian National Committee on Refugees and Victims of Political Persecution (CNCR),[53] headed by Senator Cairine Wilson. Its own newly appointed secretary, James R. Mutchmor, was a charter member.[54] This committee of "Canada's righteous," as it has been described,[55] acted as a modern equivalent of those mediaeval Jewish *shtadlonim* who once represented Jews in gentile courts.[56] Its mandate was to loosen the rigid immigration restrictions through quiet lobbying in the corridors of power. Local presbytery committees across the nation were encouraged to give the matter "careful and constructive thought" and to work toward the "creation of a favourable public opinion" in order to strengthen the senator's hand in Ottawa.[57] The senator's hand certainly needed strength-ening, since, as is now known, behind the scenes in the capital city, an "unofficial, unholy triumvirate" consisting of the Immigration Branch, the federal cabinet and the Department of External Affairs was doing everything in its power to prevent Jewish refugees from setting foot on Canada's shores.[58]

A few presbyteries began issuing statements. On September 16, 1938, for example, the Montreal Presbytery deplored "the continued and bitter persecution of the Jewish people" and called on the "citizens and Government of Canada to do everything in their power ... to help the per-secuted and hopeless [by admitting] as large a number as possible" to the country.[59] Similar resolutions were passed by the Cobourg and Kingston presbyteries in Ontario.[60] Jewish refugees were specified for the first time in a Board of Evangelism and Social Service report in 1939, no doubt in reaction to the nationalistic St. Jean Baptiste Society in Quebec, a body openly hostile to immigrants in general and Jews in particular.[61] The sud-den creation of a much larger Jewish crisis with Hitler's depredations, end-ing "all illusions about Nazi moderation,"[62] had helped to bring the Jewish dimension of the refugee issue into sharper focus. In 1939 also, as a result of pressure from the Sub-Executive of the General Council,[63] which in turn was responding to the National Committee in Ottawa, pro-refugee motions were introduced in the many regional conferences of the church from coast to coast.[64] Virtually all were adopted. In Manitoba, the peppery Howse played no small part in persuading his fellow church delegates to line up in support. Presbyteries and individual congregations also pro-duced pro-refugee resolutions for public and political consumption; in his study of Canada's refugee policy, Gerald E. Dirks cites one such plea from the Lambton Presbytery, Ontario.[65] Even small groups, such as the Women's Auxiliary of St. Paul's-Avenue Road Church, Toronto, the Women's Missionary Society of the United Church, Welwyn, Saskatchewan, and the Women's Missionary Society of the United Church, Chilliwack, British Columbia, wrote letters to Liberal cabinet ministers. A remark made by David Rome, the archivist of the Canadian Jewish Congress, is apropos: the women might as well have saved their breath![66]

During the war years, when patriotic feelings came into play, and anti-Germanism became a new component in the Canadian consciousness, the cause of the refugees required renewed justification. Hence, when the Board of Evangelism and Social Service commended the National Committee and its work once again to the church in 1940, stressing the "tragically changed conditions in Europe," it was necessary to argue that

"German-born" refugees (i.e., Jews) would make desirable immigrants.[67] The fact that many of the refugees were children lent a poignant character to the crisis, and, in the eyes of the church, rendered both outrageous and ridiculous the obstructionism of Ottawa in demanding the death certificates of vanished parents before the children could be awarded sanctuary.[68] As a small contribution to alleviating the situation, the United Church declared itself willing to settle one hundred such small victims, both Jewish and Christian, in suitable homes "if and when child refugees are admitted to Canada."[69] Inevitably, once war began, other concerns occupied centre stage. However, in 1941, the board once again recorded its opposition to all who are "imbued with hatred of the Jewish people," although not without adding the reflection that Christian attitudes today will determine "the strength of the Christian Gospel message among Jewish people tomorrow."[70]

In 1943 the same board called for the deliverance of Jews stranded in a nervous Portugal, one of the remaining neutral asylums in Europe.[71] Hopes for international Allied action had been raised only to be dashed by the Anglo-American Bermuda Conference, which released its long delayed final report on November 19, revealing itself, like its predecessor Evian, as simply a colossal sham designed to thwart rather than assist rescue.[72] Consequently the church, in conjunction with the National Committee, endorsed a nation-wide petition on behalf of the refugees, especially those in Portugal (although Jews were not specified), for distribution among its rank and file.[73] At least one presbytery (Middlesex, Ontario) caught the spirit, voting to support Senator Wilson.[74] From his Bathurst Street pulpit in Toronto, Gordon Domm assailed the opponents of a more charitable rescue policy, accusing them of antisemitism; his sermon was published in the *Observer*.[75] Unhappily, even the proponents of rescue could be accused occasionally of this vice, judging from stray comments such as Mutchmor's warning to a Winnipeg correspondent in an otherwise sympathetic letter that "Organized Jewry is busy and ... will need watching."[76]

Claris E. Silcox

Of the various players in the drama, a single figure commands particular attention: Claris Edwin Silcox (1888-1961). The son of one of the founding fathers of the church union movement in Canadian Congregationalism, Silcox was ordained in the American Congregational Church, a denomination in which he served four pastorates, but became intimately associated with the United Church of Canada, on which he wrote an important study.[77] A graduate of the University of Toronto, Brown University and Andover Theological Seminary, the first half of his career was spent in the United States and the latter half in Canada. During his American sojourn, he worked for the Rockefeller Institute of Social and Religious Research. The fateful year of 1934 witnessed his return to his own country. Widely travelled in both Europe and the Americas, he prided himself on possessing an international perspective that few churchmen of his generation could rival. He also possessed strong opinions, activist instincts, and a taste for ethical issues. Intellectually, he was a child of the social gospel.

It was during his American days that he grew interested in Jewish-Christian relations and the problem of antisemitism. In January 1929, he organized the first seminar on Catholic, Protestant and Jewish religious differences at Columbia University, and in May 1934, the first Canadian seminar on Jewish-Gentile relations, which met in the King Edward Hotel, Toronto. In 1934 also, he became the general secretary of the Christian Social Service Council of Canada, the predecessor of the Canadian Council of Churches,[78] and an ecumenical body deeply involved in social and moral questions;[79] this was the occasion for his final homecoming. In 1938 he joined the executive of Senator Wilson's National Committee as one of its most ardent and zealous members: in fact, he was one of its progenitors.[80] Queen's University awarded him an honorary doctorate in 1939. In 1940 he resigned from his first office to become the director of the Canadian National Conference of Christians and Jews.

A man of his times, Silcox was by no means free of false predilections; indeed, a not-so-subtle odour of Christian sanctimoniousness can be sniffed even in his calls for dialogue and his tracts against antisemitism.[81] Nor was he free from certain dubious and cliché-ridden assumptions about Jews and Judaism of a type often found in popular western literature.[82] Nor were his social views always above reproach, as his opposition to the introduction of family allowances in Canada as "a bad thing biologically" serves as a notorious example.[83] Nor were his opinions on the Middle East, which came to fruition in the post-war years, devoid of bias. A hostile 1956 article on Zionism actually caused its author to fall under suspicion as a possible antisemite himself, or at least as a Christian in the grip of residual antisemitism.[84] Because of these feelings, Silcox was criticized for glibness and historical inaccuracy—his ignorance of the nature and history of the Zionist idea was certainly abysmal—by his Jewish allies in Canada.[85]

Nevertheless, on some public issues Silcox was manifestly ahead of most Christians of his day. Like the avant-garde British Anglican theologian James Parkes,[86] and like the great American Protestant theologian Reinhold Niebuhr,[87] he believed that the Jewish passion for social justice constituted the "supreme contribution of the Jews ... in the field of religion."[88] It was natural, therefore, for Silcox, who regarded Hitler as a man destined to make the name of Germany a "stench in the annals of history," to rally to the side of the embattled Jewish people.[89] From his vantage point in the Social Service Council, he established a personal bond with the Canadian Jewish Congress, addressing its third plenary session in Montreal in 1936 on the need for "new techniques" in the struggle against the ever-assiduous and inventive antisemites.[90] When the Wilson committee was formed in 1938, he was instrumental in securing non-Jewish support and in promoting its cause among the churches.[91] Among other things, a day of prayer was planned, and a Parkes visit to Canada was arranged. Plunging into action, the champion of the refugees attempted to turn the tables on the nativists who railed against the racial dilution of Canada's "native" stock. In a radio address later published in a Quaker journal, Silcox defended the German Jews as better Anglo Saxons than the Anglo Saxons:

> And, after all, what do we need most on this continent—the Anglo-Saxon blood or the Anglo-Saxon spirit? Is it not primarily the Anglo-Saxon spirit, the love of freedom, the capacity for self-discipline, the regard for fair-play, the intellectual eagerness, the respect for cultural and scientific attainment, the political *savoir-faire* that knows how to deal with all kinds of minorities? Is it not this which we most need in Canada? And where in all the world are we more apt to find it than among those refugees now seeking a new home?[92]

Anglo Saxon democracy was certainly imperilled, but not at the hands of Jews; indigenous fascist groups, some of them composed of "racial" Anglo Saxons, posed the true danger. As a result, the Secretary of the Social Service Council was forced to devote most of this time to combating their influence, which meant combating antisemitism, since, as he recognized clearly, the latter was the spearhead of the totalitarian assault on his treasured democratic institutions.[93] This sent him on the stump in western Canada in 1939, where he helped to organize local refugee committees, attracting considerable attention in the media.[94] If the antisemites succeed, he told his audiences, democracy will fail; if they fail, the democratic way of life might manage to weather the storm.[95] The message was especially pertinent in Alberta, where the doctrines of Major Douglas had many disciples:

We find people in our own country who seek to lay the blame for all our economic woes on the Jews, they circulate the lies of the Master-prevaricator, Goebbels. They disseminate the report that the Jews control the finances of the country when there is not a single Jew on the directorate of any Canadian bank. They claim that the Jews control the basic industries of the country, whereas except in a few light industries, the charge might more truly be laid against our Scottish industrialists! They claim that the Jews never do any pioneering work whereas they landed in the New World a century before any Anglo-Saxons settled here, and they were with Wolfe on the plains of Abraham.

... as a Christian people, we do homage to the King of Kings and Lord of Lords. Let us show Him who was the Son of God and the son of a Jewish mother ... that for many of these poor people, His half-brothers and half-sisters, there is yet room in the clamant and crowded inn ... even in this vast and underpopulated Dominion, where these persecuted souls ... may at length find sanctuary....[96]

A public address in Convocation Hall at the University of Toronto on March 21 of the same year examined the reasons for Canada's aborted response, including intellectual and moral confusion, labour fears, farming fears, business fears, Quebec xenophobia, Nazi propaganda (especially in Quebec, Ontario, Manitoba and Saskatchewan) and, of course, latent antisemitism in the nation at large.[97] A feeble policy, he declared, citing a pre-World War I general, always works harm. Other speeches issued in succession from his pen, most finding their way into print. Silcox was also co-chairman with Maurice Eisendrath of the increasingly vocal Committee on Jewish-Gentile Relationships, Toronto, through which a Christian campaign against antisemitism was mounted involving lectures and the dissemination of anti-Nazi literature, particularly in United and Anglican churches.[98] Moreover, Silcox strongly opposed the decision of the National Committee to expunge references to the Jews from its wartime petition: the result of pressure from its more nativist Winnipeg branch.[99] He believed, though others dissented, that such an omission rendered the petition useless.

Neither as a preacher-educator nor as a lobbyist was Silcox really successful, at least in the short run; the government remained intransigent, and public opinion could not be mobilized to an extent sufficient to crack its resolve. Therefore, he can be read as a courageous failure, breaking his lances, like Robert Browning's poetic protagonist, against the dark tower.[100] Even in the United Church, he was on the periphery, a somewhat marginal figure who stood outside its usual courts and ministries. Yet, for all his flaws, some of them serious, he embodied as much as anyone the conscience of Christian Canada, and his labours, as well as those of others, eventually bore fruit in the post-war era when the nation finally experienced a change of heart and liberalized its immigration policies. The personal anguish that he endured in the death of his wife, his son and his daughter while engaged in his campaign only magnifies his stature.

The Holocaust

To what extent was Canada's largest Protestant denomination aware of Hitler's "Final Solution" while the machinery of death was still in operation? The truth, the real truth, dawned slowly. However, some United Church members seem to have believed the worst almost as soon as whispers from eastern Europe filtered through Nazi camouflage to ears in the west. On October 11, 1942, Howse employed a lurid but not inappropriate analogy in the Winnipeg Civic Auditorium: "The scourge has fallen upon defenceless people as perhaps earth has not seen it since at the seige of Jerusalem a savage soldiery in one night ripped open the bellies of 2000 Jews to see if they has swallowed the gold of the temple."[101] When the World Jewish Congress released its inside information concerning the true nature of the Final Solution during the following month, the notion of deliberate total destruction became less incredible. On April 15, 1943, Silcox wrote of a "holocaust"—the use of this term was noteworthy—in Europe, and lamented the fact that so few brands had been plucked from the burning.[102] On May 15, 1943, Kenneth Leslie of the Fellowship for a Christian Social Order, a group of mostly United Church social radicals, spoke of a "war against the Jews" with 2,000,000 dead in a "sadist festival of hell" at a FCSO conference in Metropolitan United Church, Toronto.[103] Finally, on September 15, 1944, the *Observer* put aside its earlier doubts and published this confession:

> For some time we were reluctant to accept at face value the accounts which occasionally leaked out of the atrocities perpetrated by the Nazis against conquered people.... But Lidice changed all that.... There have been statistics ... that of three million Jews in Poland, all but one hundred thousand have been exterminated by the Nazis. The publication of these figures did not arouse the conscience of the world, perhaps again because we were defending ourselves against propaganda. But now that reputable American correspondents ... give us eye witness accounts of the scientifically brutal way in which men, women and little children were destroyed in mass murder gas chambers, there is no escaping the conviction that in our own generation there has been carried out the greatest murder plot of

all ages. The story told by correspondents of Lublin's extermination camp in Poland ... is ... horrifying beyond description.[104]

Apparently, Jewish reports alone were insufficient to convince sceptical Canadians; American reports, however, were a different matter. This was unfortunate, to say the least, but it should not be judged too severely, since, as the Holocaust historian Michael Marrus has pointed out, no one at the time, including Jews themselves, were predisposed to believe the unbelievable: "To a degree, everyone was in the dark."[105] Hearing, manifestly, is not the same as knowing, a more complex process. Information is one thing, knowledge is another; at last, however, the church *knew*!

By confirming the worst fears of the alarmists, the revelation vindicated those who had caught the scent of evil in the German Reich from its inauguration, and had warned against it. From the first signs of persecution, the dark essence of the Nazi system was noted and denounced in the official press of the United Church of Canada, and, on occasion, in its boards and courts, as well as from its pulpits and at public meetings. This happened despite the initial allure of the new European social order for a segment of its membership. Furthermore, the struggle of the church against antisemitism grew more resolute with the realization that the disease was not restricted to the far side of the Atlantic Ocean, but existed in Canada as well. As German anti-Jewish measures grew more extreme, this struggle intensified. Even before the war, on both the local and national levels, the United Church leadership displayed a keen interest in saving Hitler's victims, both Jews and non-Jews, in the face of the popular anti-immigrant sentiments and policies of the era. This interest deepened as the crisis mounted. "Among the Protestant Churches, the United Church of Canada was the CNCR's greatest ally"—so, at least, one study claims.[106] To be sure, no sustained mass outcry erupted on behalf of the refugees among the church rank-and-file; that deplorable fact must be acknowledged. Only sporadically, as with a public rally in Winnipeg against early Nazi anti-Jewish violence in April 1933 ("one of the biggest single-purpose demonstrations in the history of the city"[107]) and with the post-*Kristallnacht* rallies across the nation on November 20, 1938, did anything occur resembling mass protest in Canada, and these occasions probably involved more Jews than Christians. As a religious community, the United Church at large was silent, but not that silent. Institutionally, if editorials, letters, resolutions and sermons count for anything, and if speech is the opposite of silence, it was not silent at all. Far more was said than the post-mortems of our day have acknowledged.

IV

The Church of England in Canada

THE CHURCH OF ENGLAND IN CANADA, like the United Church of Canada, had many areas of restricted vision. Too many of its clergy harboured anti-Jewish ideas far longer than either conscience or historical sensitivity should have allowed, filling the pages of Anglican religious literature with inaccurate and antiquated images offensive to modern scholarship.[1] Examples abound. In the words of one traditionalist, the Pharisaic ancestors of rabbinic Judaism were legalistic, merciless and blind creatures whose religion was nothing more than a "monstrous creation of human ingenuity ... a system from which the light of God and the love of God had been shut out."[2] Such, in all probability, was more or less the state of conventional Anglican opinion, not only in the pre-war era but also during the war itself. Even the haunting presentiment of mass murder did not constitute a reason to refrain from attacking the Pharisees in columns and sermons as the representatives of the religion that had "crucified Christ."[3] Anti-Judaism was a legitimate posture for Christians to adopt, and apart from exceptional church figures such as James Parkes in England, no one thought that it bore any relationship to antisemitism. What did the stigmatization of a vanished religious party in ancient Judaea have do with Adolf Hitler and his stigmatization of Jews in modern Germany? Nothing, as far as most of the church was concerned.

Some Anglicans, moreover, at least in the volatile thirties, felt the same measure of attraction to the new social order in Europe as did some United Church members, even (in one case) for its harsh approach to the much-mooted Jewish problem. They were pro-German. Two were famous, although English rather than Canadian, but in the Anglicanism of the time this fact is almost beside the point. The Church of England in Canada regarded itself as an extension of the Church of England proper, and held the prelates, deans and theologians of the mother church in great esteem. Their moral authority among Canadian Anglicans can only be

---

Notes to this chapter are on pp. 152-156.

described as immense, judging from the number of times that the archbishops of Canterbury and York, not to mention lesser lights, were cited
in the branch church. A.C. Headlam, bishop of Gloucester and chairman
of the Church of England's Council on Foreign Relations, and W.R. Inge,
the famed "gloomy dean" of St. Paul's Cathedral, London, gloomy
because of his sceptical approach to some cherished orthodox doctrines,
both adopted a somewhat soft approach to fascism and its concomitants.
Since the two men were eminent intellectuals—Inge was an expert on
neo-Platonism—as well as ecclesiastical statesmen, their views received
respectful attention, even across the seas.

Headlam and Inge

Bishop Headlam, writing in 1933, reacted to early accounts of Nazi Jew-
baiting by warning the German Jews that violence begets violence and
that their own subversive attitudes and activities in Christian society
explained and almost justified the heavy hand that the new Reich had
decided to raise against them.

> We all condemn the folly and the violence of the attacks upon the Jews
> in Germany, and the violence with which the members of the Socialist
> and Communist parties are being treated, but to both Jews and Socialists
> some words of warning are necessary. Many Jews were responsible, par-
> ticularly at the beginning, for the violence of the Russian Communists;
> many Jews have helped to inspire the violence of the Socialist communi-
> ties.... Those of alien nationality who receive the hospitality of other
> countries ought to recognize that wisdom and gratitude alike demand
> that they should become healthy elements in the population. So in the
> same way our English Socialists at present are violent in their attacks
> upon Germany, and are proposing to boycott German goods. We cannot
> help remembering that they have shown little desire to condemn the far
> worse atrocities which have been perpetuated [perpetrated?] in Russia,
> that both in Germany and in England they have often threatened the
> same things, that they are proposing to break up and destroy our inher-
> ited social life with all of its traditions, that they attack our religion. It is
> they who first of all made the appeal to violence.... If it is legitimate for
> the Socialist or Communist to employ force to carry out a revolution, it
> is equally legitimate for a Nazi.... Again, although we think they are
> wrong, we have respect for the Jew who faithfully adheres to his religious
> customs, but many Jews take no interest in their own faith, are free-
> thinkers, and use their Judaism very largely as a basis for attacking the
> Christian faith.[4]

If Hitler has been unkind, his victims must have deserved their blows! So, at least, this outburst implies. Jews, communists and socialists, including British socialists, all seem to have been more or less one and the same to the anti-socialist Tory bishop. An influential figure in English Anglicanism, Headlam was predictably hostile to the German anti-Nazi Confessing Church and a personal rival of the much less pro-German George Bell, bishop of Chichester, who pleaded the cause of the anti-Nazi German Christians, including Martin Niemöller and Dietrich Bonhöffer.[5] To Headlam, writing in 1938, the recently imprisoned Niemöller was simply a "troublesome clergyman" who deserved his incarceration, whereas the German clergymen who supported the Nazi regime were simply good "orthodox" evangelical pastors.[6] The bishop of Gloucester was not a supporter of fascist politics in Britain, although Sir Oswald Mosley's Jew-baiting British Union of Fascists (Blackshirts) was enjoying its heyday, but his ecclesiastical and political conservatism was certainly tainted with anti-Jewish and authoritarian feelings. Nor was he the only upper-class Englishman at the time to be so affected. A tremendous fear of communism fed an almost fashionable (in some circles) admiration for German anti-Sovietism and seeming defence of "Christian" civilization.

Inge was more moderate. In 1936 *The Canadian Churchman* published a series of short articles from his pen analyzing the new ideologies of the day, including communism, fascism and National Socialism, for the benefit of local Anglicans. These "substitutes for religion" are dangerous to Christianity, the British dean believed, particularly communism; nevertheless, fascism had "saved" Italy from communism, and thus commands a degree of admiration—Mussolini was "easily the biggest man in Europe."[7] As Mussolini is explained by Mazzini, the father of Italian nationalism, the dean continued, so Hitler is explained by Fichte, the father of German nationalism. If the West does not like Hitler, the West has only itself to blame. The resurgence of German nationalism after 1918 was more the fault of the victorious allies, especially the French—"Poincaré and Clemenceau are responsible for Hitler"—than of the Germans themselves.[8] Inge himself, as he took pains to explain, was neither a fascist nor a Nazi, nor did he approve of concentration camps, Jew-baiting or sabre rattling.[9] However, he was a British isolationist who regarded the Duce and the Führer merely as overheated nationalists who had good as well as bad sides. After all, Germany was a great nation, and great nations do not allow themselves to be ruled by monsters. If unpleasant things were happening inside its borders, neither Hitler nor his subjects should be accused unduly. The German leader was really the product of French, British and

American lack of fair play. As late as September 1938, Inge seems to have regarded France rather than Germany as the cause of evil in Europe.[10]

"Liberty-loving Anglo Saxons"

Anglican opinion in Canada did not readily accept this kind of philo-Germanism, even from highly placed overseas churchmen. Even more than the United Church, the Church of England in Canada was profoundly attached to the imperial connection and consequently to British ideas and institutions, which were seen as the quintessence of the Anglo Saxon racial and spiritual heritage. As political democracy in its parliamentary form was an important part of this heritage, no true Anglican could turn easily to non-democratic ideologies without betraying both his or her Anglicanism and his or her essential, if derivative, "Englishness." Although "our old system has been seriously weakened," declared John C. Farthing, bishop of Montreal, in 1933, and although some Canadians "are anxious to throw over the existing order of things, and are willing to try Socialism, Communism, Fascism, Hitlerism, or any other.... We Anglo Saxons will never consent to the loss of our liberty."[11] Canadians tempted to take such a disloyal step were blind and foolish. When the Italian-Abyssinian conflict erupted in 1935, *The Canadian Churchman* took a different view from Dean Inge of the man who had "saved" Italy. "We must think of the Italian nation as drunk with the wine of war, made forcibly drunk by its own government, not of its own choice."[12] The fact that Italy was angry at Britain as a result of British opposition to the Duce's dream of a new Roman empire did not help his reputation in Canadian Anglican eyes. Mussolini became one with Hitler. In 1937, Farthing addressed his synod in uncompromising tones:

> Fascism, whether it is under the form of the paganism of Nazi Germany; or the ruthless militarism of Italy, as seen in the rape of Ethiopia, culminating in the appalling massacre of Addis Ababa, which will go down as one of the most inhuman in history, and as the darkest blot on our modern civilization; is everywhere the negation of all for which Christ stands. In Germany it has now come out boldly as pagan, which it has been in spirit since its inception; in Italy it still seeks to hide its barbarity under the mantle of the Church, while its leader ridicules the principles of Christ.
>
> The propagandists of these systems are found in every country in the world, and with wonderful enthusiasm are working night and day, hammering at our gates, and burrowing under the foundations of every

institution, seeking to destroy all that we cherish most.... Do we realize
... what a perfect hell such a condition of life would be to us liberty-
loving Anglo-Saxons?[13]

Not quite the darkest blot on modern civilization, however; that distinction, as the church came to realize later, was reserved for the
destruction of the European Jews. But the bishop's prognostication of
hell was on the right track.

"Us liberty-loving Anglo Saxons!" This refrain, echoed again and
again by Anglican writers, can be regarded as a visceral Anglican response
to the rise of totalitarianism throughout the entire pre-war and war periods. An imperial patriotism detected the "menace of fascism" almost from
the moment of its inception, and, in spite of the Anglo Saxon "love" of
democracy—fascist methods suited the "truculent German bully" rather
than the "English sportsman"—the menace was almost as great in Britain
(and Canada) as in Germany and Italy.[14] When the Italian fascists started
to ape the anti-Jewish tactics of the German fascists, Anglican disaffection
with Italy's so-called saviour was complete.[15] Nor did the emergence of
imitation organizations in Canada pass unnoticed by local Anglicans.
Adrien Arcand's headline-grabbing Quebec "Blueshirts" drew Bishop
Farthing's fire for their unChristian and unBritish antisemitic spirit and
policies, as well as for their insurrectionist threats, even if Arcand, curiously and no doubt insincerely, professed loyalty to the British Empire.[16]
If democracy was to survive, eternal vigilance was necessary. Like termites,
the enemies of freedom were chewing away.

Indigenous to all forms of modern fascism is the leadership cult, with
its short-circuiting of representative institutions in favour of a mystical
rapport between the leader and the nation. Believing that their politicians
had failed, some Canadians—no one knows how many—longed for such
autocratic leaders as a panacea for the national ills in a troubled time. This
option was rejected in Canada, but the spell cast by the European dictators was difficult to counter. While the brutal side of the National Socialist
revolution in Germany was evident from the beginning, a curious but by
no means unique tendency to distinguish between the Führer and his fol-
lowers also appeared in Anglican as well as in other Christian circles.
"What we have to fear ... is not Hitler himself, but some of the wild men
behind him, the sadistic perverts, the nationalist-maniacs, the bull-headed
young men who want excitement at all costs, whom Hitler himself no
doubt has considerable trouble in controlling."[17] In retrospect, this blindness is not so surprising, since many Germans shared it, and since their
ruler was a consummate actor who had mastered many parts. However, in

mainstream Anglo Saxon Canadian Protestantism, Hitler was seldom idealized, least of all among Anglicans; rather, his mystical leadership was distrusted and occasionally dissected with merciless clarity. The evocative sermon "Follow Me," preached by W.J. Gilling, the chaplain of Trinity College, Toronto, before a 1938 conference of Anglican youth, is a good example. To Gilling, the totalitarian state, draped with the trappings of divinity, had an appetite for blood not unlike Huitzilpochtli, the savage god of the Aztecs.

> Take any meeting in Germany today where the Fuehrer is to speak. There are songs, the roll of drums and martial music. Slowly in the intense beam of the limelight advances the figure of the Fuehrer, guarded by his SS men, escorted by his adjutants, advancing with martial air and military step until they reach the platform. The party-banners surround him, the crooked cross envelopes him, and they behold their god—the saviour of the Germanic peoples, the builder of the greater Reich. The human sacrifice is, it is true, usually conducted off-stage. In prison cells and concentration camps is spilled the blood, is exacted the anguish which shall glut the appetite of the Man-God.[18]

Overwrought? No.

"That ancient race"

From the dawn of the Nazi era, the Anglicans were not delinquent in condemning the shameful treatment meted out to the German Jews, even if their condemnations were often laced with old-hat anti-Jewish ideas, as well as pietistic hopes for their conversion.[19] A 1935 report of the [Anglican] Montreal Jewish Mission drew attention to German neopaganism in order to underscore its guiding philosophy that "Christ alone is the final solution."[20] In light of subsequent events, a more unfortunate term could not have been chosen. A Good Friday pastoral letter in 1938 from the archbishop of Toronto, Derwyn Owen, who was also the primate of Canada, reflects the same duality:

> The return of Good Friday reminds us once more of the debt which we owe the Jews, and of our responsibility to share with them ... that which we have ourselves found in Jesus Christ. The presence in the world today of all that is meant by the term "anti-Semitism" and its consequences, gives to the Jews a new claim on our sympathies. As people who profess and call ourselves Christians we have witnessed with horror and regret the sufferings and injustices which have been done to them. This distress also lends urgency to the need of evangelism among them....[21]

To the archbishop, conversion was the cure for the material as well as the alleged spiritual problems of the Jews, including the menace of anti-semitism. Many Anglicans clung to this simplistic view, even during the war years, as did many non-Anglicans. But the material problems were not minimized.

Throughout the entire Hitlerian tyranny, the British church, which was closer in any case to the European continent, and thus better informed than its daughter institution, supplied the latter with up-to-date reports and apropos editorial comment. Following the British lead, the Canadian Anglicans dutifully decried the Aryan laws and their harsh consequences in the new Reich.[22] When, in the mid-thirties, Hitler's regime was on its best behaviour because of the forthcoming Olympic games, the editor of *The Canadian Churchman* asserted that it was "high time that the public opinion of the world was aroused at the condition of the Jews in Germany," pointing to their "pitiable" and "doomed" situation.[23] James G. McDonald was cited approvingly: "It is being made increasingly difficult for Jews and 'Non-Aryans' in Germany to sustain life. Condemned to segregation within the four corners of the legal and social Ghetto which has now closed upon them, they are increasingly prevented from earning their living. Indeed more than half of the Jews remaining in Germany have already been deprived of their livelihood. In many parts of the country there is a systematic attempt at starvation of the Jewish population."[24] Once the Olympics have ended, the editor continued, the Jews expect a new terror, not without reason. Judging from the intensifying denunciations of Nazi policy in Canadian Anglicanism in the latter half of the decade, they were not alone in their expectations. In New Brunswick, Archbishop J.A. Richardson of Fredericton addressed his diocesan synod on the "appalling persecution of the Jews in Germany," reminding his hearers of the need for Christian remonstration.[25] Even doggerel verse was employed to stir the conscience of the faithful:

> If Jesus lived in Germany
>   And plied His craft today,
> Doing His Honest carpentry
>   In His own perfect way,
> Oh! would He find His workshop wrecked
>   By some mad Nordic crew—
> His windows labelled: "Men, beware!
>   Within there works a Jew?"
>
> Oh! you who name the Name of Christ,
>   And claim to walk His ways,

> Can you join the Jews' oppressors
> In these last evil days?
> If you persecute His people
> Your [sic] pierce His heart anew—
> They were His kinsmen here on earth;
> Your Lord was born a Jew![26]

Kristallnacht confirmed the fears of a new terror and focused Anglican attention on antisemitism and certain related evils to an unprecedented degree. As the world moved inexorably toward a clash of the titans, this preoccupation with the crimes of the German state toward both Jews and Christians—the church struggle was also a constant concern—acquired a more impassioned tone. On the front cover of its February 23, 1939 issue, *The Canadian Churchman* featured in bold print a call for its readers to pray for the "Jews of all lands"—the "stunned, desperate, tortured victims of demonic hate," many of whom were being "slowly starved out of existence."[27] Antisemitism, the readership was told, is inherently unChristian, and anathema to a religious community nurtured on the ethical and spiritual insights of ancient Israel.[28] At least, it should be anathema, but, as Conrad Hoffman had said earlier (in part I of a republished speech),[29] the most tragic aspect of the European situation resided in the fact that so many European Christians were contaminated with the same disease as the National Socialists and were assisting the persecutors. Not only European Christians, moreover: Canadian Christians were also contaminated. The circulation of "venomous" anti-Jewish literature on the home front was deplored by the Anglicans with equal vigour.[30] Correctly suspecting Nazi propaganda behind the current antisemitic movement in Quebec (Arcand and his ilk), Archdeacon F.G. Scott of Quebec City wrote to the *Montreal Gazette* to express his outrage and that of a "large proportion" of the citizenry: "Narrowness and bigotry must not be allowed to take root in Canadian soil."[31]

These condemnations were not isolated. As early as April 1933, the Synod of the Diocese of Montreal recorded its "sincere sympathy" for the suffering Jews of the new German Reich.[32] The local Jewish mission began its 1934 report by alluding to their "bitter persecution."[33] On September 20, 1934, the Lower House of the General Synod of the nation-wide church passed an unequivocal resolution:

> *Resolved*: That, the Upper House concurring, the General Synod of the Church of England in Canada extend to the Jewish people throughout the world its profound sympathy in view of the present world situation respecting that ancient race. That the General Synod has an adequate

sense of the great debt that the world owes to the Jewish people with their contribution to human knowledge in the realms of Science, Literature and Religion. Above all, it would acknowledge with deep thankfulness that the great treasury of revealed truth, the Old Testament Scriptures, was given and preserved through the instrumentality of the Jewish people; and it is ever mindful of the profound significance of the fact that Jesus Christ, our acknowledged Lord and Saviour, was, after the flesh, the Son of David. It deprecates as being a denial of the principles of Christianity, and therefore abhorrent to Christian people, the ill-treatment of the Jews, or any other people, by nations, communities or individuals on account of their race or religion....[34]

The Upper House (of Bishops) did concur.[35]

With these dignified words, the Anglican assembly declared its antipathy to the anti-Jewish measures across the Atlantic Ocean. Words, of course, are merely words and serve an expressive purpose only, and resolutions are merely resolutions, more often than not a means of evading action rather than a call to arms. They are easily ignored and soon forgotten. Yet, having placed itself on the side of the Jews, the church had committed itself morally to their assistance; the logic was inescapable. In the year of *Kristallnacht*, two diocesan synods, Niagara and Rupert's Land (Manitoba), reiterated Anglican sympathy for the Jewish plight, attaching, in the case of the latter, a rider pledging material aid for Jews in flight from Hitler, including a "place on the earth where they can live in peace and enjoy the freedom which is rightly theirs."[36] Predictably, in light of Anglican evangelical interests, the pledge of material aid was accompanied by a pledge of spiritual aid or the pious hope that the Jewish fugitives would discover a place of spiritual refuge in the Christian faith. This, however, was probably a motherhood statement; practical help was the obvious imperative of the hour. A number of highly placed Anglicans participated in the wave of protest rallies across Canada in the aftermath of the Nazi pogrom.[37] In Toronto, J.E. Ward, the rector of St. Stephen's Church, addressed a packed Maple Leaf Gardens on behalf of the Anglican primate.[38]

Every last refugee?

Canada, as we have seen, was in neither a pro-immigrant nor pro-refugee mood in the 1930s. For the Church of England in Canada, with its strong Anglo Saxon ethos and its fervent imperial loyalties, the suggestion that the nation should suddenly open its gates to masses of non-Anglo Saxon, non-British, non-Christian and frequently destitute strangers constituted a moral test of no small proportions. How did the Anglicans respond? Certainly, they shared the typical hesitations and apprehensions of the age, as well as its worst prejudices. Immigration, according to one expert, if permitted at all, should not be allowed on an indiscriminate basis; national (and doubtless racial) origin must be considered as "cheap men ... drive out dear men" according to "Gresham's law of population."[39] While this curious restatement of Gresham's law was never endorsed by any ecclesiastical body in Canada, a decided preference for immigrants of British stock, indeed, an anxiety concerning the consequences of a decline in the ratio of British to non-British immigrants, is clearly present in the various recommendations of Anglican officialdom throughout the pre-war period. Thus the "English-speaking" churches were urged in 1933 to form a council on British migration in order to assure the British government of their "united and unwavering" desire "to have more and yet more British people settled in Canada."[40] A renewed effort was made in 1937 to encourage a higher number of British settlers because of their "disturbing" recent decline in relation to European, especially south European, immigrants.[41] The Department of Immigration was urged to be vigilant in making certain that a "proper proportion" of the newcomers were British.[42] This concern was not regarded as reprehensible in any way during the proud days of empire, although any such proposal would draw instant castigation in the anti-racist and multicultural Canada of today. To preserve its general linguistic, ethnic and even racial character was the right and even the duty of every nation, according to received wisdom, and measures to secure this goal were in no wise to be considered as malignant.[43] The Anglicans simply took this principle for granted. So, in fact, did many others.

The British priority, however, was soon challenged. Troubled by the mounting persecution of Jews and "non-Aryan" Christians in Austria and Germany, the Anglican watchdogs began to have second thoughts. The refugee crisis posed a counter claim. In September 1938, the year of the failed Evian Conference, the Social Service Council of the Church of England in Canada confirmed the 1936 manifesto signed by thirty-one ecclesiastics[44] by passing its own resolution imploring the government to explore the question of "selected" Jewish immigration "so far as is possible and desirable."[45] When the cabinet ignored this and similar exhortations, the fact did not pass unnoticed. One of the participants at the inaugural meeting of the Canadian National Committee on Refugees and Victims of Political Persecution at the Chateau Laurier, Ottawa, was

H.H. Clark, priest-in-charge (later dean) of Christ Church Cathedral, Ottawa, and later primate of Canada.[46] During the same month, *The Montreal Churchman* republished an article from the *Australian Church Standard* excoriating the Australian government for dragging its feet on the refugee question. The implication was obvious:

> What is in the Government's mind is not clear, but we are somewhat perturbed by reading from time to time of what seem to be special measures directed against Jewish immigrants.... The desperate plight of European refugees should give them a prior claim.... At the same time, we may express our regret that signs of anti-Jewish sentiments are becoming apparent in certain quarters.[47]

Did Australia also have recalcitrant bureaucrats as well as recalcitrant politicians? Like their Australian cousins, some Canadian Anglicans were becoming suspicious.

In 1939, the year of the ill-fated *St. Louis* and other disasters, the Social Service Council reiterated its support for Jewish admissions, whether British or non-British:

> In this matter our Church, through its Council and through the Primate and other leaders, has let it be known that we regard this problem primarily on humanitarian and Christian grounds. It presents especially a call to the Christian Church.... The matter is one of deep-set prejudice in the mind [*sic*] of most people ... large sections of opinion, within the membership of the Churches as well as without, are inimical to the Jews and to the possibility of further Jewish immigration in any proportions.... The whole mass of (Nazi victims), Jewish and Christian, in their suffering and humiliation, in the breaking up of their families, in the deprivation of every individual, political and religious right, reveals a situation that has not been known since mediaeval days or the worst days of the Ghetto.... Canada requires several million more population. Among these people are thousands who can be provided for, and provide for themselves, in this vast country, in spite of depressed conditions.[48]

While they continued to prefer British immigrants, the Anglican policymakers gradually became more concerned with the preservation of British institutions and ideals than with the preservation of British racial hegemony. It was the Anglo Saxon *idea* that counted; Anglo Saxon *blood,* in the final analysis, guaranteed nothing. In fact, some Anglo Saxons, notably the leaders of the Canadian Communist Party, actually possessed subversive tendencies. Moreover, every subversive foreign language paper published in Canada was matched by at least one subversive English paper. "What ... must we as Anglo Saxons do?... We must change our attitude from one of self sufficiency and superiority, and we must acknowledge the potential values of these new compatriots (i.e., non-British immigrants). We must not destroy their native cultures but fuse them in a wider Canadian tradition."[49]

This debate over immigration policy, which, on a deeper level, was really a struggle against nativism, grew more vehement as the refugee crisis grew more acute. Refugees, of course, are not ordinary immigrants, and the niceties of ordinary immigration policy with its calculated quotas do not or should not apply. To some Anglicans, the carefully phrased qualifications of the official resolutions with their emphasis on selection and reasonable numbers were odious. Did not the Christian conscience require more, especially in the wake of the *St. Louis*? "What must our warm-hearted King and Queen ... be thinking as they read of that shipload of persecuted Jewry being sent back to Germany, and then recall the vast open spaces of the Canada they have just seen and, we believe, have learned to love?" asked a correspondent in *The Canadian Churchman*.[50] That his voice was not solitary is demonstrated by the spate of offers to adopt refugee families following the drama on the high seas, including one from a Toronto congregation,[51] perhaps prompted by a pro-refugee resolution of the local diocesan synod.[52] The government, however, rejected these applications.

Cecil J. Lamb, a small-town rector in Ontario, minced no words in castigating the selfishness of Canadians opposed to helping the Jews of Europe:

> The horror of the plight of the refugees was emphasized a month ago when a shipload of 907 homeless and despairing people, driven from their country by the Nazis, were refused a haven in South America. For three weeks they went from port to port, and because no nation in the so-called generous West was willing to receive them, were in danger of being dumped again on German soil.... I am going to suggest that we in Canada can take—if we have the courage and humanity to do so—every last refugee, man, woman and child in Europe ... there is no reason to believe that the rank and file will be any inferior—indeed they may be superior— as a group to millions of people who are already here, some of them foreign-born and others of our own "good American or Canadian stock." ... Our regulations—at least as far as the Jews are concerned—are almost prohibitive.... We are our brother's keeper whether we like it or not.[53]

Every last refugee? Lamb was not only far ahead of public opinion, but also ahead of much liberal opinion, as the ensuing squabble revealed. "Why do we not allow them to come? We have plenty of '*Lebensraum*,'" he repeated in 1941 when the *Einsatzgruppen* were conducting their massacres in eastern Europe in the wake of Hitler's legions in order to create a Germanic *Lebensraum*.[54] Why not, indeed? Unfortunately, as W.W. Judd, the general secretary of the Social Service Council, found himself arguing, public fears and apprehensions as well as political bureaucratic mean-spiritedness and sheer logistical objections had to be reckoned with by the pro-refugee forces.

> Churches, like other bodies, unhappily, sometimes have to deal with facts and practicalities.
>
> Is there not always a tension between idealism and realism, between hopes and facts?... In this instance, if we can get the Canadian Government ... to open the door even a few inches we shall do well and we shall be helping some of these sorrowful peoples. A demand at this time for a wide open door would in the end help to seal it fast.[55]

W.W. Judd

Canon William Wallace Judd (1883-1981), a native of Hamilton, Ontario, a graduate of Trinity College, Toronto, a parish priest in St. Catharines and Hamilton, a headmaster of King's College School in Windsor, Nova Scotia, became the social conscience gadfly of his church after he assumed charge of its Council for Social Service in 1936. Like Silcox, he was also an ecumenical statesman and a self-taught expert on Jewish-Christian relations in Canada. Inspired by William Temple, the brilliant socialist archbishop of both York and Canterbury who attempted to relate Christian principles to the social order,[56] Judd evidently stood in the same tradition of Anglican social radicalism as his British mentor. This tradition, however, formed in nineteenth-century Britain, had little apparent impact on the Canadian church,[57] although socialist and even Marxist circles seem to have existed in Toronto, Montreal and elsewhere among the Anglican intelligentsia in the 1940s.[58] Judd subscribed to Temple's famous maxim: "The art of government in fact is the art of so ordering life that self-interest prompts what justice demands."[59] This explains his appeal to realism with its "facts and practicalities" as he struggled to persuade the Canadian government to soften its anti-immigrant, anti-refugee policies. It was in the interest of Canada to admit newcomers prepared to invest their sweat in the economy. Moreover, as Judd must have known, national self-interest rather than humanitarianism had moved former Canadian governments when refugees from persecution had been admitted in the past, such as the Mennonites and the Doukhobors.[60]

Facts and practicalities, however, did not appeal to the idealists. While the nation might benefit from an influx of Jewish refugees—did not the great refugee waves of the past (Spanish Jews, French Huguenots, English pilgrims, United Empire Loyalists, etc.) bring unanticipated gifts to their countries of refuge?—a "truly Christian nation," *The Canadian Churchman* proclaimed, can never disregard the victims of history even if their succour serves no other end.[61] This noble sentiment was inspired by Conrad Hoffman's "Good Samaritan" plea for Christians to play a similar role in the modern world.[62] Judd believed in the Good Samaritan principle as fervently as Hoffman, but he also knew that governments are rarely susceptible to altruistic appeals unless they are tempered by some non-altruistic considerations. A pragmatist, who knew with whom and with what he was dealing, and an altruist, who believed that Christians could do better and that a Christian state could do very much better, he approached his task with both instincts, but his style was that of a lobbyist rather than a crusader.

A member of Senator Wilson's National Committee from its foundations, the Anglican emissary devoted himself to pestering governmental authorities, including the prime minister himself. His post-Evian letter to King (October 12, 1938) on behalf of his church was a gentle attempt to extract more than lip service to the refugee cause out of the cabinet: "The Council for Social Service of the Church of England in Canada ... realizing the great distress of these unhappy people, asks the Canadian Government to continue to explore the possibilities of help for them."[63] Together with Archbishop J.C. Roper of Ottawa and others, he struggled to dismantle the immigration web.[64] The problem, in his view, was one of deeply ingrained prejudice, and it was the task of the church to remake or at least to reeducate—the Social Service Council saw its role as educational—Canadian society in this and other matters in light of the "vision and the dream."[65] Thus he juggled the great code words of the day—Christianity, humanitarianism, democracy, national prosperity—hoping that one or the other would melt the public heart. His efforts increased in the war years, as the crisis deepened and the paucity of Canadian admissions grew more scandalous: "Under pressure our Canadian Government has admitted *a very few of these* [refugees and victims of political persecution] but, in the opinion of your Council, might be far more generous."[66] Canada simply had to rise to the occasion.

In 1943 things were more pitiful and desperate:

> At the present moment there are some 10,000 to 15,000 (refugees) in Portugal who have escaped over the Pyrenees.... Those rescued make room

for more to escape from conquered countries. Every one rescued is a life saved. There is here a challenge for humanity's sake, for sweet charity's sake. These, today, are among the offended "little ones" [many of the refugees were children] of the world for whom Christ spoke.[67]

The pathos of the situation also excited the sympathy of the 1943 Anglican General Synod. Almost certainly at Judd's instigation, both houses resolved to "earnestly entreat" the King government to offer immediate sanctuary to the victims of persecution, especially those stranded in Portugal, without regard to "race, creed or condition," and to ease their entry by suspending the immigration laws due to the exigencies of the hour.[68] Similar resolutions were passed during the same year—the year of the failed Bermuda Conference—by the diocesan synods of Niagara and Rupert's Land.[69] Unlike Silcox, Judd did not believe that the decision to omit any reference to the Jews from the National Committee's wartime petition rendered it useless: another sign of his pragmatism as well as his internationalism.[70]

However, Canadian opinion was in a sluggish and torpid state: "We, in our secure western world, have become very complacent as a people," Judd confessed ruefully.[71] None knew better than he that the struggle to admit refugees, especially Jewish refugees, was a struggle against the stream. Still, in the old canon's retrospective opinion twenty years after the war, his church at least had faced the refugee crisis firmly.[72] To an extent, it had, although less so than the mother church, the Church of England— in Britain, "there was no shortage of condemnation by Church leaders ... of the Nazi persecution of Jews" or personal offers of asylum to Jewish refugees[73]—but, alas, without much success. Despite repeated wartime entreaties from the British government, neither the Dominion nor the various colonial governments felt able to respond: the empire, as far as its politicians and bureaucrats were concerned, was already filled to capacity.[74]

The Holocaust

Intimations of the destruction itself and of its horrors started to appear in the Anglican press as well as in other ecclesiastical channels almost as soon as the fires of Auschwitz began to burn in the terrible year of 1942. Cyril Garbett, archbishop of York, warned English Anglicans of "cruelties and atrocities" in Poland "so ghastly" as to defy belief, and his words were reprinted and circulated in *The Canadian Churchman*.[75] Temple, by this time archbishop of Canterbury, described "an eruption of evil [such] as the world has not seen for centuries" at a public meeting in Albert Hall,

London, and an account of his speech also found its way into the Canadian Anglican press. According to the Anglican primate, the "fury of the Nazi evil" was concentrated so much on the Jews that "it was hard to resist the conclusion that there was a settled purpose to exterminate them."

> "What else," said Dr. Temple, "is the explanation of recent occurrences in France? At first it seemed possible to explain the German demand for the surrender of Jewish refugees in unoccupied France as due to a need for additional labour-power; for at first only men of working age were demanded. Later, women were claimed, with the option of leaving their children ... not expecting ever to see them again.... But now the children also are being deported, from two years old and upwards...." Dr. Temple said that there was every reason to fear that a large proportion of those who were being deported were destined for the ghastly ghetto in Eastern Galicia, where thousands of Jews have already perished. He claimed that the Government should do whatever was possible for their relief.[76]

By this time, the British government, in conjunction with ten other Allied governments, had issued a public condemnation of Germany for carrying into effect a policy of annihilation, thereby validating the fears and rumours. Anthony Eden's statement in the British House of Commons on December 17 not only had the most dramatic effect on that venerable assembly that a former prime minister, David Lloyd George, could remember in his lifetime, but also had a similar impact on British public opinion.[77] In Canada, as in the United states, the impact was considerably less dramatic, as anti-refugee attitudes remained as intransigent and the government as adamant as ever. Still, the veil had been raised, even if doubts persisted.

Further reports on events in Europe continued to be published on a regular basis throughout 1943. Once again, the British archbishops publicly condemned the Nazi policy of "cold-blooded extermination" and appealed to their own as well as to the Dominion governments to offer sanctuary within the imperial domains to all who might still be rescued from the European hell.[78] In Canada, A.P. Gower-Rees, archdeacon of Montreal and rector of St. George's Church, drew this picture at an interfaith rally at Temple Emanu-El in the same city on May 28:

> Friends, at the moment ... revelations have brought home to us the horror of Nazi rule.... The greatest crime in history is now being perpetrated—the murder of a nation and the deliberate extermination of Jews, particularly throughout Europe. It is not possible to give a correct estimation of the extent of the fiendish operations of the Nazis. But you have already been told ... that no less than two million out of 3½ million of Polish Jews have

been done to death. The remainder seemed doomed to torture and death.... This is a horror unprecedented in the history of the whole world. It is a blood bath on a gigantic scale, to which no parallel can be found.[79]

Like the British archbishops, Gower-Rees concluded his speech with a call for rescue and sanctuary.

To what extent this perspicacity was echoed in Anglican pulpits of the day will never be known. No one can determine what was said or not said in innumerable sermons, parish newsletters and other media during these dark years. As Archbishop Garbett declared, the Holocaust defied belief, and undoubtedly many Anglicans, like many others, including many Jews, did not believe it. Yet Gower-Rees was not the only Anglican in Canada to grasp the true enormity of events in Europe. Occasional synodical resolutions during the war years show that Anglican eyes were not totally blind nor Anglican ears totally deaf. In response to a ringing condemnation of the "unspeakable and inhuman treatment" suffered by the European Jews, the Diocese of Niagara, for example, decreed [May 1943] (a) that antisemitism is "contrary to natural justice, incompatible with the Christian doctrine of man, and a denial of the Gospel"; (b) that "every possible step ought to be taken at once to rescue from massacre the Jews in enemy and enemy occupied countries"; and (c) that Canada should offer sanctuary to "Jewish and other refugees."[80] During the same summer, the Diocese of Montreal forwarded to the federal government a similar resolution urging a "large-hearted attitude" on the part of its officials towards the escapees.[81]

As in the case of the United Church, no sustained mass outcry on behalf of the Jews ever erupted among the rank and file of the Church of England in Canada. The post-*Kristallnacht* protest rallies across the nation included Anglican representatives, but the rallies were interfaith rather than Christian. As in the case of the United Church also, most Anglicans, like the proverbial Laodiceans in *Revelation*, were neither "hot nor cold" but somewhere in between. Most, however, were not all, and those who did speak spoke loudly, sometimes clamorously. Nor did only a few highly placed Anglicans break the silence: church journalists, ordinary priests and lay people also made their individual and collective voices heard. In particular, evangelical Anglicans immersed in Jewish missions, especially those possessing Jewish origins themselves, strove to publicize the Jewish plight. Frequently, events were read incorrectly, and wrong conclusions were drawn, but the night and fog in Europe were obfuscating. Once the fires of imperial patriotism were stoked and German totalitarianism was identified as the mortal foe of Anglo Saxon democracy, Canadian Anglicanism became less silent. To save the Jews was to save the honour of the British Empire and the principles of the Christian faith. This blend of British loyalty and Christian humanitarianism had its counterpart in the United Church, as well as in other Protestant denominations, but it was especially strong in the Church of England in Canada. In such an hour, there was no scope for antisemitism.

V

The Presbyterian Church

IN JANUARY 1938, JOHN BUCHAN, Lord Tweedsmuir, novelist and governor general of Canada, lectured the General Council of the Alliance of Reformed Churches on the erosion of morals in contemporary society. Pharisaism, he informed his audience, signifies a loyalty to conventions that have lost their "binding spiritual force" and thus can supply "no basis for virtue."[1] No doubt, like everyone else, the Presbyterian viceroy was alluding to biblical rather than present-day Jews and intended no harm.[2] Usually an astute man, he did not realize the inappropriateness of his metaphor in the Nazi era, or the irony of attacking the Pharisees for moral turpitude when their spiritual descendants were feeling the oppressor's lash. Like the minor strain of literary antisemitism (typical of the World War I era) that infects his marvellous novels, the comment was unthinking rather than malicious.[3] For Canada's most gifted governor general was far from being an antisemite, nor was he in any way supportive of the German Third Reich and its anti-Jewish violations; to the contrary, on the testimony of his prime minister, Lord Tweedsmuir's sympathies were strongly directed towards the European Jews, and, unlike the vacillating Mackenzie King, he favoured their admission to Canada.[4] However, as a devout Presbyterian who worshipped regularly in St. Andrew's Church across from Parliament Hill, he was aware neither of the folly of such homiletical speech nor of its role in the long historical denigration of Judaism as an immoral and unspiritual religion, setting up the Jews for persecution. One cannot blame him too much for reiterating an old canard, but, in 1938, Pharisaism was by no stretch of the imagination the major obstacle to moral reform. Of course, a blind adherence to dead conventions, which is antithetical to the real spirit of Pharisaic Judaism, was another matter.

Lord Tweedsmuir's small sophism, however, was mild in comparison with certain other Presbyterians of the day, including two Toronto clergymen who did not hesitate to draw extravagant theological lessons from

---

Notes to this chapter are on pp. 156-160.

Jewish misery in Europe. In the same year, and in the wake of *Kristallnacht*, John Inkster, the Scottish minister of Knox Presbyterian Church, Toronto, the largest congregation in the denomination, declared from his pulpit that the German pogrom had its seeds in the same spiritual obtuseness that had caused the ancestors of Hitler's victims to reject and crucify Christ:

> it is sad to see the Jews turning in every direction and seeking sympathy and help from man instead of God; instead of confessing their sins and asking God for forgiveness for themselves, especially the sin of unbelief and denial of Christ; instead of asking God to lift the curse which is resting upon them today and grant them His salvation.[5]

Presumably, the blows of the storm troopers were a divine visitation! In 1940, a year of intensified suffering, another prominent Toronto minister, John Pitts of Calvin Presbyterian Church, also invoked the same crime-and-punishment mythology in one of his sermons. Having conceived of the messianic age as an age of Jewish domination rather than one in which all nations would serve God on equal terms, he told his congregation, the Jewish people failed to recognize the true messiah with his message of universal righteousness, spurning and crucifying him—Pitts seems to have assumed that the crucifiers were Jewish—"in their blindness."[6] Jewish history, as a result, has often been "very black indeed," so black that the black news from the other side of the Atlantic Ocean should astonish no one. Hitler merely confirmed the ancient curse.[7] Neither Inkster nor Pitts approved of the Nazi molestations. Both were sincerely anti-Nazi, and sincerely deplored the savagery in Europe.[8] Both, however, wrapped themselves in old fatalistic anti-Jewish myths in their attempt to elucidate the current troubles of the Jews to their flocks. Today, their "biblical" sermons only serve to show why classical Christian theology requires serious revision.

In solidarity with this body of moribund ideas, but far less negative and judgmental, stood a tiny group of pietists devoted to the conversion of the Jews. Like their Anglican counterparts, these (largely Toronto) Presbyterian evangelicals took the trouble to instruct themselves in Jewish affairs, gleaning information from local Jews about the vicissitudes of their lives both in Canada and in Europe. In this manner they acquired a sensitivity to the harsh reality of antisemitism unusual among Canadian Christians. Certain conclusions followed. Christians who seek to convert Jews must treat them with "kindness and goodwill."[9] The kindness and the goodwill were not merely strategic; they were elements of a necessary ethic, and without their leavening presence evangelization was false as well as futile. "During the last few years," declared their guiding light Morris Zeidman in 1938, "we have had to engage, not only in preaching the Gospel to the Jews, but also in combatting anti-Semitism among Christians."[10] Antisemitism among Christians? This recognition alone elevated Zeidman above the mainstream. A Jewish convert himself, his career incorporated two concerns: the saving of Jewish souls and the saving of Jewish bodies. Should Christian kindness and goodwill fail, and antisemitism was the indisputable proof of such failure, not only would the church forfeit a golden opportunity to evangelize large numbers of new Canadians, but the Jews themselves would be cheated both spiritually and socially.

Morris Zeidman

Morris Zeidman (1894-1964), a native of Czestochowa, Poland, came to Canada in his youth following a political escapade in tsarist days involving young Jewish socialists that almost terminated with a prison term in Siberia.[11] He embraced Christianity in Toronto, attracted by a small mission to the Jews known as the "Christian Synagogue" established in the city by the General Assembly of the Presbyterian Church in Canada in 1908.[12] Graduating from the University of Toronto and Knox College, he was ordained in due course and dispatched to the maritimes for a brief assignment in the pastorate. Subsequently, he returned to Toronto and the site of his conversion, now renamed the Scott Institute (after John McPherson Scott), in order to become its superintendent. There he spent the balance of an innovative and energetic inner-city ministry.

Because of his Polish memories, Zeidman entertained no illusions about the menace of antisemitism and possessed a good nose for detecting its odour in his new homeland.[13] Nor was he the first Jewish Christian to discover its poisonous presence in the religious community that he had joined: a painful discovery for the young convert. However, he rose to the occasion without losing his faith. During the xenophobic and inflammatory thirties, when Bible-thumping demagogues such as Charles Coughlin and Gerald B. Winrod were on the warpath, claiming biblical sanction for their diatribes against Jews, Zeidman did what he could to defend them:

> There are others who are simply slandering Jews and telling all sorts of untruths about them. Somehow they manage by unscrupulous lies to distort facts and invent malicious stories of Jewish plots ... which only exist in the minds of these sensational, racketeering, jazz imitating, gospel

teachers that are preaching (in the words of St. Paul) "another gospel which is not a gospel" but a Gospel of Hate. The time for keeping quiet has passed. They are not only slandering the modern Jew but are besmirching the names of the patriarchs. They are sapping the life of the Church like a canker. If we do not cut that canker out of our Church in America it will be nazified, like the Church in Germany. No, we cannot remain quiet. If we should, the very stones would cry out.[14]

Winrod was an American Protestant fundamentalist. When he arrived in town in order to preach in the Peoples Church on Bloor Street, Zeidman, a fundamentalist himself, picketed the service.[15]

A capable administrator, the superintendent guided the Scott Institute through the stormy seas of the Great Depression, when financial support was tenuous and ecclesiastical support was tepid. Increasingly, his organization turned to that social relief for which it and its successor institution, the interdenominational Scott Mission, became noted, perhaps the only significant social action on the part of Canadian Presbyterianism during this troubled period.[16] Its original purpose was not abandoned, even if the success rate in conversions was not high, so that Zeidman's personal relations with the Jewish community remained strained, in spite of his constant efforts at amelioration.[17] Not surprisingly, considering his Jewish origins, both he and his activities were regarded with suspicion,[18] but his relief work as well as his practical assistance to Jewish survivors immediately after the war won some commendation.[19] Information as well as social action was his forte. It was in the pages of his many reports, articles and speeches that Canadian Presbyterians and other Protestant evangelicals were reminded most frequently and forcibly of the Jewish plight and the evils of National Socialism. In addition to regular Presbyterian and Scott Institute publications, his warnings of impending doom were published by *The Evangelical Christian,* a non-denominational journal, and *The Pentecostal Testimony* of the Pentecostal Assemblies of Canada, a denomination in which the pietistic Zeidman had many friends, and in whose churches he frequently preached.[20] Fear for his own family in Poland spurred his wartime efforts. The fear was well founded; as he was to learn in the course of time, his mother, brother, several sisters and their spouses and children perished at Treblinka.

Two citations capture the flavour. With the *St. Louis* and other vessels packed with fleeing Jews in mind, Zeidman began his 1940 mission report as follows:

The year 1939 will go down in Jewish History as the blackest in the annals of our people. Harrassed [*sic*] and dispossessed and in despair, they wander all over the world, knocking at the doors of nations. Few have been admitted. Few have found refuge, but thousands have been turned away to wander in no man's land. Others sail the seven seas aimlessly, month after month, under the most deplorable, unsanitary conditions aboard their crowded ships, seeking a haven.[21]

The self-styled Hebrew Christian never doubted that he himself was still a Jew and that the afflictions of the Jews were his afflictions as well. In an article on antisemitism in *The Evangelical Christian*, his sense of personal identity emerged with a vengeance as he denounced gentile pride—"Some (Christians) are even proud of the fact that they are Gentiles, if for nothing less than that they can boast that they are not Jews"—as the root of this particular sin, exemplified so powerfully among the so-called Aryans.[22] Reacting to a "Gentiles Only" sign on the Queen Elizabeth Highway in Ontario, Zeidman enlarged on the theme: "The 'Gentiles Only' is merely a translation of the 'Nazi Aryans Only'.... The teachings of Mein Kampf, the fruits of the 'Gentiles Only' and 'Aryans Only' doctrine have brought misery, destruction and death unto Europe."[23] Canadians must not behave as Nazis, but as their antithesis. Antisemitism is unCanadian as well as unChristian.

Perhaps because of the patriotic fervour of the war era, perhaps because of his personal gratitude toward his adopted nation, the Polish immigrant never forgot to doff his hat before British virtues in his summation of the struggle: "On the one hand we have the Nazis, Fascists, Communists, Falangists, Iron Guards, Black Guards, Rexists, Croix-de-Feu and their friends and sympathizers, with their totalitarian, dictatorial and neo-pagan ideals; and on the other is the British Empire with her Dominions, and English-speaking people, with Democracy, the fruit of Bible Christianity, and the culture and civilization that sprang from and were based on the Bible."[24]

Persecuted Christians

Despite its own internal crisis following the trauma of schism, the continuing Presbyterian Church in Canada was soon swept into the mounting global crisis, forcing its leaders to "survey the world situation,"[25] and to formulate a response. Zeidman's political sentiments were shared by others. Almost from the beginning of the Nazi era, the church's official journal, *The Presbyterian Record*, adopted an anti-German stance, castigating anyone inclined to sympathize even slightly with Germany's resentment of the Treaty of Versailles. Thus Richard Roberts of the

United Church, who, of course, was also strongly anti-Nazi, was criticized for suggesting that the current ferment was not wholly the consequence of German perversity.[26] After Germany's barbarous behaviour during the First World War, the editorialist declared, the victorious Allied powers should not have been expected to "bring forth the best robe, the ring, and the shoes, and kill the fatted calf."[27] Two years later (1936) the critics of Versailles were denounced again, with the economist John Maynard Keynes as the target of editorial wrath.[28] Since the *Record* was as pro-British as it was anti-German, it was also swift to justify British rearmament as soon as the drift toward war became apparent. The "proud pre-eminence" of Great Britain among the peace-loving nations was described as the best hope for international concord, and God was praised for the fact that British instincts, unlike German instincts, were not prone to aggression.[29] Few Presbyterians were pacifists.

Preachers as well as editors sounded the note of imperial patriotism. T. Christie Innes, who had succeeded Inkster as minister of Knox Church, Toronto, lamented the rise of totalitarianism in Germany and Italy from his pulpit, comparing this modern calamity to the ancient plague of locusts recounted by the prophet Joel, which left only the "utmost desolation" in its wake—a strikingly apt illustration, as matters transpired.[30] Among the victims of the modern locusts were the Jews, whom the preacher did not fail to mention.[31] At the same time, rather than the persecuted Jews, the persecuted anti-Nazi Christians of Germany, particularly Martin Niemöller, seem to have captured the larger share of his attention, stirring most of his outrage. Ultimately, both sets of victims were linked together, but for many Canadian Protestants—not merely Presbyterians—Hitler's assault on the German churches was a stronger proof of the iniquity of his regime than his assault on the Jews. Certainly, a passionate concern with the German church struggle revealed itself in the ranks of Canadian Presbyterianism virtually from the outset.[32] As Protestants of Calvinist lineage, the Presbyterians were particularly influenced by the anti-Nazi utterances of the great Swiss Reformed theologian Karl Barth, who composed the defiant Barmen Declaration[33] of the Confessing church and who was dismissed from the University of Bonn in 1934. It was Barth who warned the German churches not to confuse the Word of God with the word of man, as some German theologians had done, attaching revelatory significance to national and racial categories such as blood, *Volk* and soil.[34] As fascism, in both its German and Italian forms, was wedded to the false deities of nation and "race," it was anathema to true Christians, especially to the spiritual descendants of Calvin's Geneva with their lofty doctrine of God's sovereign majesty and powerful distrust of idolatry: the human mind, Calvin had written, is a "perpetual factory of idols."[35] As early as 1933, therefore, with Barth as their luminary—there was a strong Barthian theological strain in Canadian Presbyterianism in any case—the Presbyterians had made up their minds about the German Third Reich and its attempt to create a new state church under direct governmental jurisdiction.[36] They also had only contempt for the Aryan laws and the attempt to divide the church as well as the nation along racial lines. From their point of view, the spirit of the Reformation was dead in its German homeland.[37]

These judgments were reiterated constantly. F. Scott-Mackenzie, W.H. Leathem, James D. Smart, G.D. Henderson and others embroidered the anti-Nazi theme.[38] Preaching in St. Andrew's Presbyterian Church in Ottawa (the church attended by King as well as Lord Tweedsmuir), Leathem compared Barth to John the Baptist as a man "sent from God" to awaken the German churches from their spiritual torpor, summoning them to repentance.[39] Several months later, the same minister castigated the "Spirit of anti-Christ" that was overwhelming German Christianity: "the clouds lie dark and heavy over Christian Germany.... Hitler's latest device ... is to starve out the great living elements of German Protestantism which resist him.... That Germany is moving not towards a merely subservient Church ruled by the State, but to something definitely anti-Christian is clear from the authority of Rosenberg,[40] who is the deadliest foe of Christianity in the whole country ... this sinister figure rises up as a threat to all that is true and good in German life. Side by side with this goes on something akin to the deification of Hitler."[41] Did King, soon to become prime minister again after Bennett's defeat, hear Leathem's sermon? In light of his later and quite different reactions to Hitler, one doubts it.

As the church struggle deepened in Germany, the possibility of any Presbyterian sympathy for the new European social order was snuffed out. A totalitarian neo-paganism that trampled on men such as Niemöller deserved only condemnation and would receive nothing else from decent Christians. "What can We do for Christian German Refugees?" was the title of an address by a German exile, Dr. Frank Bohn, before an audience of Canadian and American church editors in June 1936: "The expulsion or migration of those who for their faith or nationality or both have suffered in Germany ... constitutes one of the tragedies of the time and confronts the Christian people everywhere with an opportunity of brotherly sympathy and service."[42] "Karl Barth is To-day's John Calvin," proclaimed Professor Henderson.[43] If Barth was seen as a modern Calvin, Niemöller was seen as a modern Luther, with his latter-day "Ich kann nicht anders, hie stehe ich, Got helff mir, Amen"[44] against a new religious and political tyranny.[45] Was this mounting antipathy toward the National Socialist state and stream of sympathy for its Christian victims, including refugees, matched by a corresponding sympathy for its many more Jewish victims, including refugees? Or, as Robert W. Ross has argued in an American setting, did the Protestant, especially Presbyterian and Lutheran, preoccupation with the German church struggle deflect North American attention from that other simultaneous and more terrible struggle?[46] In the case of Canadian Presbyterianism (and, as we shall see later, in the case of Canadian Lutheranism), the relative scarcity of references to the Jewish plight in contrast to United Church and Anglican sources supports this hypothesis.

The rabbit and the snake

Like the modern Calvin himself, who confessed after the war that he had not seen the *full* dimensions of the National Socialist evil—"We were hypnotized by it as a rabbit by a giant snake"[47]—and therefore had not protested sufficiently against its treatment of the Jews,[48] most of Barth's Presbyterian admirers in Canada also missed something significant in Hitler's *Novus Ordo Saeclorum*, at least at its inception. The first apparent public mention of something amiss in the new Germany appeared in the Women's Missionary Society journal *Glad Tidings* in 1935, which reprinted a prayer for the conversion of the Jews that included a petition for their delivery from "persecution, misrepresentation, and ill-will"— a classic pietistic stance.[49] Not until May 1936 did an article on their situation appear in the *Record,* prompted by James G. McDonald's highly publicized League of Nations resignation.[50] McDonald's "astounding disclosures" had a ripple effect in the church. Presumably influenced by the high commissioner's action, the Presbytery of Chatham, Ontario, chose this moment to forward a resolution to the General Assembly calling for a new rapport between Jews and Christians:

> WHEREAS, the Christian Church has never approached the leaders of
>   Judaism with a view to creating a spirit of Love and Friendship
>   between them; and
> WHEREAS, there is an increasing appreciation of Jesus and His Message
>   in modern Judaism,
> THEREFORE, the Presbytery of Chatham humbly overtures the
>   Venerable the General Assembly to invite the leaders of Judaism to
>   meet leaders of the Presbyterian Church in Canada, to be appointed

by the General Assembly, with a view to developing a deeper spirit of Friendship between Judaism and Christianity and thus to allay the long estrangement between Jews and Christians.[51]

The presbyters did not allude to current events, so that their resolution remained general and devoid of real significance. How the deeper spirit of friendship was to be developed was never specified, and one suspects that the Chatham Presbyterians scarcely knew themselves. For technical reasons, the document did not reach the floor of the General Assembly, and nothing transpired.[52] No other presbytery broke its silence. Indeed, only a few months later, as if nothing had happened, the *Record* saw fit to publish a callous sermon preached by C.M. Kerr, the minister of St. David's Presbyterian Church, Halifax, which hinged on this reflection: "Have you ever considered that the Germans are now treating the Jews exactly as the Jews once treated other peoples whom they thought might contaminate them? That is to say they set out to exterminate them."[53] With the Final Solution still invisible on the horizon, the language of extermination was premature, if prescient. But nothing can excuse the observation.

On *Kristallnacht*, however, the snake unleashed its coils, and the destruction was impossible to ignore. Not all Presbyterians responded as did Inkster and Pitts. Disgusted reactions started to reappear in the press and elsewhere, dwelling on the distress of those in flight, sometimes with considerable poignancy.[54] In Britain, Neville Chamberlain's policy of appeasement suddenly lost credibility. In Canada, the government's anti-refugee attitude was denounced as "stupid," "un-Christian" and "inhumane."[55] The Presbyterian Church also sent its representatives to the large interfaith protest rallies across Canada.[56] Even Presbyterians dominated by fixed ideas found it difficult to shrug off the dramatic rise in the number of Jews frantic to leave the territories of the Third Reich at all costs. In common with other Protestants of British stock, as well as most Canadians of the day, the denomination was not eager to admit religious, ethnic and racial aliens to Canada, especially aliens associated, rightly or wrongly, with political radicalism. It was better not to upset the national applecart. However, the cries of the persecuted could not be drowned out. Prior to *Kristallnacht*, a 1937 report on [Jewish] children trapped in Spain, many of them orphans, had caused a stir.[57] Now, the clamour rose an octave higher. "To what place of refuge shall these people [i.e., persecuted Jews] turn?" asked the *Record* in January 1939;[58] the answer was obvious: the Dominion of Canada. "Canada as a nation must not be wanting at this time in such a grave crisis when man's brotherhood has such a splendid opportunity for expression."[59] The appeal was moving, but, while the editorial writer was thinking of all of Hitler's Jewish victims, he was thinking particularly of Jewish *Christian* victims, whose number he estimated, no doubt erroneously, as half a million. Two months later, as Hitler devoured Czechoslovakia, the editorial call was repeated:

> Nearly one and a half million people living in indescribable misery are knocking at the doors of the world for mercy. That knock is heard loudly upon Canada's door and in the name of our common humanity it must not continue unheeded.... It seems reasonable to expect much from Canada on account of her unoccupied and sparsely settled areas and limited population.... Suffice it to say that as a Christian nation we ought not to stand upon ceremony or be daunted by material consideration. Help is needed. Let us give it and at once.[60]

On this occasion, there was no special emphasis on saving Christians.

In the early summer of the same fatal year, without mentioning Jews, the General Assembly fell into step with Senator Wilson's National Committee and adopted a resolution in favour of a "wise and well-controlled immigration policy" as required by the exigencies of the hour and the "impulses of humanity."[61] The Presbyterians, however, had no C.E. Silcox or W.W. Judd to agitate on behalf of the refugees or lobby the government, with the result that their efforts never coalesced into a real campaign. Still they were not entirely mute. Adolf Keller, secretary of the Central Bureau for Relief of Evangelical Churches in Europe, was invoked in 1940: "The Refugee is the modern leper, for he has no home, no fatherland, no bread, no papers, no rest, no refuge.... Perhaps the travail of this time will bring forth a new world—but will the Refugee live to see it?"[62] Armenians, Syrians, Ethiopians and Chinese constituted some of Keller's modern lepers; Jews, curiously, were not specified, although almost certainly Jews were implied. Nor were the Jews named in a 1941 column on the European relief agencies that located the gravest situation in unoccupied France.[63] Keller reappeared in 1942 in order to single out the European nations most in need of material assistance because of the waves of "hapless exiles"—once again, not Jews specifically—pouring across their frontiers.[64] The reluctance to single out the latter was strategic, but it also diluted the plea. At least one Presbyterian of the day other than Zeidman was not reluctant, however: William Orr Mulligan, minister of Melville Presbyterian Church in Montreal, who joined Archdeacon Gower-Rees in denouncing the Nazis at Temple Emanu-El (May 29, 1943) and in calling for the admission of 100,000 Jewish refugees without delay.[65] By this time, of course, the murder industry was in high gear, even if not everyone accepted the fact.

Mulligan, who was the convenor of his presbytery's committee on immigration, was not among the skeptics.

The national church also grew less reluctant. A month later, the General Assembly made another attempt to rally support for Hitler's victims, approving without amendment a resolution drafted by the Presbytery of Saskatoon:

> WHEREAS, never before, perhaps in the history of Christianity has the ancient race of Israel been tortured and persecuted as at the present time, and
>
> WHEREAS, the Protestant Churches of Europe have gone on record as being sympathetic to that race, and anxious to be of help to them in the dreadful predicament in which they find themselves in almost every part of Europe, and
>
> WHEREAS, as far as we are aware, no Church in Canada has taken a like stand,
>
> WE, THEREFORE, petition the Venerable the General Assembly to go on record that we, as a Church, are sympathetic to the Jewish Race in their trials and persecutions in every part of Europe, and we further petition the Venerable the General Assembly to communicate with the Government of Canada, urging it to do all in its power to mitigate the suffering of God's ancient race, to open the doors of our Dominion to a fair share of the refugees as opportunity presents itself, and to provide as far as possible for the immediate necessities of such refugees as may come to us from time to time during the war, and in the immediate postwar period. And we would still further petition the Venerable the General Assembly to urge the people of our Church to denounce anti-Semitism wherever found, and to remember at all times that "The Author and Finisher of our Faith" was born of Mary, a Jewish maid.[66]

At last, the church faced reality, although the claim that no other Canadian church had acted reveals, to say the least, a remarkable lack of attention to the other denominations. As a relatively small body, the Presbyterian Church in Canada did not carry much political weight, especially when compared to the considerably larger United and Anglican churches. In the person of one individual, however, it did. One Presbyterian at least, the paradoxical and enigmatic William Lyon Mackenzie King, prime minister of Canada, not only held the reins of power in his hands, but took his religious faith seriously.

W.L. Mackenzie King

That King was, or thought he was, a devout Christian is indisputable; his diary entries confirm this, and, while a suggestion of hypocrisy and hints of a double life can be detected in its pages,[67] there is no reason to doubt the authenticity of at least his early typically Victorian religious professions: "My whole desire in this life is to serve Christ and I will endeavour to accomplish it"; "I hope to be able to do more for Christ, to love him more and more"; "I feel I must not waste a hour but improve my time in every possible way so that I may make my life ... a blessing to others," etc.[68] The young King even considered becoming a Presbyterian minister,[69] but deflected his religious convictions into politics instead, in which arena, according to his less than sympathetic biographer C.P. Stacey, he saw himself as "a man of destiny, appointed by Divine Providence to carry on his grandfather's work."[70] (His maternal grandfather was the rebel William Lyon Mackenzie.) The man of destiny or "knight of the Holy Spirit," as another political historian, Joy Esberey, has described him, intermingled Gladstonian liberalism—according to Esberey, he possessed a "Gladstonian feel for the 'politics of virtuous passion'"[71]—and evangelical pietism, with both its lofty ideals and its self-righteous proclivities. To such a mind everything invariably is simplified, enabling God's knight to see himself in mortal combat with the powers of evil,[72] who, in King's case, were usually and simplistically identified with his political enemies.[73]

On the subject of Jews, the prime minister seems to have shared a degree of conventional gentile Anglo Canadian Protestant prejudice—stray antisemitic remarks can be found in the diaries[74]—although he claimed to disavow the more savage views of the great intellectual guru of his youth, Goldwin Smith, and, apparently, Thomas Eakin, a former principal of Knox College, Toronto.[75] Perhaps, as H. Blair Neatby suggests, ambivalence best described King's mental frame: "he thought of them [the Jews] as aggressive and clannish and disturbingly prominent in international finance ... at the same time, he deplored any overt discrimination against them."[76] If the latter was true, he was better than his quite unambivalent director of Immigration, Frederick C. Blair, who certainly did not deplore overt discrimination.[77] Hitler's persecutions troubled King, especially after the Munich pact and *Kristallnacht*.[78] "I feel Canada must do her part in admitting some of the Jewish refugees," he confided to his private diary immediately following the latter event, when, for the moment at least, his heart softened.[79] Hitler himself, however, did not trouble him, as his much cited diary account of his pre-Munich visit to Germany reveals:

> I am convinced he [Hitler] is a spiritualist—that he has a vision to which he is being true.... I believe that the world will yet come to see a very great man—mystic in Hitler. His simple origin & being true to it in his life— not caring for pomp—or titles, etc., clothes—but reality—His dictatorship

is a means to an end—needed perhaps to make the Germans conscious of themselves—much I cannot abide in Nazism—the regimentation—cruelty—oppression of Jews—attitude towards religion, etc., but Hitler ... the peasant—will rank some day with Joan of Arc among the deliverers of his people, & if he is only careful may yet be the deliverer of Europe. It is no mere chance that I have met him, & von Ribbentrop & Goering & the others I did—it is part of a mission, I believe ... "Divine Commission Fulfilled" says Hitler etc.... He is a pilgrim—his love of music—of Wagner Opera—his habits abstinence, purity, vegetarian, etc., all evidence of the mystic who is conscious of his mission & lives to it.[80]

The monumental folly of these lines, read in the harsh glare of subsequent history, simply beggars description, as does the inelegance of the prime ministerial prose. King was not the only western statesman to be duped by the consummate actor in Berlin, but his spiritual impressionism, together with his own sense of personal destiny, served him ill when faced with another man of destiny. Hitler's "virtuous" traits duplicated most of his own self-appointed virtues, as Esberey notes: "A man who had so much in common with Mackenzie King ... could not be other than 'eminently wise.'"[81] The virtuous Führer successfully extinguished the prime minister's better judgment, whatever the evidence of the ears and eyes, blotting out the cruelty of the German government, at least temporarily. In light of these illusions, it is possible to understand why King's Christian solicitude for the Jewish refugees surrendered so readily to the dictates of politics and national expediency, and why his deputy Blair, incidentally another Presbyterian, was able to work his nativistic will without much interference.[82] The prime minister's intoxication with Hitler may also have contributed to the Evian fiasco.[83]

The Holocaust

Compared to its United Church and Anglican counterparts, if we except the passages already cited, the Presbyterian press reported little about the fate of the Jews of Europe once war had begun. Only *The Hebrew Evangelist*, a tiny paper published by the Scott Institute, did its best to inform its small readership of what was happening across the seas. In 1941 it carried an account, reprinted from Italian sources, of a massacre of five hundred Jews in Jassy, Romania, as a "horrifying example of Nazi savagery."[84] This was the time of Marshal Ion Antonescu and his Iron Guard, a dictatorship as antisemitic and brutal as its German patron. The same issue also described anti-Jewish excesses in Lithuania, organized by the Nazis with the assistance of "Lithuanian quislings,"[85] and endorsed a description of Hitler by a former moderator of the Church of Scotland, Norman Maclean, as the "greatest persecutor of the Jews that ever existed."[86] It also alluded to the Warsaw ghetto and the evacuation of Ukrainian Jews.[87] Other British voices, including William T. Elmslie, general secretary of the Presbyterian Church in England, and Sir Robert Vansittart, were cited occasionally in the *Record* to the same effect.[88] Even in 1943, when the Riegner revelations had become public property in Britain and North America, only sporadic references were published, and these did not suggest the true scale of things.[89] Yet, as the preamble to the 1943 refugee resolution of their General Assembly demonstrates—"never before ... has the ancient race of Israel been tortured and persecuted as at the present time"—the Presbyterians were not oblivious to the sinister reports issued by the World Jewish Congress. This does not mean, of course, that they understood their true deadliness. Like other Canadians, they wrestled with belief and disbelief, with disbelief usually gaining the upper hand.

"There was much that was unknown," wrote William Fitch, a later minister of Knox Church, Toronto, following the war: "No one knew of the systematic extermination of the Jews under Hitler."[90] This judgment, however, depends on how knowledge is defined; the information was available, but its reception was resisted. Zeidman, thinking of his family, described the emotional seesaw in heartfelt terms:

> All during the war, the family and I were praying daily for those unfortunate ones in Poland who were under the Nazi occupation and oppression. We had heard, and read in the newspapers of the wholesale murders and tortures, the beatings, the crematoriums; but we had hoped against hope that these were only war atrocity rumours, and that surely such bestial, inhuman treatment, and such deliberate destruction of non-combatant Jewish men, women and children was inconceivable, unless the Nazi occupational authorities had gone insane, and were working for their own destruction and annihilation. We kept on praying daily at our family worship for dear ones and loved ones, for friends and relations, for Jews in particular, and for people generally who were suffering at the hands of the Nazi degenerates. The children in our home had saved their pennies and laid them aside, designated for the poor people in Poland. I had saved up my own discarded clothing and set aside clothing that had been sent to our Mission for that purpose, so that when the war would be over, I could immediately proceed with the much needed help and comfort for those who had survived.[91]

Knowledge is not a simple matter; as this narrative illustrates, it is possible both to know and not know at the same time. The Presbyterian

Church in Canada was not silent with respect to the Jews, but it was less vocal and less involved than the larger United and Anglican churches. Various reasons suggest themselves: the lack of a high profile champion, a preoccupation with denominational survival, the dominance of Barthian theology with its peculiar blind spots, and too narrow and exclusive a concern with the German church struggle—the image of the suffering Christian had a more visceral appeal than the image of the suffering Jew. All diverted attention from the Jewish plight. Yet, the Presbyterians were as anti-Nazi as most Protestants of British descent, and there is no evidence to suggest that antisemitism was more widespread in their ranks than in the rest of Canadian society, in spite of the antiquated anti-Jewish theological ideas cultivated by some of their more conservative preachers. In his determination to prevent his fellow churchmen as well as his adopted country from turning a deaf ear to the cri de coeur of his own people, Morris Zeidman came as close as anyone to embodying the spirit of Presbyterian humanism. Moreover, the Jewish connection which he personified created a natural empathy, proving that "Jews for Jesus" are not driven necessarily by Jewish inauthenticity, as is sometimes alleged and to which a certain kind of convert tends to lend credence.[92] Some shafts of light broke through the prevailing shadows, and these should not be forgotten.

VI

Baptists and Evangelicals

THE BAPTISTS, INCLUDING THE SO-CALLED "modernist" Baptists, were no worse and no better than other Canadian Protestants on the subject of Jews and Judaism. They simply reflected the general misconceptions and endemic ignorance of Jewish history and religion that pervaded the Christian world in pre-Holocaust times, as well as certain anti-Judaic sectarian strains. Christian triumphalism made itself heard in all its flagrancy, including the charge of deicide:

> But I read the shameful story
> How the Jews abused their King,
> How they killed the Lord of Glory,
> Makes me angry while I sing.[1]

Evangelical Baptists such as T.T. Shields, the minister of Jarvis Street Baptist Church, Toronto, intermingled familiar fables and clichés about the Jews from the store of antiquity with stock conversionist appeals:

> When Pilate said to the Jews of his day, "Will you crucify your King?," They said, "His blood be on us, and upon our children." And it has been! Oh, it has been! The Jews have already reaped a terrible harvest whatever their future may be. Their isolation, their place in history, the fact that no nation can assimilate them, that there is no possibility of obliterating their distinctiveness, whether in Germany or in France, or Italy, or Britain, or Canada, or America ... they stand out identified as the children of those who shed the blood of the Lord Jesus,—and His blood has been upon them! The awful record of their sufferings from then until now attests to the fact.
>
> Oh, my Hebrew friends who hear me by radio, turn ye to Jesus of Nazareth. He is the solution to your problems....[2]

Both the verse and the sermon were published in 1933, a fateful year in Jewish and German history.

Notes to this chapter are on pp. 160-165.

The Canadian Baptists, however, did not admire fascism, which some discerned in three forms: Italian, German and Roman Catholic or Vatican "totalitarianism."[3] Because of their strong assertion of the free church principle, a cardinal tenet of the radical strain in Protestantism, they were instinctively suspicious of Nazi plans for a national German Protestant church under the patronage of the state, leaving, in the words of one observer, Protestant Germany answerable "not to the voice of God, but to the voice of Hitler."[4] This early mistrust of Hitler's intentions seems to have alerted them to other aberrations in the new German Reich, particularly the Aryan laws and the persecution of the Jews. In contrast to the Canadian Presbyterians, the German church struggle did not establish a near monopoly over the Baptist mind; from the outset, the Jewish plight received equal attention. Baptist apprehensions crystallized when the church was faced with an international crisis over the question as to whether Canadian as well as British and American Baptists should attend the World Baptist Alliance congress scheduled [actually rescheduled] to meet in Berlin from August 4-10 in 1934. A fierce debate erupted both inside and outside Canada regarding the suitability of this location.[5] Would a Berlin meeting intimidate the visiting Baptists, driving them into a "cowardly silence" on such burning issues as church-state relations, nationalism, racism and world peace?[6] Some certainly thought so. On the other hand, would their hosts, the German Baptists, who wanted the congress as much as the Nazis themselves, if for different reasons, be mortally offended if it were cancelled? In the end, the World Alliance leaders decided to witness to their religious convictions, especially in the political arena, in a land in which free church and democratic values were accorded scant respect. "Whoever thinks that for Baptists to hold a World Congress in Berlin implies approval of anti-semitism, or any weakening in their view of our Lord's authority and of the Christian faith as supernatural and interracial, knows little of them and credits others with similar lack of knowledge...."[7]

To judge from subsequent reports, the delegates, at least in their own eyes, acquitted themselves well in Germany, even protesting against Nazi oppression without interference from their hosts in the German capital itself.[8] Hitler, a skillful window dresser, had guaranteed freedom of deliberation to the visitors. Naturally, the free speech was double-edged; it included an obligation to listen to pro-Nazi addresses.[9] Moreover, a number of overseas Baptists willingly accepted Reichsbishop Ludwig Müller's personal invitation to visit his headquarters in order to receive pleasant blandishments.[10] The German Baptists themselves had mixed feelings about the new social order in their country. Initially pro-Hitler, because he had warded off the twin perils of communism and atheism, they were inclined to defend the National Socialist revolution with the same ardour as many other Germans.[11] Even in the late thirties, despite growing reservations about what the "positive Christianity" of the regime really signified, especially the determined efforts of positive Christians to turn Jesus into an Aryan, they were still inclined to find more good than evil in Hitler: "Before 1933 we were not able to proclaim the Gospel as well as we can now."[12] Most non-German Baptists, both in 1934 and in 1939, when the Baptist World Alliance held its next congress in Atlanta, Georgia, were, to say the least, sceptical.[13]

T.T. Shields

No Canadian Baptist was more vehemently anti-Nazi on every conceivable ground than the fearless and bellicose Thomas Todhunter Shields (1873-1955). A native of England, Shields emigrated to Canada in his youth, where he followed his father into the Baptist ministry, and where, in due course, he assumed the pastorate of the imposing Jarvis Street Church in downtown Toronto. The history of his stormy pastorate, which lasted almost forty-five years, and the tumultuous and divisive role that he played in Canadian Baptist history, are not relevant to this study.[14] A master orator and organizer, as well as a commanding figure in other respects, Shields was a quintessential fundamentalist, although, interestingly, he had no use for dispensationalism, a popular brand of fundamentalism that divides world history into a succession of ages.[15] He had no use for various other "isms" as well, particularly for Roman Catholicism, which he regarded as the "curse of Canada" and against which he railed incessantly.[16] Catholicism for him constituted an evil power comparable only to the other evil powers of the age: "Nazism and Fascism and Communism and Japanese imperialism and Roman Catholic Jesuitical totalitarianism ... are heirs of ... the lake that burneth with fire and brimstone."[17] Indeed, the Roman church in his eyes was nothing less than a fascist "fifth column" in Canada, and Prime Minister King was nothing less than the pope's lackey in his menial subservience to Quebec and its Catholic hierarchy.[18]

Not Roman Catholics themselves, but the Roman "system," as Shields repeatedly insisted, was the object of his ire. This system in his opinion was bent on world conquest, and thus conspiratorial and diabolical in character, as well as the foe of all true religion, to wit, evangelical

Protestantism. In a manner reminiscent of past wars of religion, he did not hesitate to demonize another Christian communion and link it with National Socialism. Paradoxically, however, in light of the unreconstructed anti-Jewish theology that had lodged itself in his head, Shields did not demonize the Jews. Anti-Catholic and anti-Nazi, he was also sincerely anti-antisemitic, perhaps in part because of his hatred of the Third Reich. The Baptist preacher harboured no illusions concerning the new political order in Germany and its ruler, directing his fury against those who did, especially the proponents of disarmament and appeasement. Hitler was an "utterly satanic personality,"[19] he was another Ben-hadad[20] with his escalating demands and military encroachments,[21] he was a "modern Sennacherib,"[22] he was an "execrable murderer,"[23] he was the "most infamous deceiver and murderer of all time,"[24] he was a latter-day Pharaoh (in his enslavement of the Jews),[25] he was of the Antichrist,[26] etc. War was obviously coming, Shields believed, and pacifism was both foolish and anti-Christian, whether promoted by liberal Baptists or other Protestant modernists such as G. Stanley Russell of Deer Park United Church, Toronto, or popular cults such as the Oxford Movement.[27] "It is utterly amazing to us how any man of moral sense and ordinary intelligence can be a pacifist."[28] Neville Chamberlain, the architect of Munich, was utterly credulous, and his government a disgrace to Britain, according to this fiercely patriotic and pro-British preacher, and loyal Britons, including Anglo Canadians, would learn to revile the day of his birth.[29] When war actually did arrive, no Canadian promoted the Allied cause with greater zeal than the Jarvis Street pastor, for whom the call to arms was virtually an injunction to join a holy crusade.[30] In his mind, 1939 was 1914 once again.

Antisemitism, as Shields saw clearly, was as much a part of Nazi paganism—he had read *Mein Kampf*—as anti-Christianity. "Did you read that story in one of the evening papers yesterday about a Jew being clubbed to death in Berlin?," he asked in *The Gospel Witness* early in 1933; "It but fulfils the threat Hitler made before he assumed power."[31] "When will the Jews' Enemy, the German Haman, Hang on the Gallows prepared for Mordecai?" was the title of a sermon preached in Massey Hall in the wake of *Kristallnacht*—the Jarvis Street Church had been destroyed by fire, possibly set by local Nazi sympathizers, or so its members speculated. It shows Shields at his best and his worst.

> I will begin my exposition [of the Book of Esther] ... by remarking that
> THE ANTI-SEMITISM AND EXTREME RACIALISM OF OUR DAY
> ARE UTTERLY ANTI-CHRISTIAN, contrary to the spirit and genius of

the Lord Jesus Christ.... This whole notion of racial superiority is a fiction which flatters human vanity. I am by no means sure that the boasted "Aryan" purity of the blood that flows in German veins can be absolutely demonstrated.... The alleged superiority of the Aryans to the Jews, I say, has no foundation in fact.... Let us remember that the attitude represented by modern Germany and Italy, and of a great many people in this country and in the United States—the anti-Jewish, anti-Semitic attitude is anti-Christian. It is not of God.... The whole programme of Hitlerism is against God! We cannot take the bloody hand of Hitler, who is the devil's chief representative on earth, in friendship. I will not.... Did you think what you read on Friday was right? The burning of synagogues, the destruction of property, the persecution of a people for something for which they had no responsibility, that they were born Jews.... We regret the assassination of a man in Paris by a frenzied youth—who himself perhaps was driven half out of his mind by the suffering of his people. But does that warrant the persecution, even murder, confiscation of property, of the Jews in Germany and Austria? Is there any man or woman here who can approve that? Any man in whose heart there does not rise a feeling of almost inexpressible indignation?... If I were the only man in the Empire, I would tell Mr. Chamberlain that his Munich pact was contrary to the Word of God....[32]

The best is self-evident. The worst, together with the dogmatism concerning Munich, consists of an irrelevant diatribe against Premier Mitchell Hepburn of Ontario as a local agent of the Antichrist.

Watson Kirkconnell

If Shields was the pre-eminent Baptist preacher in Canada of his generation, Watson Kirkconnell (1895-1977) was the pre-eminent Baptist intellectual. A polymath and linguistic genius who understood over forty languages and mastered several academic disciplines, notably English, classics and economics, and who published books and articles in various fields, including politics and religion, and who taught in three Canadian colleges and universities, finally serving as the ninth president of the Baptist-affiliated Acadia University, Wolfville, Nova Scotia, Kirkconnell was also a devout Baptist layman who played an active role in denominational affairs throughout his career.[33] No fundamentalist—he regarded any attempt to impose uniform creeds as an act of tyranny, and Baptists who demanded doctrinal uniformity as the "spiritual brothers of Torquemada"[34]—and therefore no admirer of Shields, whom he scorned as the "Pontiff of Jarvis Street,"[35] he belonged nevertheless to the "twice born," having, like many evangelicals, found his assurance in a moving conversion experience during his youth. Like the pontiff of Jarvis Street, however, he had his favourite demons, in his case, the communists rather than the Roman Catholics, concerning whom he developed an obsession during the war years when subversion and treason loomed large in the public imagination, and when the "Octopus of Moscow" seemed to have its Fifth Column in Canada, as well as the "Octopus of Berlin."[36] Yet he was as anti-Nazi as he was anti-communist, and his book *Canada, Europe and Hitler,* written on the eve of the Nazi invasion of Poland, was criticized by the Toronto research committee of the Canadian Institute of International Affairs for the severity of its condemnation of the German dictator.[37]

Kirkconnell also had read *Mein Kampf* (in the original German) and had formed a sagacious opinion of its author and his political and military agenda: "Even more than Communism, Naziism [*sic*] is today a force seeking to dominate the world through revolution.... No movement of our time has revealed a comparable demonic energy in penetrating and organizing all possible communities the world over, with a view to establishing the ultimate world authority of Hitler's Reich."[38] *Mein Kampf,* he acknowledged, is a powerful text, containing a kind of "pagan idealism," or "a summons to courage, effort, self-sacrifice, hard living, and duty, to walk a stony road through a night-enshrouded wilderness," but its idealism is vitiated by the "strain of brutality, ignorance, intolerance," and a Nietzschean contempt for mercy and forgiveness.[39] Ever the English scholar, Kirkconnell could not resist a literary comparison: Milton's Satan and his "defiant commonwealth" in *Paradise Lost.*

> The griefs of defeated Germany, real or assumed, have been brooded on with "obdurate pride and steadfast hate"; and infernal courage has been shown in the defiant rearming of the Reich, with all the desperate zeal of Mammon's "brigads." Hitler, the analogue of the grim Archangel himself, surrounded by his Nazi Beelzebub, Belial, Chemos, and Moloch, has from the outset been undaunted in his decision: "War, then, war, open or understood, must be resolved." But his challenge to civilization, however brave, is inherently evil and seeks the dethronement of law in favour of force on earth. He would rather, like Lucifer, reign in a hell from which all values of human personality had been obliterated by a race-state (false in its very essence) than surrender something of German sovereignty in a truly democratic international world of civilized men. Germany, under such leadership, is thus a threat to the entire world.[40]

A vivid analogy, but surely Kirkconnell was wrong; Hitler did not possess the grandeur of Milton's fallen archangel.

Antisemitism, as Kirkconnell saw as readily as Shields, lay at the heart of the new German "atavistic tribalism,"[41] and he found ample evidence of Nazi attempts to manipulate German Canadian opinion in the interest of Hitler's political and racial policies in the German language press in Canada, particularly in Bernhard Bott's Winnipeg-based *Deutsche Zeitung für Canada*.[42] To Bott, a German national and a paid Nazi agent, the Jews were the enemies of Canada as well as of Germany, and Canadians should join the Germans in the struggle against the Jewish "world enemy"—the "sworn enemy of sound Canadianism."[43] Such notions were simply "morbid and fantastic" as far as the "Scotch-Canadian" but "100 percent Aryan" Kirkconnell was concerned, and he could scarcely contain his disgust both with Bott and others like him, especially Adrien Arcand in Quebec.[44] In *Twilight of Liberty*, his wartime sequel to *Canada, Europe and Hitler*, the local Nazi Fifth Column and its antisemitic hate sheets, in German, French and English, were subjected to further scrutiny:

> Anti-Semitism is still being vigorously propagated. The Toronto police have had to deal with pretended drunks who systematically boarded street-cars and proclaimed in loud, inebriated tones that: "Of course the Jews are behind this war. Their motto is 'Onward Christian Soldiers.'" (This despite the fact that Jewish enlistment is comparatively high.)[45]

The Baptist professor's reaction to antisemitism, especially the cruder variety, was intensified during his European visit in the summer of 1939 to lecture (in Hungarian) at Stephen Tisza University in Debrecen, Hungary, when he witnessed at first hand its ravages:

> In Vienna, the evidences of violence and social ostracism were visible everywhere. Every public bench was stencilled "Nur fuer Arier"; every restaurant bore a sign "Nur Arier verwuenscht"; every shop window was neatly labelled "Deutsches Arisches Geschaeft"; every park-entrance stated warningly "Juden verboten." In the more strictly Jewish quarters of the city, I saw an ugly trail of smashed windows and smeared walls. While I was in Vienna, edicts were promulgated designed in the near future to eliminate Jews from the professional life of Germany and ultimately from commercial life as well. All means of livelihood were to be withdrawn.[46]

As a result of these experiences, Kirkconnell, a member of the board of the Committee on Jewish-Gentile Relationships[47] and an associate of Silcox and Eisendrath, adopted a strong pro-refugee stance, which he couched in Christian terms: "The present emergency is a searching test for the professing Christians of the world."[48] His poem—the polymath was also a poet—"The Agony of Israel" lamented, in his own words, the

Jewish martyrdom in Europe while deploring the reluctance of Canadians and Americans to accept Jewish refugees.[49]

> Bow your heads, all ye nations,
> And humble yourselves, all ye peoples,
> In the presence of sorrow unspeakable,
> At the sight of anguish beyond measure;
> For the sons of Israel are slaughtered all the day long,
> And the daughters of Jerusalem are violated and slain,
> And the synagogue is burned in the fire
> The place of the congregation is utterly destroyed.
>
> These are the people of Jehovah,
> The folk of the Ancient Covenant,
> Who were spread throughout the earth
> And were scattered among the nations
> Sojourners among many peoples
> And dwellers in kingdoms far from Zion.
> Yet they rendered good to the alien
> And comfort to men of many races,
> Seeking out cures for the ills of the flesh
> And healing for the bodies of mankind.
> Their words likewise were full of understanding,
> Abraham ben Ezra, and Moses ben Maimon,
> Baruch the lens-grinder,
> And Einstein, the seer of night and the stars.
> Their psaltery also brought consolation to the soul,
> Their music was balm to the spirit,
> Even the music of Meyerbeer and Moscheles,
> Of Rubinstein and Mendelssohn-Bartholdy.
> These were a people of faith and promise,
> Abundant in their gifts to all nations.
>
> But the hangmen of Haman have arisen,
> And a greater than Haman has come,
> A man whose heart is filled with darkness,
> Whose veins run with evil,
> And he has purposed to destroy them all,
> To cause them utterly to perish.
> Therefore have the streets of Warsaw run blood
> And the highways of Poland are stained with death.
> And from every satrapy and city
> He gathers the hapless ones by force,
> The innocent to a fate of horror.
> Therefore let the nations gathered against Haman,

> The peoples who war against the Agagite,
> Swear mightily to avenge the blood of the guiltless,
> To serve Haman as he has served Israel,
> And let us offer refuge to a remnant,
> Even safe refuge to the fugitive from murder,
> That the guilt of his death be not upon us also,
> The mark of his death upon our door-sill!
> For we are all bound up together in the bundle of life,
> And the Lord God will require the blood of the guiltless
> Both of him that slays and of him that stays not the slayer
> In the day of blood,
> In the day of desolation of Israel.

Not great poetry perhaps, but the sentiment is beyond reproach.

A new Gethsemane

Other Canadian Baptists, whether evangelical, fundamentalist or modernist in persuasion, shared the same powerful antipathy to the Third Reich, and the same early discernment of its true character, especially its antisemitism. "The dogs of war are straining at their leashes," cried *The Maritime Baptist* in March 1933.[50] Dogs of greater cruelty were also straining. Accounts of Jewish persecution, including the flight of Albert Einstein, became a regular feature in church news almost immediately thereafter, as the number of editorials and articles on the subject published in 1933 alone testifies.[51]

> When the world in the Great War termed the German nation Huns, the great nation along the Rhine writhed under the insult…. But if a fraction of the atrocities against Jews with which Germany is charged to-day be true, Hun is the only word that can be used to describe the Hitlerite Teutons…. The entire world is horrified by the tales of barbarism, which are coming from Germany through devious channels; it is like reading the story of the Armenian massacres again…. German Jews, from peasant to professors, are in their dark Gethsemane and the rest of the world stands powerless to interfere…. One would never imagine that the Christ whom German Protestant and Catholics alike worship was a Jew.[52]

Much heed was devoted to the Aryan laws and to the famous "*Nein*" of Karl Barth to the German Christians in the name of ecclesiastical and spiritual freedom, though Barth was not a Baptist. Much heed therefore was devoted to Christian anti-Nazi resistance, including the later "martyrdom" of Martin Niemöller.[53] The apostasy of General Ludendorff, who declared himself a pagan in 1935, denouncing Christianity as a religion designed to "help the Jewish people to domination," amazed and repelled the Canadian Baptists.[54] Sensing the link between the attack on the churches and the attack on the Jews, they did not concern themselves with baptized non-Aryans only; their apprehensions had a wider compass: "It is no use talking of brotherhood while Jews are dragged through the streets, their property destroyed, their bodies maltreated, even when their lives are spared."[55] One contributor to *The Canadian Baptist* even recognized the historic complicity of Christendom in the present plight of Hitler's Jewish victims[56]—a rare admission in the pre-war era. As the thirties progressed, the reports continued, updating the Baptist readership on the flow of events and the "haunting fear" in Germany.[57] As with the other denominational journals, these were invariably in response to the latest outrages, and waxed and waned accordingly. In their indignation, the various kinds of Baptists with their various theologies were united.

Not only Baptists, but other Protestant evangelicals joined the refrain, often quite early, and often by correlating the Bible with the daily newspaper. "The history of the Jew is the finger of God," proclaimed the editor of *The Pentecostal Testimony* in 1935.[58] "Just as we have a barometer to tell us what the weather is like, so God has His barometer and it is 'THE JEW,'" echoed another Pentecostalist writer in 1939.[59] Inspired by this notion, as well as by pre-millennialist ideas, these evangelicals could hardly ignore what was happening to God's barometer on the other side of the ocean. Interspersed among related topics—neo-paganism, Hitler as messiah, Hitler in prophecy (a favourite theme), the swastika versus the cross, the savagery of Dachau, etc.—were accounts of Jewish destitution and misery in Germany and other parts of continental Europe, the expulsion of Jewish professors, Nazi hatred, the mounting flames of ideological antisemitism, and the antics of Julius Streicher.[60] Frequently, they were accompanied by the dire prediction that, in persecuting the Jews, Germany will reap what it has sown, i.e., its own inexorable destruction.

There were, of course, less prescient evangelicals. Oswald Smith, the pastor of the non-denominational Peoples Church in Toronto (the church that invited Gerald B. Winrod to preach from its pulpit, drawing the wrath of Morris Zeidman), penned an idealized description of the new Germany following a visit in 1936: a Germany from which all fear and insecurity had vanished, in which people were suffused with hope and joy, in which everyone greeted everyone else with a smile, and on which heaven itself seemed to smile.[61] In Hitler's new Germany, moreover, according to the impressionable Canadian, such evils as Spiritualism, Russellism (i.e., Jehovah's Witnesses), Bolshevism and sodomy had been stamped out, while Jewish schoolteachers who violated the honour of young schoolgirls under their supervision received their just deserts: "I have nothing against God-fearing Orthodox Jews," Smith declared, "and would be the last person to make their hard lot still harder. But their brothers who have abandoned their faith have betrayed them and become their worst enemies."[62]

Smith's German utopia did not impress other Protestant evangelicals in Canada. Harsh reality shattered the idyllic vision of smiling Germans bathed in sunlight. Writing in *The Evangelical Christian,* a non-denominational Canadian journal that served as a forum for conservative and fundamentalist opinion, an American Presbyterian cited European sources to describe the entrapped Jews of Austria and the "program of liquidation" that awaited Jews and Jewish Christians alike: "The spirit of anti-Semitism is the spirit of the Anti-Christ and the battle is now joined between the forces of Satan and his hosts and the forces of Christ and his Church."[63] Only an evangelical would have selected the language of Armageddon to interpret current events, but the human imperative was unambiguous: the Jews, whether Christian or non-Christian, had to be saved. A moving editorial accompanied his plea.[64] Most but not all Canadian evangelical churches caught the spirit. One searches in vain the pages of *The War Cry,* the bi-weekly publication of the much-respected Salvation Army, for references to the Jewish plight throughout the pre-war era. Except for a single short editorial on General Ludendorff,[65] virtually nothing reflected contemporary events in Europe. Its many edifying tales of personal conversion are perennial, and completely detached from the hurly-burly of a world falling into ruin. Why did an organization dedicated to humanitarian relief apparently not hear this particular cry for help? Perhaps the peculiar policy of the Army, its deliberate avoidance of politics and chosen neutrality in order to concentrate on its special mission, answers the question. Perhaps also the reason lies somewhere else:

> When it seems as if the Jews are about to be annihilated by their enemies, they will cry to God in agony of soul to save them from destruction. God will answer their cry and give divine deliverance. Their Messiah will suddenly descend from heaven and smite and utterly destroy their enemies (Ezekiel 38:18-22). It will be a victory and deliverance greater than any of those recorded in the history of the Jews from their beginning as a nation.
> ... But the most amazed of all people will be the Jews themselves. They will be astonished not only at the great victory, but at the Victor Himself. As they behold Him, they will see that their Deliverer is nail-pierced![66]

With such theological quietism, why should anyone lift a finger? Christ will intervene.

"Gardens of the damned"

Kristallnacht had the same traumatic effect on the Baptists as it had on most other Canadian Protestants. "How thrilling to read of the President of the United States saying plainly and bluntly and courageously that it would be nothing short of cruel and inhuman treatment to compel defenceless refugees from Germany to return to their own land!" thundered Shields from his temporary pulpit in Massey Hall, as he denounced the prevention of some Jews escaping from Hitler—"doctors, lawyers, bankers, professors"—from entering Quebec during the previous week.[67] Distant Moose Jaw, Saskatchewan, produced a resolution, penned by the local Baptist minister, calling on the Canadian government to allow a "generous quota of these unfortunate Jewish refugees" to enter the country.[68] The flight of the latter from hostile Germany to hospitable Belgium "across trackless moors, or through dark forests" was described in graphic detail in *The Canadian Baptist* early in 1939.[69] Baptists being Baptists, the reporter could not refrain from dwelling on the "spiritual needs" of the Jews, lamenting their inability, because of their impoverished state, to purchase "Gospel and Testament."[70] But this consideration was almost an afterthought.

The *St. Louis* was not the only ship to stir remonstrations. In a curiously prophetic radio address delivered only seventeen days before that ill-fated vessel left Hamburg for Havana, Cuba, with its cargo of Jews, Kirkconnell recalled another tragic steamship filled with Armenian refugees from Turkish oppression after World War I on which he himself had been a passenger. It too had been forbidden to dock in any [Mediterranean] port, reminding the Canadian of the "weirdly accursed ship of Coleridge's Ancient Mariner."[71] Today, he continued, the cafés of central Europe—the "gardens of the damned"—were filled with new refugees, only trapped on land rather than on the seas. "Whether their despairing screams will be heard in time, will depend on the nations of the so-called Christian world, of which Canada is one."[72] Not only the cafés, however, for still another "forlorn" ship[73] with three hundred Viennese Jewish refugees on board had caught his eye when travelling the Danube during his Hungarian visit: neither the Czechs nor the Hungarians would admit its passengers, moored near Bratislava for three months,[74] awaiting their fate. When the scandal of the *St. Louis* broke, *The Canadian Baptist* wept:

> There are few things more terrible than the plight of the shipload of banished Jews who sail the Atlantic coast forbidden to land anywhere. Cuba refused them sanctuary and the United States has coastguard ships trailing

the ocean vessel to prevent attempts to land illegally by jumping over-
board and swimming to shore. The fugitives are in such sorry state that
many would gladly risk the terrors of the sea rather than be returned to
the appalling conditions of Germany.... With most of their property con-
fiscated and other lands, in the grip of economic difficulties, offering no
haven, the poor people are in a desperate condition.... How the horrible
condition can be remedied no land has discovered yet; in the meantime
the cry of Israel is heard in the whole world.[75]

In response to such editorials, as well as to Cairine Wilson's National
Committee, the various segments of the Baptist communion began to
urge a more open-door policy on the part of the nation, passing resolutions to this effect. They employed the same mix of moral and pragmatic
appeals as did the other churches when addressing politicians on unpopular issues. The largest convention, that of Ontario and Quebec, produced the following:

> Whereas there is still needed, on a vast scale, amelioration of the lot of the
> refugees and potential refugees, whether Jewish or Gentile, in Europe:
>   And Whereas some steps have already been taken to provide sanctuary
> for certain of these refugees in Canada;
>   Now Be It Resolved that this Baptist Convention do urge upon the
> proper governmental authorities the desirability of admitting to Canada of
> carefully selected individuals or groups of refugees, as being desirable, not
> only from humane and ethical standpoints, but also because such immi-
> gration should prove a valuable addition to our national economy, by
> introducing skilled workers and new arts, crafts and industries.[76]

The resolution was adopted and forwarded to the Canadian government. Almost identical resolutions were approved by the United Baptist
Convention of the Maritime Provinces and The Baptist Union of Western
Canada.[77] The cabinet, of course, paid no more attention to the Baptists
than to anyone else, as did the opposition parliamentarians. Subsequent
pro-refugee church petitions also proved futile.[78] So did individual pleas,
for example, that of F.M. McCutcheon, minister of First Baptist Church,
Montreal, before a largely Jewish audience:

> The heart of the Christian world has been startled and appalled by what
> we have been hearing of in Europe.... The condition of the Jews today
> offers the paradox of being themselves, by their laws, always considered a
> refugee [sic], and now are refugee people on a large scale.... We
> [Christians] owe too much to the Jewish race to forget you in this time of
> persecution.... I agree perfectly with the editorial comment in a recent
> issue of Toronto Saturday Night, in claiming that Canada should open her

doors to these refugees. The only things that would give us the right to respect ourselves is taking every conceivable step ... for the rescue of as many as possible of the victims from the hands of the murderers; and everything we fail to do is just so much more added to our guilt as accessories to the murderers.

There are hundreds of thousands who could still be rescued from the Gestapo if any nation on the face of the earth were willing to grant them sanctuary ... our immigration laws are part of the wall which encloses those wretched victims which they cannot break through or climb over and against which they will ultimately be shot or clubbed to death by the disciples of Mein Kampf.[79]

In the meantime, the evangelical press, which included some Baptists, pressed hard for rescue. Many evangelicals, as we have seen, tended to regard the Jews as the divinely appointed hinge of history, and therefore searched for providential lessons.[80] However, they also mingled moral and pragmatic arguments:

The plight of Jewish refugees in Germany has excited the pity and stirred the conscience of the world.... Canada has a responsibility in this respect. There are vast spaces of this great Dominion without population of any kind.... It is not suggested that all the Jews who find themselves compelled to flee from Germany should come to Canada, but the Dominion should do its share in providing a home for the homeless.... A nation that calls itself Christian has a responsibility towards those less fortunate than itself. Canada has been blessed abundantly in basket and in store.... All that it lacks is population.... Such a course would have the blessing and favour of Almighty God.[81]

In other words, both parties would benefit. The same issue of *The Evangelical Christian* included a substantial article on the same theme by a Victoria minister, J.B. Rowell, replete with up-to-date information.[82] "With the facts concerning the modern persecution of the Jew before us, let us unite our effort and influence against the monster which seeks, not only to annihilate the Jew, but to demolish the citadel of Bible truth and Christianity."[83] A noble exhortation, but the citadel of Bible truth and Christianity contained certain intolerant elements of its own. When the *St. Louis* was in the news, *The Evangelical Christian* rebuked local Jews for creating Christian inhospitality in Canada by failing to respect the Christian "Sabbath," e.g., the Sunday taboos of Protestant society. "If the Jewish rabbis of our city [Toronto] were to gather together a group of our best Jewish citizens, with a group of Gentiles interested in the Jewish welfare ..., they could quickly stop many of the things that are fast promoting bitterness."[84] Once again, something not far removed from antisemitism spoiled the good will. Other examples of the same failing leap to the eye. The Canadian Pentecostalists, for whom the Jews were God's barometer, were not always saved by this belief from anti-Jewish canards of their own, especially when influenced by German Pentecostalists torn between their religious and political loyalties.[85] However, no trace of antisemitism can be found in the following supplication, published in January 1940:

WHY PRAY FOR THE JEWS

1. No people have contributed so much to the happiness and success of mankind as the Jew. It was the Jew who passed to the world the ten commandments which have formed the foundation for the good laws of all lands. From him we have received the finest things that we possess in ethics and morals....

2. When we survey the progress that has been made down through the years, in science and art, we find that the Jew has been the world's finest contributor. For the pleasure and culture which these contributions have given us, we have much to thank him for.

3. Although the Jew has been hounded and persecuted from country to country, we never find him planning revenge, but rather returning good for evil.

4. When his rights in Palestine were unjustly challenged by the repudiation of the Balfour Declaration, he did not rise up and threaten the government, but in the face of this terrible shock the Jews lifted up their voice ... calling the attention of the world to their sad plight....

5. When dictators and God-defying powers have crushed and pillaged them, we hear them crying out of their great distress: "We have faced hard problems before and have overcome them; we are ready to face the present...."

6. While the Jews are reaching out imploring hands, beseeching the sympathy of fellow-beings, we hear their leaders urging them on, saying: "Victory must and can come only through the Jews themselves.... It is the imperative duty of every Jew to remain true on every occasion ... to those noble principles that have made our race."[86]

A plea for rescue? Indubitably.

When the war began, some of the most vigorous campaigns to pluck as many Jewish brands as possible from the Nazi conflagration through private rescue operations and money-raising campaigns were staged by Canadian (and American) Protestant evangelicals, especially Hebrew Christians. Their sometimes frantic agitation helped to spur other evangelicals during the war years. Full- and half-page advertisements with arresting titles—JUST RETURNED FROM EUROPE (A Picture of the Appalling

Sufferings of Jews and Jewish Christians), THE AGONY OF ISRAEL, THE AGONY OF ISRAEL IN DEVASTATED EUROPE, THE TRAGEDY OF ISRAEL, HITLER'S POLICY OF EXTERMINATING THE JEWS, A CRY FROM THE ABYSS ... OVER TWO MILLION JEWS ARE DEAD—appeared intermittently in *The Evangelical Christian*, sponsored by the Canadian Advisory Refugee Council of the International Hebrew Christian Alliance. They seem to have been written by Jacob Peltz, the general secretary of the organization. "During the past six years," he declared, "the Alliance, under God, has saved thousands ... who otherwise might have starved, despaired or committed suicide."[87] How much truth this claim contained cannot be fully determined; one suspects inflation, and, in fact, there is little doubt that Peltz was guilty of exaggeration.[88] But, if he is to be taken at his word, the Hebrew Christians poured whatever funds they succeeded in raising into refugee hostels in Europe, including Britain, where continental refugees had been interned. Dreams of conversion, of course, were never far from their minds—"Thousands of Jews are coming to Christ even through their suffering"[89]—but the victims were not to be ransomed because of the waters of baptism; they were to be ransomed because of their humanity. The appeal for money continued throughout the war years. In Vancouver, the local Christadelphians collected money from their members for Jewish relief, which they transmitted to the Jewish External Welfare Fund.[90] Like many fundamentalists, the Christadelphians were ardent Christian Zionists for whom the Jews and Jewish history are a source of constant fascination.[91]

The Holocaust

Perhaps because of a tendency, peculiar to biblicist forms of Christianity, to see the world dualistically and the war as a "gigantic and unprecedented battle between the forces of Christ and anti-Christ,"[92] the evangelicals, both Baptist and non-Baptist, were the first Canadian Protestants to sound a note of what can only be described as cosmic alarm at the drift of things in Europe. Their acute sense of radical evil caused them to express their forebodings in hyperbolic language, including the language of extermination; unfortunately, as matters transpired, what they said proved not to be hyperbole at all. Already, in 1940, comparisons between Hitler and Genghis Khan were being drawn, and gas ovens were being mentioned.[93] Alexander Marks, another Hebrew Christian, in his address before the 1940 Pentecostalist Convention in Saskatoon, drew the attention of his audience to the opening of "hell's gates" in Europe: "Stricher [*sic*], the notorious Jew baiter in Germany, says that the night on which all the Jews of the world will be murdered will be the holiest night in the history of the world.... Hitler and his men will have to give an account before the living God."[94] Hitler was a latter-day Haman, declared another evangelical, A.S. Loizeaux, in 1941, only more diabolical; he was engaged in actual annihilation.[95] The following year, in one of his anti-Catholic sermons, Shields included a horrifying tale involving a concentration camp that featured a crematorium.[96] "Before the end of the present year," prophesized *The Evangelical Christian* with considerable acumen in the summer of 1942, "the world will witness such an orgy of destruction as has never been seen since man appeared upon the earth, with the exception of the Flood, which carried humanity away leaving only eight persons."[97] The world, in fact, did not actually witness this orgy, but was certainly to learn of it in due course. A stream of articles in *The Pentecostal Testimony* by Morris Zeidman warned of impending extermination.[98]

By 1943, when the terrible news was out, the Baptists, particularly the biblical literalists, were perhaps less surprised and less sceptical than some other Protestants; their prophetic and apocalyptic mode of thinking had prepared them for the devil's cloven hoof. "There has never been a doubt of the attitude of Baptist people regarding the satanic persecution of the Hebrew race," wrote J.H. Rushbrooke, recalling the distaste felt by his co-religionists at the prospect of meeting in Berlin a decade earlier: "In the excitement of military events we are apt to forget the calculated malice which is steadily seeking the destruction of a great race to which mankind owes an incalculable debt."[99] A subsequent report in *The Canadian Baptist* (February 1) alluded to the death of two million Jews in the "Nazi Crucifixion of Europe."[100] The July 1 issue employed the term "holocaust" in referring to surviving European Jews:

> Five million Jews of occupied Europe are face to face with extermination. An official statement from the Inter-Allied Information Committee states that measures of extermination against Jewish communities are being intensified and that the Nazis intend to wage war against them "until the Jews have been wiped off the face of the earth." Poland has been transformed into one vast centre of Hebrew annihilation. In Czecho-Slovakia no day passes without some unfortunate Jew being whipped or dragged off to slave labor.... In Yugoslavia 99 per cent of the country's Jewry are now dead together with 86,000 refugees who had sought asylum there from other countries.[101]

In January 1944, Kirkconnell solicited Baptist signatures for the National Committee's petition to the Dominion government on behalf of Hitler's victims not yet consumed by the Holocaust:

The tempest of terror and cruelty that has swept over Europe in the past five years paralyzes the imagination. Millions have perished in circumstances of appalling agony and millions more stand in the shadow of death.... Britain, into the narrow limits of the United Kingdom, has already admitted some 700,000 refugees to share her limited rations, but Canada has kept her door almost completely locked against them. How can we, in our relative prosperity, justify this attitude of refusal?... It may be objected by some that a high proportion of those seeking rescue are what one of my small daughters once accidentally called "the Refujews." The charge is a fact, for this ancient people has been specially marked down for extermination by the Nazi regime; but to be influenced by the charge is to be guilty of dark intolerance.[102]

The age of innocence regarding Nazi intentions had long since ended.

In light of these and other declamations, it cannot be said that either the Baptists, both modernist and fundamentalist, or the evangelicals in other denominations sealed their lips about the Jews of Europe. Even the silent Salvation Army offered to aid continental refugees ("race" and religion unspecified) in 1939.[103] As in the case of other Canadian Protestants, no mass outcry erupted from the rank and file, but the Baptists were not large numerically in any case, nor were the other conservative churches. Yet their representatives were also present at the post-*Kristallnacht* rallies across the nation,[104] and some Baptists, notably Shields and Kirkconnell, were extremely outspoken. To both men, as to other Protestants of the day, imperial patriotism and Anglo Saxon liberty served as a powerful stimulus of anti-Nazi sentiment, especially once the fighting was under way. As with the Presbyterians, no Baptist Silcox or Judd emerged to lobby the federal politicians, although Kirkconnell almost performed this function, nor did the regional Baptist conventions provide as good a forum for unified fronts on key issues as the more centralized polities of the United, Anglican and Presbyterian churches. The Baptists, and most non-Baptist evangelicals, were congregationalists and frequently individualists as well. This was both a strength and a weakness in the battle for public opinion.

Individualism promotes freedom of expression, as the history of religious non-conformity proves in ample measure. At the same time, individualism is fraught with hazards, especially when blinded by strange obsessions and religious narrow-mindedness. Had the courageous but irascible Shields not made his name a household joke by lashing out ad nauseam at the imagined evils of Roman Catholicism and Protestant modernism, as well as wasting his energies, as Kirkconnell said, in "barren attacks on other men,"[105] his defence of the Jews and criticism of

Canada's restrictive immigration policies might have received a wider and better hearing. In Ontario, at least, his voice commanded attention beyond the stone walls of his downtown church, and local politicians more than once found him a force to be reckoned with. The great fundamentalist preacher was newsworthy, especially during elections, when his hatred of the ruling Liberals was unleashed—he made no secret of his Tory sympathies. Tory or not, on at least one question, he was more liberal than the Liberal cabinet of his day.

VII
Lutherans, Mennonites
and Quakers

Lutherans

AT THE HEART OF THE LUTHERAN TRADITION stands the inescapable figure of Martin Luther himself, the father of the Protestant Reformation, if it can be said that the spiritual revolution of the sixteenth century had a single father, and a man who, whether a "Mr. Valiant-for-Truth" or the arch "disruptor of Christendom," was indisputably an elemental force on the historic stage.[1] In Lutheran eyes, Luther was and remains a great religious hero: perhaps not one of the saints of the Christian church, but nevertheless not someone to be lightly impugned. When the *Toronto Star* published a harshly critical article in 1934 entitled "Luther's Influence for Good and Evil," castigating the reformer for a series of misdeeds, including "cowardly cringing" before the German princes at the time of the peasants' rebellion, a sharp rebuttal to the unidentified author's attempt to demolish Luther's "fine character" swiftly appeared in *The Canada Lutheran*.[2] When, a decade later, *The Canadian Churchman* published a bitter anti-Luther, anti-Lutheran and anti-German diatribe by the no longer pro-German Dean Inge, blaming the reformer for the war, disbelief and anger overflowed in the Lutheran press:

> We don't recall ever reading anything about Luther and the Lutheran Church quite so nasty. If the "gloomy dean" was trying to be sensational he really outdid himself.... Some of his statements ... are downright ridiculous nonsense. We refer especially to those which would describe the work and person of Luther as a curse to the world, and responsible for this present conflict, and the Lutheran Church as essentially and exclusively German—and decadent—with the addition that the sooner Lutheranism dies the better it will be for the world....

Notes to this chapter are on pp. 165-172.

Let the little dogs bark and big wolves howl against him. Because he identified himself so courageously with the truth in Christ, he is impregnable. Luther still stands and will, because the Truth still stands and will.[3]

Luther and the Truth therefore belonged together: a conviction that made serious criticism of Luther extremely difficult, if not impossible. The tremendous defensiveness of the editorialist with respect to both the reformer and his country was no doubt shared by many Canadian Lutherans, especially those of German descent. Lutheran Germany had become the enemy, and, with the dangerous simplifications and ugly passions that war always breeds, to be both a Lutheran and a German in wartime Canada, no matter how remote the German connection, was to feel acute discomfort. Non-German Canadian Lutherans were not caught in this peculiar bind, particularly those of Norwegian and Danish extraction who possessed ample reason to be anti-German themselves, but even they could scarcely deny Luther's German identity nor the German origins of Lutheranism. Had the Lutherans of the day chosen to notice the strident antisemitism that disfigures some of Luther's later writings, and to reflect on this literary corpus in light of Hitler's mounting oppression of the European Jews, they would have suffered an even greater discomfort.[4]

The Lutheran tendency to defend Luther against attack by non-Lutherans, including other Protestants, naturally reinforced whatever blind spots regarding the man himself and his faults that already existed in Lutheran ecclesiasticism. Hence his rhetorical savaging of mediaeval Jewry remained unscrutinized by the majority of modern Lutherans, and the broader anti-Jewish slant to his theology remained sacrosanct. As far as modern Jews were concerned, the only real attention that the Canadian synods paid to their situation prior to the war arose from the familiar pietistic interest in Jewish missions, which was sufficiently widespread among the different branches of Lutheranism to support the intersynodical Zion Society for Israel. A body with nineteenth-century European roots—one is reminded of Franz Delitzsch and the *Mission unter Israel*[5] in imperial Germany[6]—the Zion Society for Israel drew strong support from the various Canadian churches, especially the pietistic Lutheran Free Church, the Norwegian Lutheran Church of America and the United Danish Evangelical Lutheran Church. In keeping with the logic of this enterprise, Christians were enjoined to express their gratitude for their own salvation at Jewish hands by converting the Jews to Christianity:

Christ for the Jews, I hear some say,
"Are they not cursed and cast away?"

No, "God forbid," we plainly read,
Let Gentile-Christians well give heed.

"The Jews for Christ! Christ for the Jews."
This slogan we would gladly choose;
From them to us salvation came,
To them we now must Christ proclaim.[7]

Whatever its offense to Jewish readers, this verse at least had the merit of disavowing the malediction motif of historic Christendom, which is more than can be said about much of the popular theology of the period. Such was the strength of the pietistic strain in Canadian (and American) Lutheranism that money was collected for the purpose of saving Jewish souls in the Lutheran churches throughout the entire war, although the number of Jews in the world available for eventual evangelization became smaller with each passing day. This "fervent religiosity" combined, in the German case, with a "naive nationalism," was part of the baggage brought by Lutheran immigrants to North America during the nineteenth century.[8] Even when German Lutherans resisted Hitler during the *Kirchenkampf*, according to the historian Uriel Tal, they opposed the persecution of the Jews in the Third Reich mainly because it prevented the latter from "seeking redemption" at the hands of the persecutors![9]

Luther's land

Among North American Lutherans of German origin, initial reactions to Hitler's Germany were either ambivalent or laudatory, even inspired by a "secret delight" that the land of the Reformation—"Das deutsche Land ist vor allem Luthers Land"[10]—had recovered from its military defeat and was "'turning the tables' on its enemies with a new display of military might and industrial growth."[11] That this was indeed the case is demonstrated by an account of a German visit in the summer of 1935 by J.H. Reble, president of the Evangelical Lutheran Synod of Canada. Reble, it seems, had some "pleasant surprises."[12]

> Everywhere in village, city, or open country were signs of industry and frugality. On the city streets there were no beggars. In the rural sections there were evidences of bounteous harvest. The German farm is a thing of beauty. Every foot of the ground is cared for like a garden or a park. Forests are planted with the care of a fruit orchard, and there are flowers everywhere. Every side of the city street is usually lined with four-story residences, packed together like great apartment houses. And down that stretch as far as the eye could see were tiers of flowers. On every balcony,

suspended from the sill of every window, were flowers of red, blue, yellow and pink.

I received the impression that the great majority of the people are following and supporting the "Fuehrer" because they realize that the political party strife ... corruption ... open debasement of literature, of amusements, and of society by the injection of immoral and unmoral influences would ruin their country entirely—and Adolf Hitler, the man with a vision, of strong convictions and love for his country would be the right "Fuehrer" to lead them from darkness into light, out of a period of despair into a new future of light and hope....

Germany is re-arming but for defensive purposes only. There is no talk of war.... There are no strikes, no hold-ups any more. Whereas from 1918-1933 one was not safe in the streets of Berlin or any other large city after dark, now one can go about unmolested at any hour of the day or night....[13]

One bad sign, alas, spoiled this lovely idyll:

But it is true that certain actions in creating the "Reich-Church," the propaganda of influential leaders in the new Germany for the German Faith Movement; denying the Old Testament and the letters of St. Paul, and trying to "create" a religion that is native to the soil, and the demand of many public school teachers that the stories of the Old Testament and the teaching of Paul be discarded and Jesus only taught as a hero caused a great storm of resentment and re-awakened the spirit of Luther.[14]

This was certainly disquieting, but Reble reassured himself with the thought that such shocking anti-Christian proposals drew no support from the rulers of the new Germany.

The report reveals much: what was happening to the Jews apparently escaped the Canadian visitor's attention, as it escaped the attention of that other Canadian cleric Oswald Smith a year later; what was happening or threatening to happen to the German Protestants most certainly did not. How could Reble have seen the one and not the other? The reader of today wonders, but a predisposition to regard tales of Jewish persecution across the seas as simply anti-German propaganda was common in the German Lutheran churches of Canada and the United States.[15] Such Lutherans still smarted from residual anti-German sentiments following the First World War—Berlin, Ontario, for example, was renamed Kitchener, after the British general Lord Kitchener—and their insecurities no doubt contributed to this mindset. Reble himself, incidentally, despite his Germanic affections and his willingness to believe the best of Hitler (in 1935), was fervently loyal to the British Crown, pledging his allegiance to the "common cause of the peoples of the British Empire" when war with Germany was declared in 1939.[16]

In fact, the anti-Christian rumbles in Luther's land that disturbed the president of the Evangelical Lutheran Synod of Canada during his German excursion had reached his ears prior to leaving Canadian soil, as the minutes of the 1934 annual convention of his church disclose: "In the Land of the Reformation the Lutheran Church is passing through great tribulations.... Being a free Church in a free country, independent of State or any other worldly authority, the Evangelical Lutheran Synod of Canada appreciates the situation in which the Lutheran Churches of Germany find themselves and sympathizes with them."[17] Great tribulations? Undoubtedly, the strange phenomenon of neo-paganism or "new heathenism" with its Lagardian[18] attack on classical Lutheranism and its cry for a post-Christian Germany was a matter of serious concern, but apocalyptic language in the Nazi era was more relevant to the Jewish than the Christian situation. However, the Canadian Lutherans were worried. Like Reble, they comforted themselves as long as possible with sunny mirages about Hitler, if not about some of his supporters. Thus a 1937 pro-Hitler book[19] was reviewed favourably in *The Canada Lutheran* as a welcome attempt to present "the other side": North Americans, counselled its author (and the reviewer), should visit Germany and see for themselves the "effect of the Jewish boycott and propaganda upon the religious concepts affecting the Lutheran and Catholic Churches.... Like a great and skilled surgeon who performs a successful operation on an almost hopeless case, Hitler has won the boundless gratitude, the deep appreciation, the fanatic enthusiasm of a whole people."[20] Great surgeons, it went without saying, should not be vilified. Truly, as a visiting churchman informed a Lutheran gathering in Berlin in November 1937, "Deutschland hat keinen grösseren, keinen besseren Freund als die lutherische Kirche in aller Welt."[21]

Possibly not, but the reverse sentiment could not be sustained, even by the Germanophiles. Protestantism in Luther's land was manifestly under siege, and the attackers were not merely fringe anti-Christians of the neo-pagan German Faith Movement (*deutsche Glaubensbewegung*) for whom the Old Testament was an "alien, unethical and dangerous book"—in other words, a Jewish book[22]—but members of the government itself. Bad news spilled into the Lutheran press abroad. The imprisonment of Martin Niemöller was a blow.[23] The invasion of Poland and outbreak of war was a much greater blow, and one that had a salutary effect on any lingering illusions in Canada about the German leader and his regime. Political pro-Germanism fell under a shadow as the once admired new Germany became a totalitarian ogre, suppressing Christian principles that represented the supreme glory of the German nation: the land of truth was the land of truth no more![24] When Hitler's armies swept into Lutheran Norway and Lutheran Denmark in April 1940, Norwegian and Danish Lutherans in Canada were filled with patriotic anger and deep anxiety for the "martyred" nations and their captive churches, although some were unwilling to assign too much blame to Germany because to do so would "tear asunder" the bonds of Christian and Lutheran fellowship.[25] Lutheran suffering was German as well as Scandinavian. But the Scandinavian Lutherans soon found a hero in Bishop Eivind Berggrav of the Church of Norway who defied both the German conquerors and their puppet government by refusing to acquiesce in the nazification of the state church. His resistance and subsequent imprisonment won him acclaim outside the Lutheran world, and remains a striking exception to the more usual pattern of submission to the ruling powers long embedded in Lutheran theology as a legacy of Luther's original teaching.[26] Norwegian indignation, especially against the Norwegian arch-traitor Vidkun Quisling[27]—"The day Hitler falls you die"[28]—consumed the Canadian Norwegian community.

And the Jews?

It cannot be said that the Canadian Lutherans said nothing about the Jewish plight in Germany and Nazi-occupied Europe, but they did not say much. Those who did speak were usually pietists who were interested in the Jews for religious reasons, and of Scandinavian rather than German lineage. *Hyrden/The Good Shepherd*, for example, a Norwegian church journal, reported "harrowing details of riots by students and grave ill-treatment of Jewish families" instigated by Nazi sympathizers in 1934 Romania, a nation whose natural antisemitism had been heightened by the unpopularity of Madame Lupescu, King Carol's Jewish mistress.[29] Meeting in the United States, the 1938 convention of the United Danish Evangelical Lutheran Church (which included Canadian delegates) alluded for the first time in its report on missions to Jewish persecutions in central Europe and the worldwide spread of antisemitic propaganda, concluding that the sorrows of the Jews made them ripe for conversion: "This may be the day of our opportunity."[30] The idée fixe was intensified a year later when the next annual convention improved on its predecessor by deciding that God must be working in mysterious ways: "Perhaps their present affliction will prepare the way for Christ in the hearts of the Jews."[31] Perhaps. But there were other modes of reading the signs of the time, and in the summer of 1939 the time was beginning to shorten.

The refugee crisis concerned the Canadian Lutheran churches, but, judging from contemporary comment, more as a crisis of fleeing Lutherans than fleeing Jews.[32] Did the Lutherans allow their perceptions of Jewish suffering to be coloured by the kind of theological fatalism that, following the war, persuaded certain German Protestants, including the courageous anti-Nazi Lutheran churchman Heinrich Grüber of Berlin, that the Holocaust was a visitation of divine wrath on the Jews for their sins?[33] Conceivably, they did. "Judaism has been subjected to the judgment of God," declared one Lutheran pastor in 1941 in a rare allusion to the Jewish plight in official Lutheranism.[34] Implicitly, therefore, nothing much could be done, except, of course, to offer the unfortunate Jews the gospel, a duty that the Lutherans never wearied of reiterating.[35] The European Jews were out of reach, but their Canadian co-religionists were not; Edmonton, Alberta, for example, according to one Lutheran specialist in Jewish missions writing from that city in 1943, contained approximately two thousand Jews ripe for conversion.[36] What was transpiring across the seas—"untold miseries so gruesome that we could think that all hell was let loose on earth"—had served to awaken the "true Christians," who had turned to prayer.[37] These true Christian prayers, however, seem to have had less to do with material than with spiritual rescue, or the "message of love, hope and redemption."[38]

Antisemitism drew an appropriate condemnation, especially when it sunk its teeth into Christian flesh, as when the Nazi neo-pagans referred to Jesus as a "swine" and a "Jewish tramp," and when they attacked the Old Testament, which, according to traditional Lutheran theology, was a Christian rather than a Jewish book.[39] The notion that antisemitism was a threat to Christians and Christianity as well as to Jews and Judaism did impress itself on some Canadian Lutherans, even if the lesson was slow in the learning. "Beware, Leaguers [i.e., members of the Young People's Luther League], of the spirit of hatred towards the Jews," solemnly warned the Saskatchewan-based *Shepherd-Hyrden* in May 1943, following an account of an antisemitic incident in Toronto taken from *The Evangelical Christian*. "Jesus Christ was a Jew. If you are a true believer and hence one of the blood-bought children of God, you cannot hate his kinsmen according to the flesh."[40] Such incidents, in the words of the original narrator, constitute "the first foundation stone—the enterning [*sic*] wedge—the primary trickle in Canada of the same devastating flood that is engulfing Europe."[41] But these admonitions seem to have been rare.

Of the Holocaust one can find no mention in the Canadian Lutheran church press, nor in any other ecclesiastical source during the war years. Only silence.

Mennonites

The complex reactions of the Mennonites in Canada to Nazi Germany have attracted the attention of recent Mennonite historians, especially regarding the late-arriving Russländer immigrants.[42] In many respects a special case, the Russländer stood apart from the old Kanadier and still older Swiss Mennonites of Ontario. On the one hand, their largely German identity—German was in a sense the sacred language of this form of Protestantism—and their natural affinity for things German, including German culture and the German fatherland (*Deutschtum*), inclined a vociferous minority, but still a minority, in a pro-Nazi direction; on the other hand, their Christian pacifism and the feeling of being Mennonites first and Germans second served to moderate such political sympathies, especially in the later thirties. Mennonite perceptions, moreover, were deeply affected by Mennonite experience, which like Jewish experience, was thoroughly acquainted with the blows and desolations of history. Persecuted from their beginnings, often with great savagery, persecuted in Soviet Russia in the twentieth century, many of the spiritual heirs of Menno Simons who came to Canada as refugees in the 1920s had terrible tales etched into their memories. These recent martyrdoms were related to earlier martyrdoms, although, as the Mennonite literary scholar Magdalene Redekop points out, the "Anabaptist story" and the "Russian" story do not belong to the same cycle.[43] It was only natural that many Russländer debates, including those on the Jewish situation, reflected in some measure this peculiar and highly charged historiography.

The German connection

Mennonites of German extraction, like other Canadians with German and northern European roots, were by no means uniform, especially with respect to acculturation. Whereas, for a variety of reasons, the Germans of eastern Canada (mostly Ontario), Mennonites as well as Lutherans and Catholics, had become less German and more Canadian, the Germans of western Canada, rural, communal and relatively isolated, had resisted assimilation.[44] So intense was the attachment of some western Mennonites to their German origins that any suggestion that neither they nor their churches were quite as German as they wished to believe was certain to draw an anguished refutation.[45] (In fact, as family names attest, many Mennonites of today are not German in descent at all, even among the Russländer; Swiss, Dutch, Frisian, Polish and Russian ancestors abound.)

With Germanic pride, the Mennonites of western Canada initially welcomed *völkisch* and romantic messages from afar. Despite or perhaps
because of their long odyssey from country to country and continent to
continent, they felt themselves, in the words of Jonathan Wagner, more
than ever "part of a vital German nation which transcended state bound-
aries."[46] Fichtean ideas ran rampant, at least until the beginning of the war.
"If a Volk trades its language for another, it loses its own life—its soul,"
wrote one settler in *Die Mennonitische Rundschau*, referring to the struggle
against anglicization in the Canadian diaspora.[47] Mennonite veins, according to the blatantly pro-Nazi Walter Quiring, a frequent contributor to the
local press, contain "pure German blood ... even purer (more German) and
more unmixed than that of Germans in the Reich!"[48] Perhaps Jesus, whose
"gleaming golden hair and beard bestowed on him a heavenly appearance,"
in obvious contrast to his dark-haired Jewish contemporaries, also had
German or Aryan blood. A few were willing to entertain the notion.[49]

The Russländer, among whom this racial strain of pro-Germanism was
most widely disseminated, leading to a "brief but intense flirtation" with
Adolf Hitler and his new social order, were encouraged to infer certain
lessons from their own recent sufferings during the "Red terror" [*des
roten Terrors*] in the Soviet Union, when they had been supported by
sympathetic Germans.[50] (Other Mennonites did not share these memories.) If communism is evil, that which defines itself as diametrically
opposed to communism must be good, and if the latter is also German, it
must be extremely good: so some Russländer reasoned. Since Hitler had
saved Germany from falling to the communists, Hitler was also good: in
fact, to employ an American heroic analogy, a type of German "George
Washington," the father of a new Germany.[51] Unlike George Washington,
however, the Führer was also a "God-sent man," a claim that Americans
usually have not made on behalf of their first president.[52] Writing from
Hamburg, one Mennonite observer, Heinrich Schröder, gave the German
experiment a religious glow: "The idea of National Socialism, our faith in
God the Almighty and in Jesus Christ the living one, gives us the power
to build the new Reich; a Reich of honour and respect, a Reich of freedom, peace and social bliss for all Germans who wish to dwell therein."[53]
Defender of the faith, the enemy of God's enemies, the Führer was the
object of veneration both at home and across the seas.

By no means, even among the Russländer, and even in the rapturous
early days of the new Germany, were the majority swept away by such adu-
lations. From the beginning, eastern Mennonites, especially those who
preferred English- to German-language church journals, saw the iron fist

in fascism, or the "rule of force," exalting the state above the individual, exemplified in Hitler's brutal treatment of the Jews.[54] To C.F. Derstine, the Kitchener-based world news editor of the [Mennonite] *Christian Monitor*, Mussolini was much less heinous (at least in 1934).[55] One might even wish the Italian dictator a measure of success in his attempts to protect Italy from "Vaticanism" and communism. This benign assessment was to change, however, with the Italian rape of Ethiopia. The "German Caesar," on the other hand, Derstine warned, should "turn the pages of history, and beware."[56] Tyrants perish.

Schröder's pro-Nazi ovations inflamed other German and German-speaking Mennonites in the early and middle thirties. Jacob H. Janzen of Waterloo, Ontario, disputed the former's obsessive fixation with "blood, race and language," including the view that the Mennonites themselves constituted a Volk or "mini Volk" (*Völklein*); German they certainly were, and part of the greater Germanic people and culture, but their essential unity was religious—only the Jews formed an intact Volk![57] While the God-sent man Hitler may have been God-sent, that did not mean that he should be deified.[58] The "Mennonite Moses," B.B. Janz of Coaldale, Alberta, so described because of his leadership role in the exodus from Russia in the twenties, also clashed with Schröder, defending Menno Simons and his ethic of non-resistance against modern attempts at nazification.[59] True Christians, as Menno had said, invite the blows of unregenerate rulers in a fallen world without responding in kind—true Christians, therefore, cannot be National Socialists. At the end of the decade, when the sounds of impending war were audible, Janz countered Nazi propaganda in Canada by advising his brethren to surrender their allegiance to the country that had offered them a place of refuge after their Russian flight.[60] For German immigrants to shout "Heil Hitler" was absurd. When Great Britain declared war on Germany, *Der Bote* published the speech of King George VI to the British Empire.[61] The king's portrait was the "one imperial symbol ... not out of bounds" in Mennonite schools, a consequence of Mennonite admiration for British traditions of political and religious liberty since the reigns of William and Mary.[62]

The "Jewish question"

Mennonite theology was not devoid of social gospel elements, but had swung more and more in a fundamentalist direction as part of a popular late-nineteenth-century backlash against modernism imported from the United States and championed by the Princeton theologians Charles

Hodge and Benjamin Warfield.[63] Not all Mennonites were fundamental-ists—the fundamentalist/modernist debate further fragmented an already fragmented religious community—but some of those who were could not resist repeating the anti-Jewish condemnations of the past. As the "people of the curse" (*Volk der Fluch*), according to one contributor to *Der Bote*, taking his clue from Jeremiah 24:9—"I will make them a horror to all the kingdoms of the earth, to be a reproach, a byword, a taunt, and a curse in all the places where I will drive them."—the Jews remain under its thrall, as their law signifies and as their entrapment in Hitlerian Germany proves.[64] Israel's long and unhappy exile arose from its ancient misdeeds, culminating in the crucifixion. The plight of the Jews was self-inflicted, a result of their "agelong rejection of the Lord Jesus Christ."[65]

Still, as the evangelist declared in the fourth gospel, salvation comes from the Jews, and that which comes from them may return to them if they themselves return to God by accepting the Son of God. The more difficult the times become, the more necessary and urgent this course of action also becomes.[66] Conversion is the true solution to the Jewish problem. Other Mennonites of a fundamentalist and dispensationalist temper concurred.[67] Moreover, there were hopeful signs. The growing Jewish trek back to the land of their origins after the Great War inspired dispensationalists to believe that the final act in the great Pauline drama of the ages was about to be played.[68] Is not prophecy "history prewritten"?[69] As we have seen already[70] a religious fascination with the Jews as the hinge of history can mitigate the worst in Christian scholasticism. "The Jew is in the care and keeping of God," wrote Derstine in 1934: "God yet has plans for this peculiar people. It is the duty of every Christian to befriend the Jew, to preach to him not only by word of mouth, but by love and mercy."[71] "Anti-Semitism is futile because it is fighting against God," he added in 1935, carrying the thought a step further; it is a "dangerous boomerang."[72] The Jew is "God's time-piece," declared D.D. Stoltzfus, another contributor to the *Christian Monitor* in the same year.[73] Some antinomies, therefore, were sprinkled throughout Mennonite attempts to relate the Bible to the news of the day, and it was possible to stress either side of the "Jewish question"—Jewish guilt or Jewish destiny. One could be either anti-Jewish and antisemitic or pro-Jewish and anti-antisemitic as one chose. Both attitudes were possible within the bounds of biblical literalism.

This was the Christian prism through which conservative Mennonite eyes gazed at the convulsions in Europe. In common with other Protestant evangelicals, most of the Russländer as well as the Kanadier—despite the curse motif—reacted against the persecutions of the Third

Reich. Not only was antisemitism wrong and cruel in itself, but also the Nazi spoilations were detrimental to Jewish missions in Germany, forcing them to shut down.[74] At times, however, especially during the early thirties, the prism refracted darker rays. Thus Benjamin H. Unruh, like Quiring an ardent pro-Nazi intoxicated with the new German social order, and a frequent contributor to the Mennonite press, depreciated Jewish suffering in 1935 compared to German and Mennonite suffering, and reminded his readers that the Jews (*Judentum*) had denied the "All-Highest" on Good Friday, which he described as a "crisis of all human nature, culture and history" that no "superficial idealism" must be permitted to diminish.[75] In any case, Unruh reminded his brethren, Germany was not the only nation engaged in a struggle against the Jews: "Wer kennt nicht das Buch von Ford!"[76] It was never a long step from this definition of the "Jewish question" to undisguised antisemitism.

Antisemitism, in fact, contaminated segments of the German language community during the 1930s, as a profusion of articles and letters reveals.[77] Anti-Jewish sentiments were kindled both by the fascination with Hitler and National Socialism, and by a continual stream of tracts and other writings blaming Jews for all the ills of the world, especially the communist scourge. Had not "Jewish communism" persecuted the Russian Mennonites, and had not Germany itself been dominated by Jewish interests for fourteen years [the "Jew-republic" of Weimar] until Hitler set matters straight?[78] Control of the press was an important lever of Jewish power, and, in order to appreciate the nature of this power and its dangers, Mennonites were exhorted to read the "manly" Theodor Fritsch, as well as Julius Langbehn, Houston S. Chamberlain, Paul de Lagarde and Martin Luther.[79] The tirades of Josef Goebbels against Jews and communists were reprinted uncritically in *Der Bote*,[80] as was a synopsis of *The Protocols of the Elders of Zion* in *Die Mennonitische Rundschau*.[81] Even Janzen, one of the more moderate Canadian Mennonite leaders, was favourably impressed by a Winrod composition entitled *The Hidden Hand*,[82] and Janz, another moderate, believed that the Jews were responsible for the atheistic Bolshevik revolution.[83] "Almost fifty million people have been devoured by the Jewish Moloch in Russia!," cried another Mennonite in 1938: "Hate against the Jews? Ask the millions of orphaned children in Russia, the masses of deprived, homeless, exiled, starving wanderers in the country."[84] Stalin, one gathers, was merely a servant of the Jewish Moloch. The stream flowed on.

From early days, however, even in the Canadian German language papers, dissenters swam against this obnoxious current. Dederich Ravall, an American Mennonite, attacked the antisemitic "hocus-pocus" so often found in their pages—"There is no Jewish or international world-domi-nation"—and recommended as a model for Mennonite emulation the "noble, progressive posture of the Quakers," who refused to tolerate trashy racist and anti-Jewish slanders.[85] "What do we have in common with the brownshirts?" asked another correspondent to *Der Bote*, refer-ring to a recent bloody rumble [June 5, 1934] in downtown Winnipeg between local communists and fascists in which some young Mennonites had participated on the fascist side.[86] The brownshirts, apparently, were members of William Whittaker's Canadian Nationalist Party, one of the numerous petty fascisms that littered the Canadian landscape during this period. (Incidentally, its antisemitic monthly, *The Canadian Nationalist*, was printed by Herman Neufeld, the editor of *Die Mennonitische Rundschau*.[87]) Such incidents violate the basic moral principles of the Mennonite faith and should be abhorred. Unlike their German-language counterparts, the English-language Mennonite papers (which originated in the United States[88])—the *Christian Monitor*, *The Mennonite*—never succumbed to pro-Nazi, anti-Jewish sympathies, which, in any case, were uncongenial to Kanadier- and Swiss-descended Mennonites.[89] Quiring's Nazi enthusiasms, especially his rabid racism, proved too much for even the pro-German faction, which knew that Christianity was a world and not a Germanic religion, and could not be reduced to biological formula-tions without destroying itself. "Does it really matter so much whether pure German blood flows in my veins?" wondered a Saskatchewan resi-dent: "On judgment day our saviour will not ask us whether we have unadulterated blood in our bodies, but how we stand personally to him."[90] "Salvation comes from the Jews: without Jews no Bible, no Christ, no Christianity," wrote someone else.[91] "Antisemitism is not the solution to the [Jewish] question," declared Janzen, in reply to Quiring; Canadian Germans, moreover, must not compromise their loyalty to their new promised land of Canada and its king by serving the national inter-ests of their former country.[92] A devotion to high German culture was one thing, trans-Atlantic involvement in German politics was quite another.

Jews or Germans?

With so many predisposing factors—immigrant insecurity, burning mem-ories of the Red terror and their own victimization, a martyrological tra-dition as old as the Reformation, emotional ties to Germany and things German, vulnerability to Nazi propaganda in Canada, a radical pacifist ethic (*Wehrlosigkeit*[93]) in imitation of the Christ who had disowned Peter's sword, a traditionalist theology, and a certain amount of simple credulity—it is not extraordinary that many Russländer and other Mennonites as well were slow to grasp the reality of the Jewish situation in Hitler's domains. Their own virtues stood in their way. Individual voices, including pro-Nazi voices, were allowed to speak in an open forum that encouraged a multiplicity of viewpoints. Unfortunately, the Germanophiles often dominated the debate. It was easy to fall prey to the notion, constantly reiterated by professional agitators, that the Anglo western press had been utterly biased against the new Germany from the moment of its inception, and therefore anything it said about the Jews and their persecution was either exaggerated or a tissue of anti-German lies. The bias, of course, was easily explained: Jewish interests allegedly manipulated and falsified the news, inventing slanders against the great movement led by the God-sent man to redeem the defeated and demoralized nation from its foreign oppressors and Jewish exploiters. Consequently, reports of Jewish travail were often either dismissed as anti-German fabrications or represented as necessary and legitimate acts of German self-defense.[94] Not the Jews but the Germans were portrayed as the true victims.

A good example of this sleight of hand is supplied by the manner in which the early anti-Jewish measures of the Third Reich, notably the 1933 boycott of Jewish merchants, physicians and lawyers, were doctored for Canadian consumption. *Der Bote* published a letter from a "friendly firm" in Germany acknowledging the action against the Jews but decrying its misrepresentation in "mendacious" external sources with their unrelenting "atrocity propaganda" campaign against an innocent German government.[95] If only Germany's critics would desist, such emergency decrees would be suspended at once. *Die Mennonitische Rundschau* published a similar counterattack on the non-German media and its persistent lies about Germany.[96] Apparently, German consular officials in Canada, especially the Winnipeg consul Heinrich Seelheim, regularly fed Canadian German editors sanitized versions of events in the Fatherland.[97] Until the outbreak of the war, when, for obvious reasons, pro-German agitation came to an abrupt end, Canadian Germans who trusted German rather than Anglo Canadian, American or British accounts of developments across the ocean saw things more or less as the Nazis wished them to be seen.[98] As a result, the Aryan laws failed to stir much local indignation: "Jewish professors for German students, Jewish teachers in German schools, Jewish judges on German courts, Jewish officers in German regiments: that is an offense to the German nation."[99] Steps to rectify what was regarded as an intolerable state of affairs required no justification; the German *Volk* had to defend itself against the Jewish *Volk* which, unlike the Danish, French and Polish minorities in Germany, simply refused to remain in its place, trying instead to overrun the host society. In a similar spirit, *Der Bote* reported without disapproval the promulgation of the outrageous Nazi marriage edict by the German interior minister Wilhelm Frick.[100] If the Jews suffered some abuse as a result of the new regulations, that was certainly deplorable, but no abuse was intended by the German government. According to David Toews, a Canadian Mennonite who had attended the 1936 Mennonite World Conference in Germany, the Mennonites had endured more terrible things in Russia than the Jews were enduring in the German Reich: "I believe that I speak on behalf of all our [Mennonite] immigrants when I say that, if our people in Russia had been treated only half as well as the Jews in Germany, none, I daresay, would have thought of leaving."[101]

When Toews uttered these words, the Nazi oppression was still in its rudimentary stage. Even so, other Mennonite eyes possessed a clearer vision. The Nazi whip on Jewish backs, as well as the other crimes of the regime, including the war against the German churches, were singled out and condemned in English-language circles without remission. "Germany, beware!," the *Christian Monitor* warned in May 1933, referring to the Nazi boycotts.[102] Abusing the Jews was proof of fascist "ruthlessness," as well as tampering with the freedom of the churches.[103] Germany was becoming a totalitarian state, with ominous implications for both Jews and Christians.[104] The worldwide growth of antisemitism, including the latest pogroms in eastern Europe, was truly an occasion for alarm.[105] This "rising tide of Jew-hate" was being fed by the spurious *Protocols of the Elders of Zion,* and Christians should not make themselves party to its lies.[106] As the tide turned into a tidal wave in 1938, the *Monitor,* singling out the brutalities inflicted on university students and the outrages in Austria, became agitated in the extreme.[107] The anti-Nazi Derstine served as the Mennonite sentinel.

But the pro-German faction was ill disposed to contemplate these matters, at least until after most other Canadians. In 1937, when a similar myopia blinded Quebec, one columnist in *Der Bote*, obsessed with Jews and communists, suggested that Mennonites should work "hand in hand" with Quebec Catholics, including the illiberal and anti-Protestant Duplessis regime, against these twin evils.[108] As long as this view prevailed, not much of what was happening in Europe could make an impression. Even *Kristallnacht*, despite its shock effect on Canadian and world opinion, received scant attention in the German-language Mennonite press.[109] Instead, official Nazi denials of Jewish concentration camp incarcerations were duly passed on for the benefit of the Canadian brethren.[110] Anglo American claims were merely more "hysterical" anti-German propaganda. Naturally, these Anglo propagandists suppressed the fact that not a single German Jew had lost his life during the disturbances![111]

However, Derstine thought differently:

> We very well know that there are millions of Germans who hang their heads in shame over the terrible crime the Nazis have committed against the Jews. In savagery and mercilessness it out-Herods Herod. It puts the Hitlerites in a class by themselves, sets them outside the pale of civilized nations, characterizes them as a party with which it is impossible to have honorable dealings, because they have no honour. To condemn a whole people for the impetuous act of a crazed youth; to burn their synagogues, smash the windows of their stores, destroy their homes and then compel them to pay for the damage done by a wild Nazi mob; to levy a fine of $400,000,000 and collect it at the point of the bayonet, bankrupting their miserable victims; and to close all doors of opportunity and hope for the Jews is worse than anything that has happened since Nero threw Christians to the lions. Had the Nazi leaders any imagination at all, they could have seen that such a course of action would shock the whole world and align all self-respecting people of earth against such abominable cruelties.[112]

The refugee crisis

Predictably, the Jewish refugees failed to evoke much sympathy among the German sympathizers. Most nations, declared a somewhat acidic commentator on the Evian conference in 1938, were "not as stupid about the Jewish question as people believe."[113] That is to say, most nations had more sense than to admit Jews, even nations interested in new immigrants such as Argentina, Columbia, Ecuador, Uruguay, Peru, Venezuela, Mexico and the Dominican Republic, since useful immigrants must be willing to work on the land: "Perhaps Rothschild will go to these countries?"[114] Australia, of course, had no "race" problem, and was certainly not going to be foolish enough to import one![115] The mounting crisis in 1939 had no telling effect on this attitude. If Jews were being deprived of their rights and banished from Germany, someone else maintained, the matter was distressing in Christian terms but understandable in political terms.[116] To exaggerate and misconstrue their difficulties, however, by vilifying Germany and calling Hitler a "deified demon" (vergötterter Dämon), as a recently published [English] booklet entitled Jacob's Trouble had done, was worse than outrageous: "The author [Louis Baumann] probably did not reflect on the fact that he would have to answer for these lies and distortions and for the influence of such false images on the great day of judgment."[117] This statement underscores the pathos of those Christians, Mennonite and non-Mennonite, who, having persuaded themselves that Hitler was a defender of Christian values, stubbornly clung to this conviction as an article of faith. It was published a month before the *St. Louis* set sail from Hamburg.

Again, Derstine dissented: "In Europe there are at least 7,650,000 people who are unwanted because they, by accident of birth or inheritance, happen to have Jewish blood in their veins.... In the face of these facts, what can be done?... We must relieve them in the hour of their distress."[118] Part of the relief that the editor had in mind consisted of spiritual succour in the form of Christian evangelism, but part of it was also practical:

> Committees have been formed in Great Britain and America to raise funds and in other ways to help these sufferers, and, if possible, to establish them in new homes. The Jews in America have raised $250,000 for the present year [1939] to help the refugees of their race; surely the Christians can do as much or more. Now is the time of testing, not only for the sufferers, but for Christians living in a land of liberty and plenty.[119]

The poignant prayer of a refugee rabbi was published in *The Mennonite*, a Kansas-based paper also read in Ontario.[120]

With the advent of war, the pro-German voices suddenly changed their tune, dropping their support for the Third Reich and aborting further discussion of the Jewish question. Patriotism of a different order suddenly intervened, and professions of loyalty to Canada and the British crown replaced the earlier eulogies to Hitler, which, in fact, had never found much favour in the first place, especially in the Kanadier and Swiss communities. Although withdrawal rather than engagement was the preferred strategy of these religious opponents of war and violence, some Mennonites followed the Quakers in seeking alternative modes of service to demonstrate their Canadianism and to "dispel any lingering suspicions of German loyalty."[121] Among other things, they became involved in various forms of overseas relief.[122]

As for the Jews and their fate, the usual veil of doubt and disbelief hung over Mennonite as well as non-Mennonite eyes, although scattered accounts of expulsions and pogroms intermingled with other items from the news of the world were published throughout the war years. The Holocaust itself remained concealed, or, if not wholly concealed, unacknowledged, since, unlike some of the other Canadian churches, no dramatic disclosures of the real nature of the destinations "in the east" toward which the European Jews were herded seem to have found their way into the Mennonite media. If such moments of truth occurred, they were not recorded. Only after the war did the veil lift, exposing the true face of the once-admired German Third Reich. Even Walter Quiring repented.

Quakers

Perhaps because of their tendency to discount dogma in favour of inward illumination, the Quakers have rarely succumbed to the rigid ideas of more orthodox Christians about Jews and Judaism. This has not saved them altogether from the charge of antisemitism, but the accusation belongs to a different context and a later age.[123] It also has not saved them from the charge of conversionism, but it is doubtful if they ever proselytized with an excess of zeal.[124] Historically, the Quakers contrasted themselves to the Jews much as they contrasted themselves to other Christians—as exponents of the inner light rather than the external paraphernalia of organized religion with its rites, creeds and law codes. But rites, creeds and law codes are not to be despised if they promote spiritual ends, nor are the principles and convictions of non-Quakers, provided they agree more or less with Quaker values. Thus Rabbi Maurice Eisendrath of Holy Blossom Temple in Toronto literally packed the Quaker meeting house in Newmarket, Ontario, on a Sunday evening in the spring of 1930 when he spoke on the theme: "If I were a Christian."[125] He was invited back in the autumn.

The inner light cared little for militarism, nationalism or racism—the "absurd idea of national or racial superiority"—and therefore little for the new political order across the ocean: "Are not all men equal before God?"[126] The question, of course, was only rhetorical; nothing could have been more self evident to the mystically inclined. As internationalists, the Quakers strongly supported the League of Nations, or at least its ideals, taking profound alarm at the spectacle of German rearmament in defiance of these ideals, however unfair the terms imposed on the defeated nation in the Treaty of Versailles.[127] Yet, they believed, or certainly wished to believe, that Hitler truly desired peace: "We want peace more than any other country does, for we require it to obtain bread for our millions of jobless compatriots," they quoted him as saying, drawing assurance from his assurances.[128] This belief persisted throughout the decade, not because the Quakers turned a blind eye to the mounting persecution of the Jews and others in the German Reich, but because of their faith in the divine ground of the human conscience and its inextinguishable flame. Such a faith inspired their appeals both to the personal conscience of the leader as well as the collective conscience of the nation in order to melt the power of evil in the German soul, steering the regime from its perilous course. In this spirit, the British Friends wrote an open letter in 1935 to Hitler and his subjects deploring the concentration camps and other oppressive acts that had disfigured the country: "If these drastic regulations are only temporary, surely the time has fully come to abandon them."[129] If they are permanent, then a "great nation" has shamed and dishonoured itself.

The Jewish plight

The Canadian Friend, like The American Friend,[130] was swift to sense disorder in Germany, although less swift than its American model to condemn the Nazi assault on the German Jews. The persecutions were noted, together with the ideology that informed them, but their antisemitic character eluded the Quakers, at least at the start: "The number of Christians who suffer persecution by accident of their Jewish descent is double that of persecuted Jews. To that must be added the numbers of purely Aryan Christians who are persecuted on purely political grounds."[131] This account leaves the impression that Christianity was the true target of Nazi wrath. However, James G. McDonald's sudden resignation caused the Canadian Quakers to place the Jewish plight in a wider frame with a sharper focus: "[Nazi] laws and proclamations deal a death blow not only to the Jews but to all those living in Germany who believe in liberty and the right of conscience which we Anglo-Saxons, and especially the Quakers, so firmly believe in."[132] We Anglo Saxons! By oppressing the Jews, Hitler was offending both Anglo Saxon sensitivities and Quaker principles: a potent combination. Hopefully, a "storm of protest" on behalf of "non-Aryan Germans" would sweep the world.[133] Whether it swept the world or not, the storm at least swept liberal opinion in the Protestant churches of Canada, producing, as we have seen,[134] the "Protestant" manifesto of 1936 urging the admission of a "reasonable number of selected refugees." The Quakers signed with alacrity.[135] It was the beginning of the campaign.

Following Kristallnacht, Quaker anti-Nazi fervour intensified, partly as a result of the pogrom itself and partly as a result of more reliable intelligence on internal German affairs furnished by their own international network with branches in Berlin, Vienna, Geneva and Paris. Established by British and American Friends in the 1920s, the latter was designed to radiate the "Quaker spirit" in the citadels of Europe, and thus to dispel the surrounding moral darkness.[136] These centres of illumination, especially the one in Berlin, soon attracted those in trouble, both Jews and other so-called non-Aryans anxious to escape German rule. The American Friends Service Committee (AFSC), founded in 1917 as a relief agency with close ties to the German Friends,[137] served as an important conduit to Canadian Quakerism as well. OUR BROTHERS—THE JEWS OF GERMANY is the title of the following post-*Kristallnacht* AFSC article in *The Canadian Friend:*

> It has become increasing apparent within recent weeks that Adolf Hitler and his Nazi followers will never restrain themselves by any considerations of humanitarianism in their sadistic desire to annihilate some 300,000 German citizens.... Any lingering doubts on this score must have been surrendered by the civilized world in the recent government inspired pogrom.... The fact that the victims are of Jewish or partial Jewish descent is not a factor in the thinking of Christians ... surely there can be no difference of opinion, among Friends at least, about the urgency of doing something tangible to demonstrate our fellow-feeling for these people who are, to use Hitler's phrase about the Sudetans, "God's creatures."[138]

Before the night of broken glass, the AFSC had been constrained by a desire not to compromise the excellent and non-political reputation that it had acquired in Germany as a reward for its relief efforts after World War I.[139] There was also a fear that the German Friends might be offended by public criticism of their nation; there was also a high degree of passiveness.[140] The events of November 9-11, 1938, however, overcame both the constraint and the passivity, and the Canadian as well as the American Friends abandoned earlier hesitations. At their monthly meeting in Toronto on November 16, the small Canadian fellowship agreed to approach the government of Canada in order to determine if, in any way, they could provide relief to Hitler's victims in light of the British offer to "take care of some thousands of Jews in co-operation with the Dominions."[141] After Rufus Jones, the eminent American Quaker, together with two companions, returned from an investigative mission to Germany on the heels of *Kristallnacht* (the three Americans were derided by the German propaganda ministry as three "wise men" from the west instead of the east and promised myrrh and frankincense— Nazi style![142]), his graphic account of the "veritable reign of terror" inflicted on the Jews accelerated Quaker efforts in both the United States and Canada to relieve the terrorized.[143] Jones had managed to speak with several high Nazi officials, including two Gestapo aides-de-camp and Hjlamar Schacht, Hitler's finance minister, and, while he himself cast doubt on the success of the visit—Quaker appeals certainly did not melt the evil in Nazi hearts—some temporary material aid was provided through Quaker agencies and agitation for the admission of fleeing Jews to western countries received a new impetus.

In Canada as elsewhere, a flurry of Quaker activity was generated. Raymond Booth, a transplanted American serving as secretary of the Toronto Monthly Meeting, was released from his local responsibilities in order to enable him to devote himself for six months exclusively to the refugee cause. Like other pro-refugee lobbyists of the day, he swiftly encountered the obduracy of the King government. The Canadian Friends, however, persisted in spite of constant rebuffs. One attempt on the part of a Nova Scotia Quaker to sponsor a German Jewish family with two children reveals much about the times: "When I found no admittance I wrote the King, the Governor General, Hon. Mr. Mackenzie King, and back to the immigration people till I got a final curt refusal."[144] Other Friends reported the same frustration. In every case, they were informed that existing immigration regulations did not permit such actions.

Raymond Booth

In common with Claris Silcox and W.W. Judd, G. Raymond Booth (1895-1951) deserves more than a passing nod in the chronicles of the refugee crisis at the end of the thirties. Booth came to Toronto from smalltown Indiana in 1927 first as pastor, later as executive secretary, of the Toronto Meeting of the Society of Friends, serving in this capacity until 1939, when he accepted Cairine Wilson's invitation to join her National Committee as one of its executive secretaries because of his speaking and organizational abilities."[145] However, he returned permanently to the United States a year later in order to promote the refugee cause in a larger arena. A "dynamic soul," according to an acquaintance,[146] this disciple of Rufus Jones became an early member [1935] of the Social Service Council of Canada, which brought him into close contact with Silcox and Judd. He was also a personal friend of Maurice Eisendrath. With other liberals of both faiths, he involved himself in Jewish-Christian seminars concerned with, among other matters, anti-semitism in Toronto and elsewhere in the nation.[147] An ardent pacifist and early member of the international pacifist Fellowship of Reconciliation, Booth swiftly encountered the dilemmas faced by all pacifists, whether religious or secular, whether separational or integrational, when the god of war draws his sword.[148] On one occasion, he found himself advising a deputation of Czech Jews on how to enlist in the Canadian armed forces![149] With respect to refugees, his credo was simple: "Jesus was a political refugee.... Indeed, a Jewish refugee. Even more tragic is the story of the Jewish innocents whose parents did not or could not awake and seek refuge in the night."[150] This was in the spring of 1939.

As with Silcox and Judd, his task was twofold: to keep the Canadian public, particularly the churches, informed as to the turn of events across the Atlantic, and to rouse the government on behalf of refugee suppliants, while appealing to the Christian conscience of the nation. The many accounts of his activities in the church press (not merely the small Quaker press) are ample proof of the dedication with which he attended to these responsibilities.[151] His disappointment, both with the public at large and with the bureaucrats and politicians of the day, finally overwhelmed his Quaker optimism:

> After many months of intense and nerve exhausting work on behalf of refugees, I am feeling low tonight. Perhaps it is because the end of summer is in sight with no holiday to look backward to. It may be because the old Ford shows signs of approaching journey's end. It is much more likely, however, that I am chaffing under the anti-refugee attitudes of people who ought to know better....
>
> Particularly obnoxious is the crop of anti-Semitic objections....
>
> They say, for instance, that the refugee problem is only a Jewish problem.... A scurrilous attack on refugees has coined the hyphenated word, "refu-Jews." But calling names is always the last attempt of the man who has no valid argument.
>
> They say that the Jews are communists. I know some who are. Less than one in every thirty Canadian communists is a Jew. Communist candidates in Toronto get their largest vote in non-Jewish wards, while the Jews elect Conservative candidates.... The only political generalization which one can make of the Jews is that no generalizations can be made. All the Jewish refugees I know personally have been monarchists or social democrats. Some profess to be both, a position not at all incompatible....
>
> The refugee problem is not a Jewish one, but if it were, I would want to help just the same.[152]

Booth had good cause to feel low. No matter how prudently the case for admission was stated, appealing to national interests as well as humanitarian obligations, the voices of commiseration invariably lost the day. "We have been quite disappointed in the reluctance of the government to admit refugees," he wrote, "... for some unexplainable reason the government is very reluctant to permit even those who can make a definite and immediate contribution to Canada to come in."[153] For some unexplainable reason! The Quaker was baffled. Why at least would the nation not act rationally if it could not act morally? The matter defied comprehension, at least to an exponent of the inner light. In a democracy such as Canada, rationality should prevail, for democracy has always been associated with enlightened self-interest and it was clearly in the nation's interest to rescue a people as gifted and accomplished as the Jews of Europe. What could Canada possibly have lost?

Starving children, dying Jews

The Canadian Friends continued to press for the admission of European refugee children to Canada, Jewish and non-Jewish, while collecting clothing and other items for distribution through their service centre in London to the nine thousand such children then billeted in temporary homes and camps in Britain.[154] A victim was a victim was a victim in Quaker universalism, but the Jews were victims in a particular sense: "The war has brought tragedy to many people, but perhaps none so unfortunate as those who have been driven out of European countries because of their Jewish birth."[155] Money, much of it raised by the Quakers themselves through their Central Committee for War Victims Relief[156] was forwarded to the British Friends, since, with war raging, the continent had been rendered almost inaccessible.[157] Together with the Mennonites, the Quakers promoted the purchase of special Dominion of Canada Loan Certificates that, in response to pacifist requests, the government agreed to issue in order to finance the mitigation of war-induced suffering. In this fashion, the two historic Protestant peace churches could allow themselves to invest in the national patriotic enterprise without qualms of conscience.

Quaker concerns were not confined to the European war theatre. In 1940, internment camps were established in Canada for a substantial number—4,500, according to Abella and Troper[158]—of young Austrian and German male nationals, including many Jews and non-Aryan Christians, who, while obviously victims of political and racial persecution, nevertheless were classified by the Canadian government as enemy aliens.[159] They had been shipped from Britain following the Nazi invasion of Belgium and the Netherlands, along with genuine German prisoners-of-war. The tale of their imprisonment reflects as badly on their reluctant host country as the tale of the *St. Louis*.[160] Gradually released by means of private sponsorship, they were assisted in practical ways by sympathetic Canadians, both Jews and Christians, among whom members of the National Committee, including Senator Wilson herself, and representatives of the peace movement were prominent.[161] The Canadian Friends did what they could with limited resources to lessen their tribulation, as well as that of the interned Japanese Canadians in the interior of British Columbia. Small in number and with few wealthy members, the Friends complained of insufficient funds.[162] The American and British Friends also suffered from financial constraints; however, the AFSC involved itself in the wartime flight of cornered Jews from Lisbon, the last open port in Nazi-occupied Europe.[163]

A new apprehension with respect to the starving children of Europe gripped the Quakers, who began to criticize the Allied blockade.[164] "Starvation has stunted children in the Occupied Countries physically and mentally, and even those who survive will not be able to reproduce themselves, while at the same time the German children who are well fed will grow up strong."[165] The starving children were not only Jewish; in fact, by 1943, the likelihood of Jewish children in Nazi hands living long enough in order to starve was extremely slight. Judging from the "ghastly slaughter of Warsaw's ghetto," another fate was in store.[166] In 1941 and 1942, however, the American and European Friends managed to evacuate a limited number of refugee children from France, and to ship food and other supplies to other internees.[167] These achievements required no small degree of perseverance in the face of bureaucratic and practical obstacles. For the most part, the Quaker rescue and feeding efforts met with defeat.[168]

Despite statements such as the above, little information about the atrocities was published in the Quaker press, in part, no doubt, because of the same hesitations that tied the tongues of other Canadians, but in part also because of the Quaker preference for action rather than speech. In his study of the American churches, Nawyn suggests that, as a matter of policy, the Friends chose to say as little as possible in public about the persecutions in order not to jeopardize their relief programs in Germany.[169] Their path was that of "few words and many deeds."[170] If words are good, deeds are surely better. Conrad Hoffman's verdict has already been cited: the Quakers and the Quakers alone supplied genuine practical assistance to the besieged Jews of Europe.[171] In retrospect, this was not entirely correct, since certain evangelical groups may also have assisted Jewish internees, but it was almost correct. What was true before the war remained more or less true during its course.

VIII
Conclusion

HAVING FINISHED OUR SURVEY, we return now to the judgment pronounced by Irving Abella and Harold Troper on Canadian Christendom during the refugee crisis: "As long as the churches remained silent—which they did—the government could dismiss the [CNCR] members as well meaning but impractical idealists to be patronized but not taken seriously."[1] But who or what exactly constitute the churches in this reproach? The worshipping congregations? The organizational bureaucracies? The clergy and ecclesiastical leadership? The Christian populace at large? Which segment of the Christian world has been placed in the shadows? The accusation is imprecise. This is the first problem. The second has to do with the nature of silence itself. Silence is a subtle thing, with more than one possible connotation. The Quakers, as we have seen, said little but did much, proving that silence need not signify antipathy or indifference, even if it often does. To the degree that the churches were indeed silent—for the moment, we will beg the question raised above—care must be taken in unravelling the cause. In the opinion of another critic, Robert Wright, whose indictment of the churches is equally severe, the true reason for their moral failure in the thirties and forties lay in their inability to resolve the conflict between the past with its anti-Jewish intolerance and the present with its need for toleration and interfaith co-operation.[2] An "essentially ambivalent view of Jews and of Judaism" haunted the Canadian Protestant imagination, affecting its responses to the Nazi persecution and the ensuing flight of Jews from Europe. Although antisemitism was unconscionable to most twentieth-century Protestants, it formed a subterranean current in Canadian Protestantism, occasionally rising to the surface in order to nourish Christian vainglory, Anglo Saxon nativism and, we might add, other forms of ethnic nationalism. Because of these dark eddies, Wright maintains, the churches did too little too late.

Notes to this chapter are on pp. 172-173.

Whether or not this explanation of Christian inaction is sound, or even whether the charge itself is well founded, it is certainly true that Protestant Christianity possessed a divided mind on Jews and Judaism. As we have documented throughout, mixed and sometimes contradictory attitudes characterized the various Protestant churches in Canada during the Nazi era. Even Quakerism can be accused of some ambivalence, since Jewish particularity remained a stumbling-block to Quaker universalism. However, Quaker anti-Judaism pales in comparison with the anti-Jewish theological albatross hung around the collective neck of the rest of historic Christendom, both Catholic and Protestant. The more conservative the church, the heavier this albatross. Even so, it does not follow that conservative Protestants were necessarily more antisemitic than Protestants with a liberal orientation. On the contrary, as we have seen, some of the most fervent Canadian denunciations of Hitler's persecutions and most forceful demands for Jewish rescue came from evangelicals and fundamentalists. Nonetheless, the internal tension between an inherited anti-Jewish religious legacy (Christian Zionism notwithstanding) and an ethical imperative to cast aside its dictates in a world grown dangerous for Jews was more acute for tradition-bound religious minds. In this peculiar internal tug-of-war, sometimes the one instinct prevailed, sometimes the other.

Of the non-Catholic communions, the Lutherans and the Salvationists said the least, whereas the United, Anglican and Baptist clergy and laity said the most. Part of the reason for the virtual silence of the Lutherans and Salvationists and the relative silence of many others on the orthodox end of the Protestant spectrum—Presbyterians, Mennonites, etc.—can be traced to doctrinal rigor mortis, compounded in certain cases by immigrant defensiveness, pro-Germanism and other restrictions of vision. Part of the reason for the outcries of leading United Church, Anglican and Baptist figures can be assigned to the moral activism that in one form or another determined their understanding of Christianity, even if its strength varied from denomination to denomination. But neither the silence of some Protestants nor the vocal protest of others can be explained in purely theological terms; the subject abounds with paradoxes, and simple classifications misrepresent the historical record. Claris Silcox, a son of the social gospel and the champion of the refugees, favoured Jewish quotas in Canadian medical schools and held other discredited opinions on Jews, Judaism and matters of "race."[3] T.T. Shields, a biblical literalist to the core of his being, and a believer in the Matthaean curse "His blood be on us and on our children,"[4] was a fierce critic of the obstinacy of the King government on the refugee question. A further paradox is that of the Protestant evangelicals who became arch-enemies of antisemitism and impassioned advocates of rescue after earning opprobrium in the Jewish community for trying to spread Christianity in its midst, especially when Jewish converts played a conspicuous role. Only the Lutheran pietists seem to have blinded their eyes to the moral exigencies of the hour in favour of its supposed spiritual opportunities; even they, however, decried the terror.

Still another paradox had to do with the Anglo Saxon ethos of Protestant (and English) Canada which, in tandem with its nationalistic Quebec counterpart, is held accountable for the exclusion of racial aliens during the anti-immigrant, anti-refugee 1930s. The nativism was real enough, and antisemitism was undeniably one of its fruits. Yet the same Anglo Saxon pride inspired a strain of idealism that defined itself in altruistic terms as the spirit of British fair play and democratic commitment— "us liberty-loving Anglo Saxons!" This slogan transcended mere tribalism by incorporating a profound moral obligation. The blood was treasured, but the spirit was greater than the blood. United Church members, Anglicans, Baptists and Quakers often invoked it, and even Protestants of non-British derivation such as the Lutherans and Mennonites paid it homage, although, except for the English-language Mennonites, their voices were more muted on the Jewish plight. Honour, the honour of Canada, the honour of the crown, the honour of the empire and the honour of its kith and kin demanded a noble and generous response. The code of chivalry was still in effect, at least for some Canadians. Moreover, the dominion was vast and underpopulated; its empty spaces cried out for new settlers.

The other Nazi persecution, that of recalcitrant German Protestants, especially Martin Niemöller, which troubled Canadian Protestants as soon as the fissure between the pro- and anti-Nazi factions in the German churches started to appear, also produced a paradoxical effect. In the case of the Presbyterians and the Lutherans, the German church struggle seems to have diverted attention from its concomitant, the deeper tragedy of the Jews, despite the link supplied by the racial legislation of the Reich, the Aryan laws. Christians rather than Jews became the principal suffering victims of the Nazi tyrant and the refugees whose expulsion commanded immediate sympathy and support. Both the Presbyterians and Lutherans reacted strongly against political totalitarianism and anti-Christian neo-paganism across the ocean, defending the integrity of the biblical Word of God and the great confessions of the Protestant Reformation. Neither, however, especially the latter, noticed the obvious—that the true sacrificial food of the Nazi Moloch was not Christian but Jewish flesh. The Presbyterians eventually did, but late in the day. In contrast, the German church struggle had a salutary effect on the conscience of other Canadian Protestants, particularly in United, Anglican and Baptist circles, where the two persecutions were fused into one, inviting the same general condemnation. It was a matter of no small consequence whether one concerned oneself primarily with the plight of the Jewish *Christians* or with the plight of the Jews.

Was this contrast a matter of chance, or was it dictated, at least in part, by the intellectual and spiritual characteristics of the different brands of Protestant Christianity? Presbyterianism and Lutheranism were highly confessional religious traditions and therefore more wedded to the past than less creedal forms of Protestantism. Old ideas stemming from previous ages, especially the age of Protestant orthodoxy,[5] commanded authority, and new ideas did not find easy acceptance. To make things worse, Canadian Presbyterianism was in a survivalist state of mind, having reconstituted itself after a serious schism, which made the denomination more dependent than ever on time-honoured truisms for guidance and enlightenment. Canadian Lutheranism was divided and insecure as well as stamped by the Germanic die of its historic origins and the Germanic cultural loyalties of many Lutherans in small-town Canada. In neither church did the social gospel exert any modifying influence. Confessionalism and creedalism, on the other hand, were minimal in the United Church, both because of the complications entailed in uniting Methodists, Presbyterians and Congregationalists and because of the basically non-confessional nature of both Methodism and Congregationalism, especially Congregationalism.[6] Anglicanism was as conservative in its own fashion as Presbyterianism and Lutheranism, but British heritage and liturgical rather than doctrinal conformity united The Church of England in Canada. The Baptists, whether modernist or anti-modernist, emphasized the freedom and integrity of the Christian conscience.

If preconceived ideas affected Protestant perceptions of the Jewish plight, it certainly affected the politics of rescue. Those Christians whose minds were fixated on Jewish guilt were tempted to normalize Jewish suffering—what do the Jews expect, considering their denial of Christ?—and thereby to adopt either an indifferent or fatalistic posture in face of the crisis. Shields was an exception, as was the fundamentalist Mennonite C.F. Derstine, but others such as the Presbyterian John Inkster certainly conformed to this mould. A curse was a curse was a curse, and, if the Jews persisted in their mistaken path, some form of punishment, however lamentable, belonged to the nature of things: "I will make them a horror to all the kingdoms of the world, to be a reproach, a byword, a taunt and a curse in all the places where I will drive them." Yet even this dark theology was not without a bright side. Protestant dispensationalists and Christian Zionists who saw the Jews as the hinge of history and God's barometer on earth prayed for their rescue as well as their conversion, and, in the case of a few Hebrew Christians, worked for it as well. When information about the death camps was published in the western press following the disclosures of Gerhart Riegner through the World Jewish Congress, these evangelicals with their fundamentalist theologies and satanologies had less difficulty in accepting the reports at face value than many liberal Protestants. Their "narrative tradition," to cite a popular current phrase,[7] prepared them to expect unprecedented eruptions of cosmic evil.

With this exception, it is doubtful if theology had much to do with the manner in which the various Canadian churches received the accumulating evidence of hideous crimes in Nazi-occupied Europe after 1942. The disbelief of the Christian masses, until belief was finally forced on the world in 1945, is explained more plausibly by other factors, some of which influenced Jews as well, notably the surrealistic nature of the stories themselves and their resemblance to the fabricated "Hunnish" atrocities of the First World War. Moreover, the fact that the initial news was leaked through Jewish channels did nothing to assist its acceptance in non-Jewish eyes; special pleading was suspected. Conceivably, of course, a more ancient distrust may have fed this reluctance as well. Conceivably also, a lingering unwillingness to believe the worst of Germany on the part of the two major groups in Canada with strong Germanic roots, the Lutherans and Rüsslander Mennonites, assisted their failure to discern, or at least acknowledge, the eventual fate of the European Jews. Did these once philo-German Protestants feel betrayed? Was it believable that the culture that once had inspired the reform of Christendom was doing what rumour said it was doing? It was not easily believed, especially by those who loved its language and drew their intellectual sustenance from its master thinkers, writers and artists.

When the disbelief of the churches was overcome, external and international voices played an important part. This was particularly true in the case of the Anglicans, for whom the word of the English archbishops carried enormous weight; if Temple and Garbett said that the Jews were burning, the Jews were burning. However, a few domestic voices were also instrumental. Watson Kirkconnell possessed an exceptional knowledge of

Nazi ideology and its murderous logic, and his books and other writings on the European situation did not misconceive what was in store for the new Haman's anointed victims: "he has purposed to destroy them all, To cause them utterly to perish." The Montreal clergy who addressed the interfaith rally at Temple Emanu-El in 1943 only attracted local attention, but their brief speeches on the Nazi shift from persecution to extermination signalled the dawn of a new public awareness. There is no reason to suspect these Protestants of mere emotionalism or declamation for declamation's sake; while the revelations of the Final Solution were certainly sensational, and while denunciations of the German enemy were consonant with wartime *amor patriae*, the fate of the Jews was not the paramount concern of the great majority of Canadian citizens, especially in Quebec. If it had been, the King government might conceivably have adopted a quite different policy with respect to Jewish refugees, although all speculation remains uncertain.

The growing chasm on this testy matter throughout the Nazi era between national opinion in Christian Canada and the voices of public religion illustrates a perennial problem in the study of human affairs. Religions are embedded in history and culture, but they also transcend their historical and cultural matrices. In one sense Christianity and Christendom are synonymous, in another sense they are antithetical, existing in constant tension, especially when the ideals of faith clash with the mores of society. Depending on whether Christendom as such is indicted or whether Christian institutions are, the charge of silence in the face of a terrible historical evil is both true and false. No sustained universal outcry on behalf of the beleagued refugees ever erupted from either the Christian or the Protestant rank and file, unless the coast-to-coast post-*Kristallnacht* rallies are regarded in this light. Neither Christian nor Protestant Canada spoke with a collective voice. But many Protestant pulpits were not silent, nor were many presbyteries, conferences and synods, nor were a sizable number of editorialists, bishops and academics, nor, of course, were the special envoys who devoted themselves to the refugee cause: Silcox, Judd and Booth. Here, we suggest, is where the spotlight should fall, not on the "Christian" masses of the nation. Were the churches then silent? Yes and no. What Johan M. Snoek once wrote of the Christian record in the European countries vis-à-vis the Jews could be written of Canadian Protestantism as well: "The picture is neither completely black, nor purely white." It is grey.[8]

Greyness, as any moralist knows, is a true reflection of life itself. Moral judgments are ticklish, especially after the fact, because they are coloured by hindsight and tend to assume its wisdom, and because they sometimes exaggerate the power of right moral choices to bring forth desirable results. Abella and Troper assume that, by dint of sufficient pressure, the churches could have changed governmental policy and thus have altered the tragic course of events. If Christian Canada had cried out in unison in favour of rescuing the Jews, the federal cabinet would have been forced to respond—so they seem to believe. Perhaps, but also perhaps not. The Madison Square rally on behalf of the European Jews held on March 1, 1943, and attended by 122,000 people, changed nothing in the United States. But Christian Canada is a fiction, unless one believes that all "Christians" are Christian and truly devoted to the love of the neighbour and other spiritual values. No society, whatever its religious and civic creeds and professions, is ruled by simple virtue. As Reinhold Niebuhr pointed out many years ago, human collectivities are impersonal aggregates of power, and power is morally ambiguous—"moral man" dwells in "immoral society," and, except on extremely rare occasions,[9] immoral society can be harnessed to moral goals only when its self-interest coincides with a larger good.[10] Without citing Niebuhr, Henry L. Feingold argues in a similar vein when, regarding the failure of the Roosevelt administration in the United States to assist the Jews, he makes the point that nation-states possess neither souls nor a natural sense of morality, especially as far as foreign minorities are concerned.[11] Therefore Christian Canada as Christian Canada did not and probably could not have risen to the lofty heights that some Christians of the day demanded: for example, the Anglican rector Cecil J. Lamb when he called for the deliverance of every last refugee in Europe since Canada had—as it certainly did have— "plenty of *Lebensraum*."

Morally speaking, Lamb was right; pragmatically speaking, he was wrong, unless massive rescue was demonstrably in the national interest, and the nation could have been so persuaded. However, since a sudden influx of aliens was not seen by the vast majority of Canadians as good for the country, Protestant realists committed to rescue, believing that half a loaf was better than none, chose to urge the admission of "as large a number as possible" rather than every last refugee. Despite their efforts, even this concession to the vox populi failed, but the strategy was not foolish. It was the intransigent state of public opinion rather than the alleged silence of the ecclesiastical bodies that allowed the Canadian government to dismiss the National Committee on Refugees and Victims of Political Persecution as an exercise in impractical idealism. Because of their voluntary nature, the Protestant churches were able to reach only that part of the population that attended Sunday services of worship—a minority—

and subscribed to its religious publications; over the unchurched majority, baptized and unbaptized, their influence was scant. The notion that
the churches could have bent the government in a more liberal direction
is less fanciful in the case of the more monolithic Roman Catholic community in Canada, especially in Quebec where the bishops, priests and
religious orders frequently made their influence felt in politics while dom-
inating the religious and cultural life of the province. Had the Catholic
hierarchy adopted a pro-refugee stance, the federal politicians, always
mindful of the Quebec vote, may have found the matter difficult to
ignore. But antisemitism, as we have seen, had old ideological and emotional roots in French Canada, where Catholicism and nationalism were
closely entwined, and it was an anti-immigrant, anti-Jewish petition sponsored by the St. Jean Baptiste Society that was so efficacious in stifling any
possible second thoughts on the part of the nation's rulers.

A united front involving all the churches of Canada, including the
silent Protestants and the more numerous silent Catholics, may well have
seized the public spotlight and caused the cabinet serious qualms, but
without the support of the country at large, it is unlikely that they could
have saved the European Jews. The churches of Britain—Anglican,
Roman Catholic and non-conformist—swam against the national stream,
filling the air with denunciations of the Nazi persecutions and offers of
asylum to Jewish refugees, but the British government and its bureaucracy
still managed to turn a generally deaf ear, despite the personal empathy of
Prime Minister Churchill. British society, like Canadian society, was considerably less willing than its religious leaders, including the archbishops
of the state church who sat in the House of Lords, to welcome legions of
strangers, especially when these strangers were Jews. If the finest hour of
the British churches ended in futility, is it unreasonable to conclude that
religious institutions possess only a limited capacity to sway the body
politic, even when they stand together? This is not to say that their witness is not important; had more Christian voices been raised on behalf of
the Jews, and had those that were raised been more persuasive, no one can
really predict what might or might not have resulted.

Moral appeals, however, suffer from inherent disadvantages. For one
thing, if repeated too often, their currency wears thin; for another, they
depend too much on the mood of the moment, and moods are fickle and
subject to change. The plight of the Jews in Germany excited the anger
of western observers in periodic waves, reaching a summit with the
Kristallnacht pogrom, but there were intermissions as well. Moreover,
other international events also provoked outrage during the same period,

notably the Italian rape of Ethiopia and the assorted atrocities of the Spanish Civil War, diluting the well of public indignation. Despite centuries of spiritual and social denigration, the Jews were never excluded from the Christian "universe of moral obligation" as some critics have alleged,[12] not even during the Middle Ages when they were progressively demonized in the popular imagination. While as anti-Jewish as the rest of Christian society, the mediaeval popes consistently sought to protect the Jews from Christian mobs on the rampage.[13] (Once again, the distinction between the institutional church and the baptized masses is germane.) Throughout the Nazi era, the Protestant churches of Canada never forgot that the Jewish people occupied a special place within their universe of moral obligation, but Hitler's Jewish victims were forced to compete for attention with other victims of fascism, and it was not always clear at the time which set of victims represented the most pressing claim on the western conscience.

While few Canadian Protestants, even in the pro-German, German-language communities with their nationalistic pockets, succumbed to unadulterated antisemitism of the extreme and blatant Nazi kind, few also, even in the liberal churches, understood the true dimensions of the evil and fewer still the need for Christian introspection and reform. In particular, the profound negativity towards Jews and Judaism that embedded itself in classical Christian theology after the first century was never addressed, except by rare individuals such as the British Anglican scholastic James Parkes, although its role in Jewish marginalization and victimization throughout history was not minor. It took the Holocaust to awaken the Christian mind from its dogmatic slumbers, and only today, half a century later, are the effects of the awakening slowly becoming visible in the writings of Catholic and Protestant theologians,[14] as well as in the sermonic and teaching materials used in the parishes and congregations.[15] Not only has the ancient teaching of contempt—deicide, malediction, degeneracy, carnality, diabolism—been expunged from serious Christian thought, but also its more subtle variations—supersessionism, gentilization, exclusivism, triumphalism—have been challenged, sometimes with dramatic and controversial results.[16] Mainstream Christian preachers of the present are much less likely than their predecessors to speak in facile terms of Christianity as the "crown and completion of Judaism," and to campaign for Jewish conversions. These things can still happen, of course, but the churches are wiser than in the past.

Appendix A

ON NOVEMBER 20, 1938, in the wake of *Kristallnacht*, non-sectarian protest rallies involving civic officials, members of Parliament, members of the bench, Protestant, Catholic and Jewish leaders, educators and prominent citizens were held in Yarmouth, NS, Sydney, NS, Montreal, QC, Quebec City, QC, Sherbrooke, QC, Kingston, ON, Kirkland Lake, ON, Kitchener, ON, Hamilton, ON, London, ON, Niagara Falls, ON, Toronto, ON, Welland, ON, Winnipeg, MB, Regina, SK, Calgary, AB, Vancouver, BC and in other towns and cities as well. These meetings were organized by the Canadian Jewish Congress.[1] We cite as examples several of the resolutions passed and forwarded to the Canadian government:

(1) Hamilton (attendance 2,500):

> We, 2,500 citizens of Hamilton, Ontario, assembled at a memorial and protest meeting on Sunday, November 20, and addressed by Mr. Arthur W. Roebuck, M.P.P., and others, including, Dr. Crossley Hunter, Right Reverend J.A. O'Brien, Professor H.O. MacNeill, Rabbi A.A. Feldman and Controller S. Lawrence, Mayor William Morrison, Right Reverend L.W.B. Broughall, and John Harrison express our horror at the barbarous treatment of all liberally minded persons, the Jewish race, and Catholic and Protestant Church Leaders in Germany and Austria. We join the Jewish people and the whole civilized world in mourning the innocent victims and condemn the persecution, desecration of houses of worship and destruction of property in Nazi Germany.
>
> Our hearts go out in prayer for the persecuted in Germany and Austria and for all those who are reduced to poverty and misery and who are driven into exile from their centuries-old homeland because of racial and religious differences.
>
> We, therefore, urge the Canadian Government to protest, in the name of the liberty-loving Canadian people, against the persecution of all liberally-minded persons, the Jewish race, and Catholic and Protestant Church leaders in Germany and Austria.
>
> We further urge that the Canadian Government co-operate with Great Britain and the United States of America in attempts to alleviate this terrible situation.

(2) Kingston (attendance 1,200):

> To Prime Minister Mackenzie King:
>
> We, the citizens of Kingston, assembled in mass meeting on Sunday afternoon, November 20th, presided over by the Mayor of Kingston and addressed by His Grace the Archbishop of Kingston, Most Reverend M.J. O'Brien, and Dr. R.C. Wallace, principal of Queen's University, express our horror at the outrageous treatment of helpless Jews and of Christian leaders in Nazi Germany.

Note to this Appendix is on p. 173.

Our hearts go out in prayer for the persecuted and maligned Jews in Germany and Austria and to all those who are reduced to poverty or driven into exile from their centuries-old homeland.

We respectfully submit that it is the duty of free citizens of every free and liberty-loving country to protest vigorously against the inhuman treatment being meted out to fellow beings of the Jewish race who are a minority in modern Germany.

This meeting also feels that Canada should do her share with the other members of the British Empire in providing a haven for a people known throughout the world for their consistent industry. The plight of the Jewish little children and youth makes to us a special appeal which should not go unheeded.

(3) Kirkland Lake (attendance 800):

To the Rt. Hon. Wm. L. Mackenzie King,
Prime Minister of Canada,
Ottawa.

We, citizens of Kirkland Lake assembled at the memorial and sympathy meeting called by the local committee of the Canadian Jewish Congress and endorsed by Reeve Carter and Council Township of Teck; Rev. J.E. Graham, Trinity United Church; Rev. Father McMahon, Holy Name Parish; Rev. Father Jodoin, Church of the Assumption; Rev. H.E. Sims, St. Peter's Anglican Church; Rev. C.J. MacKay, St. Andrews Presbyterian Church; Rev. Walter Daniel, Baptist Church; A.G. McCool, High and Vocational School; E.E. McDermid, Public School; Captain Wells, Salvation Army; Theo. Algar, Kiwanis Club; Neil Wilson, Canadian Legion Branch 87; B. Hynes, Lions Club; Dan Worden, Northern News; Brigadier-General A.E. Swift; Miss D. McCrea, Y.W.C.A.; Walter Little, M.P.; Rabbi Halpern, Mr. H. Garshon, Hebrew congregation; Mr. Jos. Scott, Bnai Brith; Mr. H.R. Moscoe, Canadian Jewish Congress; Mr. Jack Reid, Radio Station CJKL; which meeting was addressed by Mr. Moscoe; Rev. Daniel; Reeve R.J. Carter; Rev. Father McMahon; Rev. J.E. Graham; Rev. Father Jodoin; Rev. C.J. MacKay; Willson Woodside and Rabbi Halpern, express our horror at the barbarous treatment of the poor and helpless Jews, and the outrageous treatment of Catholics and Protestant Church leaders in Germany and Austria. We join the Jewish people and the whole civilized world in mourning the innocent victims, and condemn the persecution, desecration of houses of worship, and destruction of property in Nazi Germany.

Our hearts go out in prayer for the prosecuted, maligned peoples in Germany and Austria; to all those who are reduced to poverty and slavery, and who are driven into exile from their centuries-old homeland, because of religious and racial differences.

No expression of sympathy without alleviation of suffering can suffice in this tragedy. We, therefore, appeal to the Government of Canada and to the people of Canada that the doors of this great, freedom-loving country, which helped many exiles to find happy homes within its shores, be opened to an appreciable number of German and Jewish refugees. Let Canada be a haven of refuge to all those whose present treatment is a blot on our civilization, to all those who are hunted, starved, and morally massacred. May God help them.

(4) Kitchener (attendance 1,200):

We, the citizens of Kitchener, Guelph, Galt, Preston, Waterloo and Hespeler, assembled at a memorable meeting in the city of Kitchener, express our sorrow and horror at the barbarous treatment of the poor and helpless Jews, and the outrageous treatment of Catholic and Protestant church leaders in Germany. We join the Jewish people and the whole civilized world in mourning the innocent victims and condemn the persecution and desecration of houses of worship and destruction of property in Nazi Germany.

Our hearts go out in prayer for the persecuted, maligned, wretched Jews in Germany, to all those who are reduced to poverty and slavery and who are driven into exile from their centuries-old homeland because of religious and racial differences.

No expression of sympathy without the alleviation of suffering can suffice in this tragedy. We therefore appeal to the government of Canada and to the people of Canada, that the doors of this great freedom-loving country, which helped many exiles to find happy homes within its shores, be opened to an appreciable number of German and Jewish refugees.

Let Canada be a haven of refuge to all those whose treatment is a blot on our civilization, to all those who are hunted, slaved, and morally massacred. May God help them!

(5) London (attendance 1,000):

This great mass meeting of citizens of London, representing all classes, nationalities and creeds, civil and provincial governments, Great War veterans and labor unions, view with abhorrence the events of recent weeks in Europe, wherein scores of thousands of Jewish men, women and children have been driven from their homes and left dispossessed of their means of livelihood; expresses its deepest sympathy with the persecuted people and resolves to stand in readiness to support, through any well accredited channels, any general relief policy that may be decided upon.

(6) Niagara Falls (attendance 800):

To the Right Honorable William L. Mackenzie King,
Prime Minister of Canada.

We citizens of Niagara Falls and district, called by a local Citizens' Committee held in the Capital Theatre, Sunday afternoon, November 20, express our horror at the barbarous treatment of the helpless Jews and the outrageous treatment of Catholic and Protestant church leaders in Germany and Austria. We join the Jewish people and the civilized world in mourning the innocent victims and condemn the persecution of houses of worship and destruction of property in Nazi Germany.

We appeal to the government of Canada to co-operate with other nations in an effort to ameliorate the lot of the hundreds of thousands of refugees, seeking to escape from Nazi brutality and that the Canadian government be asked to forward the protest to the German Government.

(7) Toronto (attendance 20,000):

The world is aghast at the latest news which has come from Germany. In the hour of their unparalleled suffering we offer our fellow-Jews in Germany the assurance of our deepest sympathy and understanding. In the midst of our grief we derive a measure of solace from the fact that the civilized part of the world has come to realize that this barbarianism directed against the Jews is violence against the whole of humanity. This attitude is a recognition that we are here confronted with an issue which goes far beyond the persecution and torture of a particular minority; and that today it is civilization itself which is under attack. All Canadians—Protestants, Catholics and Jews alike—have reacted to these hideous accounts from abroad with a feeling of personal hurt. The sympathy expressed by government leaders of Great Britain and the United States and echoed by the press and spiritual and cultural leaders in Canada manifests the depth of feeling of the English-speaking peoples. This universal sense of sorrow and outrage will continue to make itself felt. Intimidation cannot prevent right-thinking men throughout the world from seeking justice for them to whom it is denied. The Jew, throughout the ages of persecution, has maintained his faith in the God of all mankind. This faith in the sovereignty of eternal justice and the ultimate triumph of eternal truth stands as the common heritage of man. It is our hope that the Canadian people having demonstrated their humane feelings will now show their moral courage by taking action together with other liberal and democratic countries to prove havens of refuge for the victims of Nazi brutality.

(8) Welland (attendance 600):

The Welland meeting passed a resolution expressing horror at the barbarous persecution and urging the Dominion government to immediately consult with the governments of other countries and to take such steps in co-operation with them to ameliorate the lot of the refugees in Germany and Austria, and to make the German people aware of the horror with which their actions have filled the civilized world. The resolution was wired to Prime Minister Mackenzie King.

Source: Information from the archives of the Canadian Jewish Congress, Montreal.

Appendix B

Statement issued by the Christian Social Council of Canada,
February 5, 1940[1]
IMMIGRATION AND THE REFUGEE QUESTION
(Approved by the Board of Directors)

The Christian Social Council of Canada has been increasingly perturbed over the apparent attitude of the government towards immigration. We believe that the war has not lessened but rather enlarged the moral responsibility of Canada towards refugee immigration, especially those now residing in England and France, and indeed within those neutral countries now threatened by Germany and her ally, Russia.

We believe that if these people are, as some seem to fear, dangerous aliens, then they are less dangerous in Canada than in Europe. If they are, as we believe, our friends, then the obligation becomes readily apparent.

In reality these victims who have withstood the brunt of Hitler's satanic fury for more than five years are our allies. More correctly, we are their allies. These who have suffered the loss of everything except life itself *would seem quite properly a charge against our war expenditure.*

Some of those in England and France, especially the children, might quite logically be brought to Canada as a gesture at least towards assisting in the problem of food supplies of the mother countries. Others in countries threatened by Hitler and Stalin should be brought, if for no other reason, in order to obviate the likelihood that they will become by force a part of the labour battalions of the enemy.

It is with increasing reluctance that we keep silence on this most pressing problem. There come times when silence ceases to be a virtue even in the name of national unity. We most earnestly press for serious consideration and action.

Note to this Appendix is on p. 173.

Notes

Introduction

1 Irving Abella and Harold Troper, *None Is Too Many: Canada and the Jews of Europe 1933-1948* (Toronto: Lester & Orpen Dennys, 1982), p. 51.
2 Ibid., p. 284.
3 William E. Nawyn, *American Protestantism's Response to Germany's Jews and Refugees 1933-1941* (Ann Arbor: UMI Research Press, 1981), p. 135.
4 We owe this observation to Professor Alan Hayes of Wycliffe College, Toronto.
5 R.G. Collingwood, *The Idea of History* (London: Oxford University Press, 1956), pp. 257f.
6 Cf. Benjamin Wall Redekop, "The German Identity of Mennonite Brethren Immigrants in Canada, 1930-1960" (unpublished M.A. thesis, University of British Columbia, 1990), p. 22.

Chapter I

1 John Herd Thompson with Allen Seager, *Canada 1922-1939: Decades of Discord* (Toronto: McClelland & Stewart, 1985), p. 195.
2 Paul Tillich, *The Courage to Be* (New Haven: Yale University Press, 1952), p. 62.
3 Ibid.
4 Donald G. Creighton, *Dominion of the North: A History of Canada* (Boston: Houghton Mifflin, 1944), p. 484.
5 Hannah Arendt, *Between Past and Future: Eight Exercises in Political Thought* (New York: Viking Press, 1961), p. 26.
6 Cf. Martin Robin, *Shades of Right: Nativist and Fascist Politics in Canada 1920-1940* (Toronto: University of Toronto Press, 1992), chaps. 1-3.
7 Lita-Rose Betcherman, *The Swastika and the Maple Leaf: Fascist Movements in Canada in the Thirties* (Toronto: Fitzhenry & Whiteside, 1975), p. 38. For a more recent and extensive examination of Arcand and Canadian fascism, see Robin, *Shades of Right*, passim.
8 Thompson with Seager, *Canada 1922-1939*, p. 224.
9 H. Blair Neatby, *The Politics of Chaos: Canada in the Thirties* (Toronto: Macmillan, 1972), p. 34.
10 Thompson with Seager, *Canada 1922-1939*, p. 313.
11 F.H. Underhill, cited in ibid., p. 314.
12 Gerald E. Dirks, *Canada's Refugee Policy: Indifference or Opportunism?* (Montreal and Kingston: McGill-Queen's University Press, 1977), p. 42.
13 After Count Arthur de Gobineau, author of *Essai sur l'inégalité des races humaines* (1853-1855).
14 See Alan Davies, *Infected Christianity: A Study of Modern Racism* (Montreal and Kingston: McGill-Queen's University Press, 1988), chap. 4.
15 Cf. Angus McLaren, *Our Own Master Race: Eugenics in Canada, 1885-1945* (Toronto: McClelland & Stewart, 1990).

16 See Esther Delisle, *The Traitor and the Jew: Anti-Semitism and the Delirium of Extremist Right-Wing Nationalism in French Canada from 1929-1939,* translated by Madeleine Hébert (Montreal: Robert Davies Publishing, 1993).

17 Johann-Gottlieb Fichte, author of *Reden an die deutsche Nation* (Addresses to the German nation) 1807-1808, was one of the fathers of modern German nationalism.

18 Delisle, *The Traitor and the Jew,* p. 63. See also Norman F. Cornett, "Lionel Groulx's rationale for French Canadian Nationalism," *Studies in Religion,* 18, 4 (1989): 407-414.

    Johann-Gottlieb Fichte (1762-1814) delivered his famous *Reden an die deutsche Nation* (Addresses to the German nation) in French-occupied Berlin in 1807. This remains one of the classic texts in the history of nationalism. Esther Delisle draws a comparison between Fichte in Germany and Groulx in Quebec: "In the manner of the post-Kantian German philosopher Fichte, who designates to the state the mission of making those who inhabit its territory into veritable human beings through its culture, Groulx designates both the nation and the state to accomplish this task" (*The Traitor and the Jew,* p. 63).

19 "There is a moment in which the self-affirmation of the average man becomes neurotic.... If this happens—and it often happens in critical periods of history—the self-affirmation becomes pathological. The dangers connected with the change, the unknown character of the things to come, the darkness of the future make the average man a fanatical defender of the established order. He defends it as compulsively as the neurotic defends the castle of his imaginary world.... This is the explanation of the mass neuroses which usually appear at the end of an era" (Tillich, *The Courage to Be,* pp. 69-70).

20 Cf. W. Peter Ward, *White Canada Forever: Popular Attitudes and Public Policy toward Orientals in British Columbia* (rpt. Montreal and Kingston: McGill-Queen's University Press, 1990).

21 Cf. Ann Gomer Sunahara, *The Politics of Racism: The Uprooting of Japanese Canadians during the Second World War* (Toronto: James Lorimer, 1981).

22 Cf. Abella and Troper, *None Is Too Many.*

23 Cf. Moshe Zimmerman, *Wilhelm Marr: The Patriarch of Antisemitism* (New York: Oxford University Press, 1986), p. 113.

24 Cf. Richard Menkis, "Antisemitism and Anti-Judaism in Pre-Confederation Canada," in Alan Davies, ed., *Antisemitism in Canada: History and Interpretation* (Waterloo: Wilfrid Laurier University Press, 1992), p. 11. See also Irving Abella, *A Coat of Many Colours: Two Centuries of Jewish Life in Canada* (Toronto: Lester & Orpen Dennys, 1990), chap. 1.

25 Menkis, "Antisemitism and Anti-Judaism in Pre-Confederation Canada," p. 13.

26 See Michael Brown, "The Beginning of Jewish Emancipation in Canada: The Hart Affair," *Michael* (The Diaspora Research Institute, Tel-Aviv University), 10 (1986): 31-38; also Abella, *A Coat of Many Colours,* pp. 18-21.

27 Menkis, "Antisemitism and Anti-Judaism in Pre-Confederation Canada," p. 15.

28 Ibid., pp. 17-23.

29 Ibid., p. 20.

30 See Phyllis Senese, "*La Croix de Montréal* (1893-1895): A Link to the French Radical Right," *Canadian Catholic Historical Studies* 55th Annual Meeting, Winnipeg, 1986, p. 92. Maurras influenced Groulx directly (Betcherman, *The Swastika and the Maple Leaf,* p. 32).

31 Senese, "*La Croix de Montréal* (1893-1895)." See also Delisle, *The Traitor and the Jew,* pp. 55-78.

32 Menkis, "Antisemitism and Anti-Judaism in Pre-Confederation Canada," p. 25.

33 Gerald Tulchinsky, "Goldwin Smith: Victorian Canadian Antisemite," in Davies, ed., *Antisemitism in Canada,* pp. 67-91; see also Abella, *A Coat of Many Colours,* pp. 105-107.

34 Ibid., pp. 75f.

35 See Phyllis Senese, "Antisemitic Dreyfusards: The Confused Western-Canadian Press," in Davies, ed., *Antisemitism in Canada,* pp. 93-111. While Senese confines her study to the western Canadian press, there is no reason to suppose that her findings do not apply to the eastern press as well.

36 Michael Brown, "From Stereotype to Scapegoat: Anti-Jewish Sentiment in French Canada from Confederation to World War I," in Davies, ed., *Antisemitism in Canada,* pp. 44-47. For a more extensive discussion of this and other aspects of the Jewish identity crisis in Canada, see Michael Brown, *Jew or Juif? Jews, French Canadians and Anglo-Canadians 1759-1914* (Philadelphia: Jewish Publication Society, 1987).

37 Ibid., p. 58.

38 Ibid.

39 Stephen Speisman, "Antisemitism in Ontario: The Twentieth Century," in Davies, ed., *Antisemitism in Canada,* p. 113.

40 Ibid., p. 115.

41 Cited in ibid., p. 118.

42 See David Rome, *Clouds in the Thirties: On Anti-Semitism in Canada 1929-1939,* National Archives, Canadian Jewish Congress, Montreal, 1979, Section 9, pp. 325-326.

43 Howard Palmer, "Politics, Religion and Antisemitism in Alberta, 1880-1950," in Davies, ed., *Antisemitism in Canada,* p. 170.

44 Pierre Anctil, "Interlude of Hostility: Judeo-Christian Relations in Quebec in the Interwar Period, 1919-39," in Davies, ed., *Antisemitism in Canada,* pp. 140-145. For a longer account, see Anctil, *Le Rendez-vous manqué: les Juifs de Montréal face au Québec de l'entre-deux guerres* (Montréal: Institut Québécois de recherche sur la culture, 1988).

45 Ibid., p. 148. For another account of the era and the Rabinovitch affair, see Abella, *A Coat of Many Colours,* chap. 8.

46 See Betcherman, *The Swastika and the Maple Leaf,* pp. 57-59. For a longer account, see Cyril Levitt and William Shaffir, *The Riot at Christie Pits* (Toronto: Lester & Orpen Dennys, 1987).

47 Robin, *Shades of Right,* chap. 9.

48 Heinrich Seelheim (German consul in Montreal in Winnipeg), cited in Jonathan F. Wagner, *Brothers Beyond the Sea: National Socialism in Canada* (Waterloo: Wilfrid Laurier University Press, 1981, p. 47).

49 For a good description of Coughlin, see Arthur M. Schlesinger, Jr., *The Politics of Upheaval* (Boston: Houghton Mifflin, 1960), pp. 16-28. Schlesinger, however, does not discuss Coughlin's antisemitism.

50 Palmer, "Politics, Religion and Antisemitism in Alberta, 1880-1950," p. 173.

51 After Major C.H. Douglas, the founder of Social Credit theory.

52 Palmer, "Politics, Religion and Antisemitism in Alberta, 1880-1950," p. 184.

53 Cf. Paul Lawrence Rose, *Revolutionary Antisemitism in Germany: From Kant to Wagner* (Princeton: Princeton University Press, 1990). The composer Richard Wagner in particular thought in these terms.

54 Hannah Arendt, *The Origins of Totalitarianism* (New York: Meridian Books, 1958), passim.

55 Arthur Hertzberg, *The French Enlightenment and the Jews: The Origins of Modern Antisemitism* (New York: Columbia University Press, 1968).

56 Cf. Jules Isaac, *The Teaching of Contempt,* translated by Helen Weaver (New York: McGraw-Hill, 1964).

57 Cf. Léon Poliakov, trans., *The Aryan Myth: A History of Racist and Nationalist Ideas in Europe* (London: Sussex University Press, 1974).

58 See, for example, Leon Schwartz, *Diderot and the Jews* (Teaneck, NJ: Fairleigh Dickinson University Press, 1987).

59 Rose, *Revolutionary Antisemitism in Germany,* passim.

60 "Patience, Luther, Hitler will come. Your wishes will be granted, and more. Let us recognize here the family ties, the blood ties, uniting two great Germans, and let us place Luther in the place he deserves, in the first row of Christian precursors—of Auschwitz" (Jules Isaac, *Jesus and Israel,* translated by Sally Gran [New York: Holt, Rinehart & Winston, 1971], p. 249).

61 For example, by James Parkes, Léon Poliakov, Rosemary Radford Ruether, Robert S. Wistrich, etc.

62 Ernst Nolte, *Three Faces of Fascism: Action Française, Italian Fascism, National Socialism,* translated by Leila Vennewitz (New York: New American Library, 1969), pp. 365-374. Ironically, despite his brilliant analysis of fascism in this volume, Nolte has identified himself increasingly with nationalistic, right-wing and revisionist ideas in contemporary Germany.

63 Arthur C. Cochrane, *The Church's Confession under Hitler* (Philadelphia: Westminster Press, 1962), p. 82.

64 "Theologisches Gutachten uber die Zulassung von Christen judischer herkunft zu den Amtern der Deutschen Evangelischen Kirche," in Kurt Dietrich Schmidt, ed., *Die Bekenntnisse und grundsatzlichen Ausserungen zur Kirchenfrage des Jahres 1933* (Gottingen: Vandenhoeck & Reprecht, 1937), p. 184.

65 Cf. Richard L. Rubenstein and John K. Roth, *Approaches to Auschwitz: The Holocaust and Its Legacy* (Atlanta: John Knox Press, 1987), p. 117.

66 Raul Hilberg, *The Destruction of the European Jews* (New York: New Viewpoints, 1973), p. 29.

67 Deborah Lipstadt, *Beyond Belief: The American Press and the Coming of the Holocaust 1933-1945* (New York: The Free Press, 1986), p. 101.

68 Dirks, *Canada's Refugee Policy,* p. 35.

69 Bernard Wasserstein, *Britain and the Jews of Europe 1939-1945* (Oxford: Clarendon Press, 1979), p. 9.

70 Rubenstein and Roth, *Approaches to Auschwitz,* p. 123. The camp that would not accept them is described in graphic detail by Henry L. Feingold, *The Politics of Rescue: The Roosevelt Administration and the Holocaust 1938-1945* (New Brunswick, NJ: Rutgers University Press, 1970), especially chap. 5.

71 Lipstadt. *Beyond Belief,* pp. 116-117.

72 The term "holocaust," from the Greek *holokaustos* and the Latin *holocaustum,* means "burnt whole." In the ancient Greek translation of the Hebrew Scriptures known as the Septuagint, it was employed to signify the Hebrew *olah,* or burnt offering. The modern usage in reference to the Nazi murders seems to have originated in France in the war period. Because of its sacrificial connotations, some writers have objected to the term, substituting the Hebrew term *Shoah,* or catastrophic destruction.

73 Cf. Arthur D. Morse, *While Six Million Died: A Chronicle of American Apathy* (New York: Hart Publishing, 1968), pp. 3f.

74 Ibid.; see also Feingold, *The Politics of Rescue*, pp. 169f.

75 "If international-finance Jewry inside and outside of Europe should succeed once more in plunging nations into another world war, the consequence will not be the Bolshevization of the earth and thereby the victory of Jewry, but the annihilation (*Vernichtung*) of the Jewish race in Europe" (cited in Hilberg, *Destruction of the European Jews*, p. 257).

76 Robert W. Ross, *So It Was True: American Protestantism and the Nazi Persecution of the Jews* (Minneapolis: University of Minnesota Press, 1980), p. 170.

77 As Deborah Lipstadt has pointed out, the public reaction was quite different in Britain (*Beyond Belief*, pp. 189-191).

Chapter II

1 See David R. Hughes and Evelyn Kallen, *The Anatomy of Racism: Canadian Dimensions* (Montreal: Harvest House, 1974), pp. 183-184.

2 Cf. John Webster Grant, *The Church in the Canadian Era* (Burlington: Welch Publishing, 1988), p. 179.

3 Nawyn, *American Protestantism's Response*, p. 34.

4 Thompson with Seager, *Canada 1922-1939*, p. 232.

5 As in his book *Strangers within Our Gates* (1909; rpt. Toronto: University of Toronto Press, 1972).

6 Nawyn, *American Protestantism's Response*, p. 42.

7 *Census of Canada, 1941*, p. 518.

8 Richard Allen, *The Social Passion: Religion and Social Reform in Canada 1914-28* (Toronto: University of Toronto Press, 1971), p. 256.

9 Grant, *The Church in the Canadian Era*, p. 103.

10 Ibid., p. 103. See John Wesley's *Thoughts on Slavery* (1774).

11 See Uriel Tal, *Christians and Jews in Germany: Religion, Politics, and Ideology in the Second Reich, 1870-1914*, translated by Noah Jonathan Jacobs (Ithaca: Cornell University Press, 1975), p. 170. Tal is referring to Rabbi Joseph Eschelbacher's public reply to Albrecht Ritschl's lectures on the anniversary of Luther's birth in 1887 in which Christ was presented as the proper spiritual and ethical model for German society.

12 Walter Rauschenbusch, *Christianizing the Social Order* (1912), cited in Robert T. Handy, ed., *The Social Gospel in America 1870-1920* (New York: Oxford University Press, 1966), p. 340.

13 Richard Roberts, "The Quiet Hour," *The New Outlook*, November 29, 1933, p. 845.

14 *Census of Canada, 1941*. p. 518.

15 T.R. Millman, "Tradition in the Anglican Church of Canada," in John Webster Grant, ed., *The Churches and the Canadian Experience* (Toronto: Ryerson Press, 1963), p. 22.

16 See H.H. Walsh, *The Christian Church in Canada* (Toronto: Ryerson Press, 1956), pp. 93-98, 172-174, etc.

17 Allen, *The Social Passion*, p. 15. However, M.J. Coldwell, the second leader of the C.C.F. Party, was an Anglican.

18 Ibid., p. 6.

19 Cf. Joseph Fletcher, *William Temple: Twentieth-Century Christian* (New York: Seabury Press, 1963), p. 284. The "people's archbishop," so named because of his

labour sympathies, was the author of a number of important books, of which the best known are *Christianity and the Social Order* (1942) and *Nature, Man and God* (1934).

20 Today, in the wake of the Holocaust, this connection has become a truism. Such post-war books as Isaac, *Jesus and Israel;* A. Roy Eckardt, *Elder and Younger Brothers: The Encounter of Jews and Christians* (New York: Charles Scribner's Sons, 1967); and Rosemary Radford Ruether, *Faith and Fratricide: The Theological Roots of Anti-Semitism* (New York: Seabury Press, 1974), reflect this claim. However, the exact nature of the relationship between Christian anti-Judaism and modern antisemitism is still the subject of debate, as well as the degree to which basic Christian beliefs, especially in the realm of christology, are affected. An impressive work of Christian theological recon-struction has been written by Clark M. Williamson, *A Guest in the House of Israel: Post-Holocaust Church Theology* (Louisville: Westminster/John Knox Press, 1993).

21 F.J. Nicholson, "The Christian Approach to the Jew," *The Canadian Churchman,* April 11, 1935, p. 228.

22 E.g., Morris Kaminsky, E.S. Greenbaum.

23 *Census of Canada, 1941,* p. 518.

24 See Walsh, *The Christian Church in Canada,* pp. 302-303.

25 John S. Moir, *Enduring Witness: A History of the Presbyterian Church in Canada,* 2nd and enlarged ed. (Toronto: Bryant Press, 1937), p. 235.

26 Ibid.

27 See Heiko A. Oberman, *The Roots of Anti-Semitism: In the Age of Renaissance and Reformation,* translated by James J. Porter (Philadelphia: Fortress Press, 1981), pp. 144-145, fn. 6.

28 Cf. "Rax Me that Bible," *The Presbyterian Record,* 62, 3 (March 1937): 87.

29 See the review of Thomas Walker, *An Exposition of the Judaism of the Home of Jesus,* in *The Presbyterian Record,* 62, 9 (September 1937): 277.

30 Rev. John Stuart Conning, "The Presbyterian Church and the Jews," *The Presbyterian Record,* 60, 1 (March 1935): 87.

31 Ibid., p. 88.

32 Chapter V.

33 *Census of Canada, 1941,* p. 518.

34 However, Anabaptist exiles in England also played a formative role in English Baptist history.

35 The term "evangelical" is actually used in different ways and can signify different things to different people, especially on opposite sides of the Atlantic Ocean. We will employ it in the broad sense indicated above, rather than in a narrow doctrinal sense. The term "fundamentalist," in a Christian context at least, has a clear doctrinal meaning. It is taken from a series of tracts entitled *The Fundamentals* (1910-1915) which assume the literal inerrancy of the lost autographs of Holy Scripture. The two terms may or may not overlap.

36 Grant, *The Church in the Canadian Era,* p. 129.

37 *Census of Canada, 1941,* p. 518.

38 Cf. Allen, *The Social Passion,* p. 69.

39 See Leslie K. Tarr, *Shields of Canada: T.T. Shields (1873-1955)* (Grand Rapids, MI: Baker Book House, 1967), pp. 91-100. Tarr's account is highly apologetic.

40 Chapter VI.

41 "Why Was Jesus a Jew?," *The Canadian Baptist,* December 14, 1933, p. 6.

42 "When Jews and Gentiles Sit Together," *The Canadian Baptist,* October 29, 1936, p. 3.

43 "This Could Not Have Happened in Germany," *The Canadian Baptist,* June 2, 1938, p. 22.

44 *Census of Canada, 1941,* p. 518.

45 Walter Freitag, "Lutheran Tradition in Canada," in Grant, ed., *The Churches and the Canadian Experience,* p. 97.

46 Grant, *The Church in the Canadian Era,* p. 240. See also Carl Raymond Cronmiller, *A History of the Lutheran Church in Canada,* Vol. 1 (n.p.: The Evangelical Lutheran Synod of Canada, 1961).

47 Walter Freitag, "Fundamentalism and Canadian Lutheranism," *Consensus,* 13, 1 (1987): 28

48 Ralph Moellering, "Lutheran-Jewish Relations and the Holocaust," *Consensus,* 8, 1 (January 1982): 29.

49 See E. Clifford Nelson, "The New Shape of Lutheranism 1930-," in E. Clifford Nelson, ed., *The Lutherans in North America* (Philadelphia: Fortress Press, 1975), pp. 453-471.

50 Moellering, "Lutheran-Jewish Relations and the Holocaust," p. 30.

51 For an account of Luther's antisemitism, see Oberman, *The Roots of Anti-Semitism,* Part 3.

52 Uriel Tal, "Lutheran Theology and the Third Reich," in Paul D. Opsahl and Marc H. Tanenbaum, eds., *Speaking of God Today: Jews and Lutherans in Conversation* (Philadelphia: Fortress Press, 1974), p. 91. See also the excellent discussion of Luther in Steven T. Katz, *The Holocaust in Historical Perspective,* Vol. I (New York: Oxford University Press, 1994), pp. 386-394.

53 See Robert P. Ericksen, *Theologians under Hitler: Gerhard Kittel, Paul Althaus and Emanuel Hirsch* (New Haven: Yale University Press, 1985).

54 Nelson, "The New Shape of Lutheranism 1930-," p. 466.

55 Nawyn, *American Protestantism's Response,* p. 87.

56 Cf. Frank H. Epp, *Mennonites in Canada, 1786-1920: The History of a Separate People* (Toronto: Macmillan, 1974), pp. 47-63.

57 *Census of Canada, 1941,* p. 518.

58 For a full account, see Frank H. Epp, *Mennonites in Canada, 1920-1940: A People's Struggle for Survival* (Toronto: Macmillan, 1982), especially chaps. 1 and 6.

59 Ibid.

60 "I tell you the truth in Christ; the truly baptized disciples of Christ, who are baptized inwardly with the Spirit and with fire, and outwardly with water according to God's Word, know of no weapons other than patience, hope, non-resistance and God's Word.... Our weapons are not such with which cities and countries are desolated, walls and gates broken down and human blood shed like water, but they are weapons to destroy the spiritual kingdom of the devil, put away ungodliness and break the flinty hearts that have never been affected by the heavenly dew of the holy word" (Menno Simons, cited in John Horsch, *Menno Simons, His Life, Labors and Teachings* [Scottdale: Mennonite Publishing House, 1916], p. 285).

61 Epp, *Mennonites in Canada, 1786-1920,* p. 404.

62 Gradually, however, this stance was modified.

63 Oberman, *The Roots of Anti-Semitism,* p. 7.

64 Nawyn, *American Protestantism's Response,* p. 104.

65 Ibid., p. 97.

66 For example, "Die Tage der Kirche in Deutschland," *Der Bote,* October 13, 1937, p. 5, and October 20, 1937, pp. 4-5.

67 Arthur G. Dorland, *The Quakers in Canada, A History* (Toronto: Ryerson Press, 1968), pp. 55-61.

68 Ibid., pp. 118-156.

69 Geoffrey F. Nuttall, *Christian Pacifism in History* (Oxford: Basil Blackwell, 1958), p. 61.

70 Hugh Barbour and J. William Frost, *The Quakers* (New York: Greenwood Press, 1988).

71 Ibid., p. 44.

72 Cf. Thomas P. Socknat, *Witness against War: Pacifism in Canada 1900-1945* (Toronto: University of Toronto Press, 1987), p. 7. The terms "separational pacifism" and "integrational pacifism" were coined by Peter Brock to distinguish the Mennonites, Hutterites, Doukhobors, etc., from the Quakers and other liberal Protestants with pacifist convictions.

73 Chapter VI.

Chapter III

1 Two years after church union.

2 *The United Church of Canada Year Book* (Toronto, 1927), pp. 116-117. Although the author of these lines is not identified, the views expressed are probably an accurate reflection of a certain element in the United Church as well as society at large during the 1920s. Hugh Dobson, a former Methodist who served as western secretary of the Board of Evangelism and Social Service from 1925 to 1951, frequently indulged in anti-semitic comments in his early correspondence, blaming the Jews for undermining prohibition and for other social evils: "I think that we should do everything in our power to knock out this Jew bunch that is trying to carry on the [liquor] export houses, " etc. See David Elliott, "Hugh Wesley Dobson (1879-1956): Regenerator of Society," in Neil Semple, ed., *Papers: Canadian Methodist Historical Society 1991 and 1992* (Toronto, 1993), p. 34.

3 In 1934, when the shadow of persecution was starting to fall in Germany, a regular columnist in *The New Outlook* charged the Jews at the time of Jesus with a "narrow nationalism" that presumed "that God had chosen them, not for responsibility and service, but to special privilege and opportunity." That the writer really meant Jews in general is evident later in his column: "How deadly upon the Jewish people themselves the effect of this attitude of mind had become the whole history of the years before and after the coming of Christ very clearly reveals." (See "When Patriotism Goes Bad," *The New Outlook,* March 2, 1934, p. 322.) Two years later, the same writer still regarded the Jews as a "bigoted people" with a "narrow" and "selfish" religion. While these epithets were attached to first-century Jewry, the piece supplies no reason for supposing that modern Judaism was in any way less bigoted and less narrow than its spiritual ancestor. (See "Mr. Black's Bible Class," *The New Outlook,* August 26, 1936, p. 797.) Even during the war itself, when the Final Solution was gathering momentum, there were still United Church members capable of responding to a rabbi's plea for better Jewish-Christian relations by charging the Jews with deicide, and consequently with responsibility for their own troubles. (See W.H. Colclough, "Gentiles Only," *The United Church Observer,* March 15, 1943, p. 10; G.G. Harris, "Christian Toleration," *The United*

Church Observer, September 1, 1944, p. 17; R.H. Baxter, "Challenges Rabbi's Statement," *The United Church Observer,* October 1, 1944, p. 13.)

Unfortunately, the bad tradition did not end with the Allied victory in the Second World War and the revelation of the crematoria. Distorted and demonized images of the Pharisees and Sadducees and their "fiendish hatred" found their way into the best-selling New Curriculum adopted by the United Church in the early 1960s for use in its Sunday Schools and in lay education, notably in Donald M. Mathers, *The Word and the Way: Personal Christian Faith Today* (Toronto: United Church Publishing House, 1962), p. 62, and James S. Thomson, *God and His Purpose: The Meaning of Life* (Toronto: United Church Publishing House, 1964), p. 128. Neither Mathers nor Thomson intended to be anti-Jewish; both, however, accepted uncritically ancient polemical texts without exploring their religious and historical setting in the antagonisms of the first century and the rivalries of Jews and Christians as the two religious communities separated from each other in the wake of the Roman War, 66-70 C.E. It did not occur to either author that these falsified descriptions had played a serious role in the evolution of both Christian anti-Judaism and modern antisemitism. Unwittingly, they lent their distinguished names to a reprehensible pedagogy.

There was worse to follow. In the midst of an acrimonious debate between A.C. Forrest, a later editor of the *Observer,* and the Toronto Jewish community concerning the geopolitics of the Middle East and the Israeli-Palestinian conflict during the late 1960s and early 1970s, a plainly antisemitic article by John Nicholls Booth, an American Unitarian, entitled "How Zionists Manipulate Your News," was published (March 1972). This exercise in bad judgment greatly reinforced a suspicion in the Canadian Jewish Congress of the presence of antisemitism in Canada's largest and most liberal Protestant denomination. The *Observer* did nothing to alleviate this suspicion when, two years later, it accepted and published an antisemitic advertisement describing "official Judah" as controlling the money of the world and conspiring to establish a Jewish world government through the power of money (March 1974). Forrest was criticized severely both within and without the United Church.

We are indebted to Jennifer Palin for her excellent (unpublished) essay "The United Church and the Jews" (Emmanuel College, 1995).

4   Cf. Robert Wright, *A World Mission: Canadian Protestations and the Quest for a New International Order, 1918-1939* (Montreal and Kingston: McGill-Queen's University Press, 1991), p. 214.

5   H.B. Hendershot, "The German Point of View," *The New Outlook,* August 9, 1933, p. 584.

6   Ibid.

7   Claris E. Silcox, "The German Psychosis," *The New Outlook,* August 16, 1933, p. 598.

8   Cited in Rome, *Clouds in the Thirties,* National Archives, Canadian Jewish Congress, Montreal, 1978, Section 5, p. 57.

9   G.R. McKean, "Why Dictatorship?," *The New Outlook,* July 8, 1938, p. 658.

10 "Editorial in Brief," *The New Outlook,* November 21, 1934, p. 1029.

11 "Warning against Fascism," *The New Outlook,* January 1, 1936, p. 11.

12 "Quebec's Blueshirts," *The New Outlook,* February 25, 1938, pp. 173-174.

13 "Wake Up, Canada," *The New Outlook,* April 22, 1938, p. 385.

14 "Citizens' Forum—Democracy in Action," *The United Church Observer,* December 1, 1943, p. 11.

15 "Editorial in Brief," *The New Outlook,* April 12, 1933, p. 301.

16 See "Facing the Storm," *The New Outlook,* May 6, 1938, p. 432: "In a vague way we agree that it is wrong to penalize the Jews, but...."

17 Silcox, "The German Psychosis," p. 598.

18 There may have been others as well. The evidence is fragmentary and survives mostly by word-of-mouth. See Richard Roberts, "If Jesus Went to Germany?," *The New Outlook,* November 15, 1933, p. 805; Richard Roberts, "German Barbarity Deplored," *The New Outlook,* May 17, 1933, p. 387; G. Stanley Russell, "Mostly About People and Churches," *The New Outlook,* December 13, 1933, p. 874; E. Crossley Hunter, "The Marks of Anti-semitism," *The United Church Observer,* March 15, 1941, pp. 10-28; Ernest Marshall Howse, "I Speak for the Jew," address delivered in the Civic Auditorium, Winnipeg, October 11, 1942, later published in *Fellowship,* monthly bulletin of the Canadian Conference of Christians and Jews. Peter Bryce, a former moderator, was one of the speakers at the mass rally in Maple Leaf Gardens, Toronto, November 20, 1938. See the *Toronto Daily Star,* November 21, 1938.

19 Cited in Rome, *Clouds in the Thirties,* National Archives, Canadian Jewish Congress, Montreal, 1977, Section 3, p. 68. However, Chappell's first name was not "Norman," and his church was not "Saskatoon United Church."

20 Reuben Slonim, *To Kill a Rabbi* (Toronto: ECW Press, 1987), pp. 145f.

21 Rome, *Clouds in the Thirties,* National Archives, Canadian Jewish Congress, Montreal, 1978, Section 4, pp. 5-6.

22 There is little doubt that the Matthaean image of the blind, legalistic, impious, hypocritical, fanatical and murderous Pharisee (Matthew 23) is a caricature inspired by Jewish-Christian frictions [in Antioch?] in the final decades of the first century. Although much remains unknown about the ancient Pharisees (or *perushim*), especially about their precise origins and even the precise nature of the movement, Christian as well as Jewish scholars today regard Pharisaic Judaism as a profound and creative attempt to relate the Torah to contemporary Jewish life by means of an oral tradition as well as a written code. Spirituality and sanctification were Pharisaic values, and, in spite of his debates with Pharisees, it is conceivable that Jesus himself shared their essential principles. Later rabbinic Judaism probably evolved out of Pharisaic Judaism, although occasional scholars have questioned this view.

23 Chapter I.

24 "Our Montreal Letter," *The New Outlook,* March 7, 1934, p. 152.

25 See John S. Conway, *The Nazi Persecution of the Churches, 1933-45* (London: Weidenfeld & Nicolson, 1968); Ernst C. Helmreich, *The German Churches under Hitler: Background, Struggle and Epilogue* (Detroit: Wayne State University Press, 1979); and Klaus Scholder, trans., *The Churches and the Third Reich,* 2 vols. (Philadelphia: Fortress Press, 1991).

26 Cf. Richard Roberts, "The City Without Walls," *The New Outlook,* May 22, 1935, p. 516.

27 See H.M. Thomas, "Beyond Luther: The Nazis and the Church," *The New Outlook,* January 24, 1934, p. 56.

28 Guy Ramsey, "God in Exile," *The New Outlook,* June 26, 1935, p. 650.

29 "The Limit Has Been Reached," *The New Outlook,* January 22, 1936, p. 73.

30 "You Must Keep in Step," *The New Outlook,* June 4, 1937, p. 509.

31 "Keeping the Money at Home," *The New Outlook,* June 24, 1937, p. 509.

32 *Record of Proceedings of the Eighth General Council of the United Church of Canada, Toronto, September, 1938,* pp. 54-55.

33 "The Canadian National Council of the World Alliance for International Friendship through the Churches views with great sorrow the spread of Anti-Semitic propaganda in Canada by various agencies at the present time. Such agitation tends to break the fundamental unity of Canadian life and threatens the status to which all elements of our population are legally entitled. We call upon the leaders of our Christian Churches to urge their people to ignore such propaganda and ... to repudiate it as utterly unChristian and foreign to the mind of Christ (endorsed on motion by the Sub-Executive of the General Council of the United Church of Canada, *Minutes,* November 2, 1937, p. 112).

34 "Scared by a Mouse," *The New Outlook,* November 18, 1938, p. 1092.

35 See Appendix A.

36 "Healthy Instincts," *The New Outlook,* November 18, 1938, p. 1095.

37 Lipstadt, *Beyond Belief,* p. 101.

38 "A New Phase in Germany," *The New Outlook,* November 25, 1938, p. 1116.

39 Cf. Margaret Wrong, "International Missionary Council," *The New Outlook,* October 23, 1935, p. 1025.

40 "Canadian Churches and German Refugees," *Social Welfare* (March 1936), p. 26.

41 Cited in Rome, *Clouds in the Thirties,* National Archives, Canadian Jewish Congress, Montreal, 1980, Section 10, p. 504.

42 "Practical Christianity," *The New Outlook,* March 11, 1936, p. 267.

43 Ibid.

44 "A Refugee Film," *The New Outlook,* October 8, 1937, p. 918. The film in question was an American production consisting of addresses by James G. McDonald and Harry Emerson Fosdick, designed to raise American awareness of both the Jewish and the Christian plight.

45 Cited in Feingold, *The Politics of Rescue,* p. 33.

46 "The Refugees," *The New Outlook,* August 12, 1938, p. 757, and October 7, 1938, p. 958. Lord Baldwin's strong appeal on behalf of the Jewish refugees was also published (December 16, 1938, pp. 1224-1225).

47 Organ of the Gestapo.

48 "Is It Nothing to You?," *The New Outlook,* February 10, 1939, p. 120. See also "Wanted—A Home," *The New Outlook,* January 20, 1939, p. 52; "The Church and Refugees," *The United Church Observer,* March 1, 1939, p. 1; and "The Refugees," *The New Outlook,* March 15, 1939, p. 4. The editorial is unsigned, but the editorialist was almost certainly the editor of the day, Gerald Cragg, later professor of church history at Andover Newton Theological Seminary and the author of two important studies of English puritanism. Cragg also taught at the United Theological College in Montreal and served after the war as the senior minister of Erskine and American United Church in Montreal. One of the authors of this book recalls him as a brilliant preacher.

49 Claris E. Silcox, *The Challenge of Anti-Semitism to Democracy* (Toronto: The Committee on Jewish Gentile Relationships, 1939), p. 16.

50 "Christian Canada and the Refugees" and "The Refugees—A Policy for Canada" (privately published). Copies by courtesy of Dr. Howse.

51 "The Refugees—A Policy for Canada," p. 13.

52 *He is Mightiest in the Mightiest,* Thirteenth Annual Report (1937), Board of Evangelism and Social Service, The United Church of Canada, p. 37.

53 Conceived at a meeting of the League of Nations Executive Committee in Montreal, October 15, 1938, and inaugurated at a conference at the Chateau Laurier Hotel in Ottawa on December 6.

54 *Let the Church Be the Church,* Fourteenth Annual Report (1938), Board of Evangelism and Social Service, The United Church of Canada, p. 30.

55 Kenneth Craft "Canada's Righteous: A History of the Canadian National Committee on Refugees and Victims of Political Persecution" (unpublished M.A. thesis, Carleton University, 1987).

56 Abella and Troper, *None Is Too Many,* p. 14.

57 Ibid., p. 52.

58 Ibid., p. 50.

59 Cited in Rome, *Clouds in the Thirties,* National Archives, Canadian Jewish Congress, Montreal, 1980, Section 12, p. 691.

60 "Presbyteries Plead Refugees' Cause," *The United Church Observer,* March 1, 1939, p. 7.

61 *There Am I in the Midst,* Fifteenth Annual Report (1939), Board of Evangelism and Social Service, The United Church of Canada, p. 55.

62 Morse, *While Six Million Died,* p. 257.

63 The following motion was presented and adopted at a meeting of the Sub-Committee of the General Council, January 31, 1939, following the report of a committee appointed to consider the persecution of the Jews and the refugee problem: "That the Sub-Executive should endorse by resolution the general terms of the pronouncement of the Canadian National Committee on Refugees; that a committee be appointed to embody the terms of this pronouncement in a draft for the United Church of Canada; that conference be had with the heads of other Canadian Churches with a view to securing a united petition to present to the Canadian Government" (*Minutes,* p. 41).

64 See *Minutes of the Fifteenth Maritime Conference,* Sackville, New Brunswick, June 6-11, 1939, p. 30; *Montreal and Ottawa Conference, Fifteenth Annual Meeting,* St. James United Church, Montreal, June 5-9, 1939, p. 1462; *Bay of Quinte Conference, Year Book and Record of Proceedings of the Fifteenth Conference,* Sydenham Street United Church, Kingston, May 30-June 4, 1939, pp. 76-77; Toronto Conference, *Record of Proceedings of the Fifteenth Conference,* Carlton Street United Church, Toronto, May 30-June 5, 1939, p. 61; *Fifteenth Session of the London Conference, Digest of Minutes,* Centennial United Church, London, May 30-June 4, 1939, p. 39; *Manitoba Conference, Digest of Proceedings of the Fifteenth Conference,* Portage La Prairie, June 5-9, 1939, p. 11; *Saskatchewan Conference, Record of Proceedings of Fifteenth Conference,* Moose Jaw, June 1-6, 1939, p. 46; *Fifteenth Meeting of Alberta Conference,* Knox United Church, Calgary, May 24-30, 1939, p. 48; *Digest of the Minutes of the Fifteenth British Columbia Conference,* Queen's Avenue United Church, New Westminster, May 17-23, 1939, p. 20.

65 Dirks, *Canada's Refugee Policy,* p. 68.

66 Rome, *Clouds in the Thirties,* Section 12, pp. 687-688.

67 *The Eternal ... The Contemporary,* Sixteenth Annual Report (1940), Board of Evangelism and Social Service, The United Church of Canada, p. 66.

68 The following letter from the personal file of Ernest Marshall Howse is illuminating:

Department of Health and
Public Welfare,
Child Welfare Division,
657 Portage Avenue
Winnipeg

File No. Misc. 224

Rev. Ernest Howse,
Honorary Secretary-Treasurer
Canadian National Committee on Refugees,
120 Maryland Street,
WINNIPEG, Manitoba

Re: Jewish Refugees

Dear Dr. Howse:

With further reference to our correspondence herein, I beg to advise that I am now in receipt of a ruling from the Department of Immigration in which they state in part, "If there is any movement of refugee children they must be orphans in the true sense of the word. If the cases which you have on record cover children that are not orphans (in the true sense of the word) there is no use in any further action being taken with respect to their admission to Canada."

It would appear, therefore, that it would be necessary for you to provide us with a *certificate of death of both parents* [italics added] of any refugee children being admitted to this country. I shall therefore be pleased to hear from you further in this respect.

Yours faithfully,
(signed) Mildred B. McMurray
Legal Supervisor

69 *Record of Proceedings of the Ninth General Council,* The United Church of Canada, Winnipeg, September 1940, p. 281.

70 *Hope in God,* Seventeenth Annual Report (1941), Board of Evangelism and Social Service, The United Church of Canada, pp. 27-28.

71 *Right Relations among Men,* Nineteenth Annual Report (1943), Board of Evangelism and Social Service, The United Church of Canada, p. 62

72 Cf. Feingold, *The Politics of Rescue,* chap. 7, and Morse, *While Six Million Died,* chap. 3.

73 "United Church Sponsors Refugee Petition," *The United Church Observer,* November 1, 1943, p. 8; "Church Endorses Petition," *The United Church Observer,* January 15, 1944, p. 11. For the text of the petition, see Paula Draper and Harold Troper, eds., *Archives of the Holocaust* (New York and London: Garland Publishing, 1991), Vol. 15, p. 243. Although the petition collected 180,000 signatures, it accomplished nothing.

74 "Middlesex Presbytery Debates Refugee Petition," *The United Church Observer,* January 1, 1944, p. 21.

75 "Jesus—A Refugee," *The United Church Observer,* January 15, 1944, pp. 11, 26.

76 Letter to W.J. Sisler, November 11, 1943, United Church Archives. In a later letter to Sisler (December 2, 1943) Mutchmor elaborated: "I know that there are no neutrals on the Jewish question. I am not opposed to the Hebrew people, but I do not regard myself as one of those who is very keen for them" (ibid.).

77 Claris E. Silcox, *Church Union in Canada: Its Causes and Consequences* (New York: Institute of Social and Religious Research, 1933).

78 The Canadian Council of Church was founded in 1944.

79 The Christian Social Service Council drew support from the United Church, The Church of England in Canada, The Presbyterian Church, The Baptist conventions, The Salvation Army, The Society of Friends, some evangelical groups and the Y.M.C.A.

80 Craft, "Canada's Righteous," p. 30.

81 See, for example, Claris E. Silcox, "A Gentile Replies," in *An Epistle to the Hebrews* (Toronto: Ryerson Press, 1938), Part 2, pp. 17-29. In this rather ambivalent article, Silcox, who is replying to an earlier article by John Cournes in *The Atlantic Monthly* (December 1937), asserts that economic rather than religious causes lie at the root of antisemitism, and criticizes Jewish exclusiveness while tending to excuse ancient Christian religious animosity. However, he calls for a deep and spiritual Jewish/Christian dialogue.

82 In the article by Claris E. Silcox, "Canadian Universities and the Jews," *The Canadian Student*, 16, 4 (January 1934): 96, one reads these words: "The Jewish mind, trained in the Talmud, developed an unusual awareness of the type of ratiocination characteristic of the legal profession, and his aptitude for the law might consequently be called racial."

83 Ibid.; see also McLaren, *Our Own Master Race*, pp. 157-158. Silcox believed that such social programs would tax away the wealth of the biologically superior middle classes to assist the biologically inferior (and non-Anglo Saxon) lower classes. This reveals the lingering influence of the once-popular eugenics movement that flourished in the pre-war era with its racial and anti-immigrant bias.

84 Claris E. Silcox, "The Crisis in the Middle East," *The United Church Observer*, February 15, 1956, pp. 5, 24-26. In this article, which was commissioned by the then editor A.C. Forrest, Silcox expressed outrage at the fact that "World Zionism" sought a Jewish state and not merely a Jewish homeland. This, in his eyes, was an essentially unjust demand. For Silcox, Zionism was nothing more and nothing better than a malevolent Jewish nationalism, and anti-Zionism a proper moral response in no sense related to antisemitism. Not only did he ignore the fact that, ever since the concoction of *The Protocols of the Elders of Zion*, at the turn of the century, the language of anti-Zionism had become the popular rhetoric of antisemitism, but he also failed to recognize that Zionism existed in different forms—cultural, religious, mystical as well as secular and political—so that Zionism and Jewish nationalism cannot be equated in simple terms. To attack Zionism in a blanket fashion, therefore, is to launch what can easily become, and usually does become, an ideological assault on Judaism itself.

Yet it is extremely difficult to regard a man such as Silcox as antisemitic, despite this and other blemishes, such as those cited by Robert Wright (*A World Mission*, pp. 222-223). Instead, he is understood better as a classical Protestant liberal for whom universal ideals are paramount, and for whom any type of particularism, including Jewish particularism, takes on the character of tribalism and thus represents a form of spiritual regression. As long as Judaism also professed universal ideals (as Reform Judaism usually did) while disavowing parochial and material interests such as the promotion of a Jewish state, it appeared as an admirable religion in old-fashioned liberal Protestant eyes. As soon as the Jewish world devoted itself to Zionist goals, Judaism was interpreted as betraying its own lofty spiritual principles. For liberals also, the underdog is always the object of sympathy. Hence, when Jews were cast as underdogs, as during the Nazi era, they had to be rescued; when, however, the tides of history turned, the matter wore a different aspect. For this reason, it was logical for individuals such as Silcox to sympathize with the Jewish victims of Hitler in the pre-war and war years, and to turn against the Jewish state after 1948. Christian ideology, of course, also entered into these judgments, namely, the ancient patristic paradigm of the "spiritual" Christian and the "carnal" Jew: something that Protestant liberals rarely discern. Silcox, like many Christians of his generation, suffered from a serious measure of intellectual, theological and historical myopia at this point. But Wright is too harsh in his condemnation of Silcox as either a bona fide antisemite himself or a panderer to the antisemitism of others.

85 See memo from Mr. Belth to Mr. Trager, June 23, 1939, Archives of Canadian Jewish Congress.

86 James Parkes was a priest of the Church of England and author of *The Conflict of the Church and the Synagogue: A Study in the Origins of Antisemitism* (London: Soncino Press, 1934; rpt. New York: Atheneum, 1977). This book is one of the most important early examinations of the historical and ideological nexus between Christian theology and antisemitism. Parkes wrote many other books on the subject, some of which have attained the status of classics. He also published an autobiography, *Voyage of Discoveries* (London: Victor Gollancz, 1969). Because of his long personal struggle against the continental antisemites while in Switzerland before the Second World War, he enjoyed the distinction of being placed on the Nazi death list in 1935. For a comprehensive study of his thought, see Robert A. Everett, *Christianity without Antisemitism: James Parkes and the Jewish-Christian Encounter* (Oxford: Pergamon Press, 1933).

87 Cf. Reinhold Niebuhr, "The Relations of Christians and Jews in Western Civilization," in *Pious and Secular America* (New York: Charles Scribner's Sons, 1958), pp. 86-112.

88 Silcox, "What We Owe to the Jews" (unpublished manuscript), United Church Archives, p. 6.

89 Claris E. Silcox, *The War and Religion* (Toronto: Macmillan, 1941), p. 15.

90 *The Montreal Gazette,* June 1, 1936, p. 3.

91 Canadian Jewish Congress files, October 17, 1938.

92 Claris E. Silcox, "Should Canada Provide Sanctuary for European Refugees?," *The Canadian Friend,* 36, 6 (December 1938): 11. Broadcast earlier on November 1 on radio CFRC, Kingston, Ontario, 7:15-7:30 p.m.

93 See the General Secretary's Report for 1938, *The Christian Social Service Council of Canada,* pp. 7-8.

94 Abella and Troper, *None Is Too Many,* p. 58.

95 Silcox, *The Challenge of Anti-Semitism to Democracy,* p. 7.

96 Ibid., pp. 14, 16.

97 Claris E. Silcox, *Canadian Post-Mortem on Refugees,* Convocation Hall, University of Toronto, March 21, 1938, Auspices of the Toronto Branch of the Canadian National Committee on Refugees (United Church Archives).

98 *Report of the Committee on Jewish-Gentile Relationships,* January 21-23, 1939, Archives of Canadian Jewish Congress, pp. 26-27.

99 Craft, "Canada's Righteous," p. 74.

100 "Childe Roland to the Dark Tower Came."

101 Howse, "I Speak for the Jew."

102 Claris E. Silcox, "Let My People Go," *The United Church Observer,* April 15, 1943, p. 11.

103 Kenneth Leslie, "Anti-Semitism—Fascism's 'Christian' Weapon," *Christian Social Action* (May-June 1943), p. 1.

104 "The Atrocities," *The United Church Observer,* September 15, 1944, p. 4.

105 Michael R. Marrus, *The Holocaust in History* (Toronto: Lester & Orpen Dennys, 1987), p. 157.

106 Craft, "Canada's Righteous," p. 103.

107 *The Winnipeg Free Press,* April 3, 1933, p. 2, cited in Redekop, "German Identity of Mennonite Brethren Immigrants in Canada," pp. 22-23.

Chapter IV

1 E.g., T.R. Herford, *The Pharisees* (London: Allen & Unwin, 1924); George Foot Moore, *Judaism in the First Centuries of the Christian Era: The Age of the Tannaim,* 3 vols. (Cambridge, MA: Harvard University Press, 1927); and Parkes, *The Conflict of the Church and the Synagogue.*

2 C.B. Mortlock, "The Christian Revolution," *The Canadian Churchman,* December 3, 1936, p. 691.

3 F.D.V. Narborough, "The Danger of Pharisaism," *The Canadian Churchman,* February 11, 1943, p. 83.

4 Cited in "Holy Church throughout the World," *The Canadian Churchman,* October 19, 1933, p. 631.

5 See Ronald C.D. Jasper, *George Bell: Bishop of Chichester* (London: Oxford University Press, 1967), p. 219.

6 Cited in Owen Chadwick, *Hensley Henson: A Study in the Friction between Church and State* (Oxford: Clarendon Press, 1983), pp. 266-267.

7 Very Rev. W.R. Inge, "Substitutes for Religion (Fascism)," *The Canadian Churchman,* April 30, 1936, p. 276.

8 Very Rev. W.R. Inge, "Substitutes for Religion (Nazism)," *The Canadian Churchman,* May 7, 1936, p. 292.

9 Ibid.

10 Cf. Chadwick, *Hensley Henson,* p. 270.

11 "Bishop's Message," *The Montreal Churchman* (August 1933), p. 1.

12 "London Letter," *The Canadian Churchman,* October 10, 1935, p. 581.

13 "Enemies of Christianity," *The Canadian Churchman,* May 13, 1937, p. 294.

14 "London Letter," *The Canadian Churchman,* August 2, 1934, pp. 461-462.

15 "Racialism in Italy," *The Montreal Churchman* (October 1938), p. 16.

16 "We are so absorbed in deploring the conditions in Europe that we do not realize that the forces which brought about those conditions are working in our city and in six provinces of Canada. The Fascists are working under the name of the National Social Christian Party, and claim to have 15,000 members in this province.... In its name this organization claims to be Christian, yet we are told that 'the major plank in their platform is Anti-Semitism.' Such a plank is neither Christian nor British. It strikes at the very root of our liberties.... We may differ in thought and convictions from ... our Jewish brethren, but not withstanding, it is ours to love and serve them to the utmost; to persecute them, to deal unjustly towards them would be to sin against Christ ("At Montreal Synod," *The Canadian Churchman,* May 12, 1938, p. 301)."

17 "London Letter," *The Canadian Churchman,* May 20, 1937, p. 308.

18 "This Holy Week our thoughts naturally turn to the sufferings of the Jewish people in Germany.... Truly the Jews have little cause to love us Christians. The blood-stained record of Christian cruelty should fill the hearts of all with shame.... Surely the attitude our Master would have us adopt to the Jews ... is one of love. Even if they happen to be our enemies, He would have us try to win them by kindness.... Therefore, whenever we are brought in contact with Jews there is a great responsibility upon us to act as Christ would have us act.... Just as it would be unfair to blame the whole Jewish race for the condemnation of Christ, so a change of mind on the part of some cannot be credited to all the rest" (E.J. Gilling, "Follow Me," *The Canadian Churchman,* December 8, 1938, p. 711).

19 A good example is the Holy Week meditation printed in the "London Letter" column, *The Canadian Churchman,* April 27, 1933, p. 262.

20 "Report of the Montreal Jewish Mission," *Diocese of Montreal Synod Journal* (April 1935), p. 100.

21 *Mission to the Jews,* Missionary Society of the Church of Canada, Good Friday, 1938.

22 "The Churchman's Digest, Summer Days" (an editorial reprinted from *The Church Times), The Canadian Churchman,* September 7, 1933, p. 533.

23 "A Chat with the Editor," *The Canadian Churchman,* January 23, 1936, p. 50.

24 Ibid.

25 Rome, *Clouds in the Thirties,* National Archives, Canadian Jewish Congress, no date given, p. 4.

26 From Dorothy M. Barter Snow, "He Was a Jew," *The Canadian Churchman,* March 5, 1936, p. 152.

27 *The Canadian Churchman,* February 23, 1939, p. 113.

28 Ibid.

29 "What is so tragic is that wherever anti-Semitism breaks out, members of the Christian churches, clergy as well as laity ... become involved and ofttimes are actually the moving spirits behind it" (Conrad Hoffman, "The German Refugees, Part I," *The Canadian Churchman,* January 26, 1939, p. 55). Hoffman was the general secretary of the International Missionary Council's Committee on the Christian Approach to the Jews, and intensely active in refugee work.

30 Editor's Note, "When Judaism Is Blasphemed," *Social Welfare* (September 1935), p. 23.

31 Cf. Rome, *Clouds in the Thirties,* Section 4, pp. 3A-4.

32 "That this Synod of the Diocese of Montreal hereby expresses to the Jewish community of Montreal and elsewhere its sincere sympathy for them in the hardships at present being experienced by the people of their race in Germany. It hopes and prays for a speedy removal of the present trouble, and the re-establishment of a condition of impartial freedom and justice" (Moved by Canon W.H. Davison, seconded by Canon A.P. Shatford. Carried. *Proceedings of the Diocese of Montreal,* 74th Annual Synod, April 1933, p. 41).

33 "Report of the Montreal Jewish Mission," *Diocese of Montreal Journal* (April 1934), p. 89.

34 Moved by Dr. Abbott-Smith, seconded by Mr. T. Mortimer, *Journal of Proceedings of the General Synod of the Church of England in Canada,* September 12-21, 1934, 13th Session, p. 117.

35 Ibid., p. 145.

36 "Report of the Committee on Jewish Work," *Diocese of Niagara Synod Journal* (May 1938), p. 114, and "The Jews," *Diocese of Rupert's Land Synod Journal* (November 1938), p. 18.

37 See Appendix A.

38 *Toronto Star,* November 21, 1938.

39 John A. Cormie, "Immigration, No Remedy!," *Social Welfare* (September 1936), p. 99.

40 *Unto One of the Least of These,* 18th Annual Report, The Council for Social Service, The Church of England in Canada, 1933, p. 9.

41 *New Paths,* 22nd Annual Report, The Council for Social Service, The Church of England in Canada, 1937, p. 8.

42 Ibid., p. 30.

43 It can be argued, of course, that the preservation of particular historical roots and political traditions on the part of a host society is a perfectly valid cause, and does not require
homogeneity of "race."

44 Chapter III.

45 *Visions and Tasks,* 23rd Annual Report, The Council for Social Service, The Church of
England in Canada, 1938, p. 29.

46 Dirks, *Canada's Refugee Policy,* p. 63. Dirks incorrectly identifies Clark as bishop of
Ottawa.

47 "The Refugees," *The Montreal Churchman* (December 1938), p. 4. No doubt Bishop
Farthing has something to do with the republication of this article in the pages of his
diocesan journal.

48 *Worship and Work in War-time,* 24th Annual Report, The Council for Social Service,
The Church of England in Canada, 1939, pp. 18-19.

49 *Wherein Dwelleth Righteousness,* 26th Annual Report, The Council for Social Service,
The Church of England in Canada, 1941, pp. 47-48.

50 W.F. Ambrose, "Letters to the Editor," *The Canadian Churchman,* June 15, 1939, p.
378. The letter was originally entitled "The Wandering Jews."

51 *The Canadian Churchman,* July 13, 1939, pp. 428-429.

52 "That this Synod urges the Canadian Government to take steps to assist in relieving the
intolerable conditions of European refugees and victims of persecution, by permitting
the admission, and organizing the settlement in Canada of some of those most fitted to
fit into Canadian life, and expresses is [*sic*] willingness to co-operate in arranging temporary hospitality or the adoption of children as required" (moved by Mr. F. Andrew
Brewin, seconded by Mr. Hugh Jones, *Diocese of Toronto Synod Journal,* 87th Session,
May-June 1939, p. 105).

53 C.J. Lamb, "Have We the Courage?," *The Canadian Churchman,* July 27, 1939, p. 442.

54 C.J. Lamb, "How Long, O Lord!," *The Canadian Churchman,* April 17, 1941, p. 249.

55 W.W. Judd, "Letters to the Editor," *The Canadian Churchmen,* February 23, 1939,
p. 121.

56 Cf. William Temple, *Christianity and the Social Order* (Harmondsworth: Pelican Books,
1956).

57 Chapter II.

58 Cf. The Anglican Fellowship for Social Action.

59 Temple, *Christianity and the Social Order,* p. 59.

60 Dirks, *Canada's Refugee Policy,* pp. 33-34.

61 "A Chat with the Editor," *The Canadian Churchman,* February 2, 1939, p. 66.

62 "It is high time that as Christians who have protested so much against Hitler's anti-
Semitism [we] should now come to the aid of the many victims thereof. Christians must
play the role of the Good Samaritan in this emergency or be justly accused of being as
the high priest of the Levite.... Six millions of people in Europe today are unwanted
because by the accident of birth or inheritance they have Jewish blood. What is to
become of them? Christendom must give the answer" (Conrad Hoffman, "The German
Refugees, Part II," *The Canadian Churchman,* February 2, 1939, p. 71).

63 Cited in Rome, *Clouds in the Thirties,* Section 12, p. 692.

64 *Worship and Work in War-time,* p. 18.

65 Cf. W.W. Judd, "The Vision and the Dream: The Council for Social Service—Fifty
Years," *Journal of the Canadian Church Historical Society,* 8, 4 (December 1965): 95f.

66 *Wherein Dwelleth Righteousness,* p. 3. Emphasis added.

67 *Judgment and Jubilee,* 28th Annual Report, The Council for Social Service, The Church of England in Canada, pp. 26-27. The number of stranded Jews in Portugal in 1943 may be exaggerated in Judd's account.

68 Moved by Dr. Cartwright, seconded by Senator A.K. Hugesson, *Journal of Proceedings,* Fifteenth Session of the General Synod of the Church of England in Canada, September 14, 1943, p. 39.

69 See the *Diocese of Niagara Synod Journal* (May 1943), p. 38, and the *Diocese of Rupert's Land Synod Journal* (November 1943) for pro-refugee resolutions. The Diocese of Niagara declared "that every possible step ought to be taken at once to rescue from massacre the Jews in enemy and enemy occupied countries," and the Diocese of Rupert's Land urged "our Dominion Government to give sympathetic consideration to the plea that Canada should play her part in affording the sanctuary needed by these people."

70 Craft, "Canada's Righteous," p. 75.

71 Cited in *Fellowship,* monthly bulletin of the Canadian Council of Christians and Jews (October 1994), p. 7.

72 Judd, "The Vision and the Dream," p. 95.

73 Anthony Kushner, "Ambivalence or Antisemitism? Christian Attitudes and Responses in Britain to the Crisis of European Jewry during the Second World War," *Remembering for the Future: Jews and Christians During and After the Holocaust,* paper delivered at the International Scholars' Conference, Oxford, July 10-13, 1988, p. 406. Besides Archbishops Temple and Garbett, the names of George Bell, bishop of Chichester, and Hensley Henson, bishop of Durham, deserve special recognition. On Henson's admirable and outspoken opposition to the Nazi regime and its antisemitism, see Chadwick, *Hensley Henson,* chap. 10. For an overview, see Richard Gutteridge, "The Churches and the Jews in England," in Otto Dov Kulka and Paul R. Mendes-Flohr, eds., *Judaism and Christianity under the Impact of National Socialism* (Jerusalem: The Historical Society of Israel and the Zalman Center for Jewish History, 1987), pp. 353-378.

74 Cf. Wasserstein, *Britain and the Jews of Europe,* p. 47. As Wasserstein demonstrates, there was a pronounced strain of antisemitism in both the British government and bureaucracy, especially in the colonial office. The role of the latter in seeking through diplomacy or force to prevent Jewish refugees from reentering Palestine, and the frequently tragic results, as in the case of the *Struma*—another voyage of the damned— was callous in the extreme. Churchill, however, was a powerful restraining force on behalf of the Jews, preventing more extreme measures advocated by some of his subordinates. In a private conversation with one of the authors in 1975, James Parkes blamed Herbert Morrison, the Labour home secretary, whom he described as an "extremely callous man," for much of the political resistance to the admission of continental Jewish refugees to Britain. Wasserstein seems to concur (p. 114), but does not regard Morrison as an antisemite: "A life long supporter of Zionism, Morrison was outspoken in his public condemnations of anti-Semitism" (p. 116). Although Britain, unlike France and Germany, never developed an antisemitic culture, antisemitism did exist on all levels in British society, not merely on the lunatic fringe. See Colin Holmes, *Anti-Semitism in British Society: 1876-1939* (London: Edward Arnold, 1979), and Gisela C. Lebzelter, *Political Anti-Semitism in England, 1918-1939* (New York: Holmes & Meier, 1978).

75 "By wholesale massacre, torture and starvation," Garbett declared, "the Nazis are delib-
   erately exterminating this brave nation" (Cyril Garbett, "From Over and Across," *The
   Canadian Churchman,* September 10, 1942, p. 509).

76 "Too Horrible to Think About," *The Canadian Churchman,* December 24, 1942,
   p. 754.

77 Wasserstein, *Britain and the Jews of Europe,* pp. 174, 176.

78 "The Empire as Refuge from Massacre," *The Canadian Churchman,* February 25,
   1943, p. 121. The archbishop's plea, however, was countered by the home secretary,
   Herbert Morrison, who declared that the wholesale admission of Jewish refugees would
   stir up latent antisemitism in Britain (Wasserstein, *Britain and the Jews of Europe,* pp.
   115-116). Like its predecessor, the Evian Conference, the Anglo-American Bermuda
   Conference on the refugee crisis (April 1943) proved to be mostly an exercise in futility, since every proposed solution encountered insuperable political obstacles. Hence,
   there was no "magnificent gesture" to the British archbishops (ibid., p. 205).

79 *Religion Pleads the Cause of Refugees,* May 28, 1943, p. 7, from the personal papers of
   Harry Joshua Stern.

80 M44 moved by the Rev. G.M.W. Smith, seconded by the Rev. D.J. Curzon, *Diocese of
   Niagara Synod Journal,* 69th Session, May 1943, pp. 33, 37-38. A copy of this resolution was forwarded to Prime Minister W.L. Mackenzie King.

81 Moved by Canon Davidson, seconded by M.A. Stephens, "Church on Refugees,"
   Canadian Jewish Congress Bulletin (August 1943), p. 2.

Chapter V

1 Lord Tweedsmuir, "Address," *The Presbyterian Record,* 63, 1 (January 1938): 12.

2 For another example, see *The Presbyterian Record,* 61, 1 (January 1934): 28: "A week
   of selfishness and a Sabbath of religious exercises will make a good Pharisee but a poor
   Christian." See also J.B. Skene, "Our Spiritual Need," *The Presbyterian Record,* 70, 4
   (April 1945): 118: "[The Pharisees] became the men of closed minds, and the enemies
   of Jesus, for they felt no need of Him."

3 The conspiracy motif, with a Jew at its core, appears intermittently in Buchan's novels,
   e.g., *The Thirty-Nine Steps.* Buchan possibly absorbed some of the popular fears of the
   First World War era, when talk of conspiracy against Britain and the British Empire filled
   the air, and when it was fashionable to distrust Jews in British society, particularly among
   the upper classes. Moreover, the antisemitic writings of Nesta Webster, later an ardent
   fascist, were in vogue. On the other hand, the conspiracy motif in the Buchan novels
   may have literary significance only as a mode of characterization. Buchan was not
   obsessed with such notions, and it would be highly unfair to regard him as an antisemite
   in personal terms. For further information, see Holmes, *Anti-Semitism in British Society:
   1876-1939,* and Lebzelter, *Political Anti-Semitism in England, 1918-1939.*

4 Draper and Troper, eds., *Archives of the Holocaust,* Vol. 15, p. 3.

5 As reported in the *Globe and Mail* (Toronto), December 5, 1938, p. 4.

6 Rev. John Pitts, "Is Hitler Anti-Christ?," *The Presbyterian Record,* 65, 5 (September
   1940): 266.

7 Ibid., p. 264.

8 "Of course, every Christian man and woman deplores and denounces the awful cruelty
   and the terrible injustice of these recent riots and persecutions [*Kristallnacht*]" (Inkster,
   as reported in the *Globe and Mail*). Notice the title of Pitts' sermon.

9 Conning, "The Presbyterian Church and the Jews," p. 87.

10 Morris Zeidman, *The Presbyterian Record*, 63, 2 (February 1938): 39.

11 Alex Zeidman, *Good and Faithful Servant: The Biography of Morris Zeidman* (Burlington: Crown Publications, 1990), p. 12.

12 Ben Volman, "'The Gospel of Hope to All': Morris Zeidman and the Relief Work of the Scott Institute 1930-1941" (unpublished paper, Knox College, Toronto, 1980), p. 2. Another converted Jew, S.B. Rohold, served as the mission's first superintendent.

13 Ibid., p. 7; see Morris Zeidman's article "Good News and Good Will," *The Presbyterian Record*, 55 (February 1930): 49.

14 Cited in A. Zeidman, *Good and Faithful Servant*, p. 21.

15 Ibid.

16 Volman, "'The Gospel of Hope to All,'" p. 10. According to John S. Moir, the Presbyterian Church chose to promote relief work by individual congregations as its official response to the Depression. The Scott Institute fed as many as 1,000 men each day (cf. Moir, *Enduring Witness*, p. 237).

17 Zeidman himself was a perennial optimist with respect to Jewish evangelization, emphasizing, in his various reports, the "tremendous inroads," "wonderful opportunities," "whole-hearted enthusiasm," "unprecedented vast fields ripe unto harvest," and so on—all portents, if not exactly proofs, of a glorious age to come ("Scott Institute Report," *The Presbyterian Record*, 58, 1 (January 1933): 23; "Institutional Work," *Acts and Proceedings of the General Assembly*, June 1933, p. 30; "The Jews and Christians," *The Presbyterian Record*, 64, 2 (February 1939): 46; and "Institutional Work," *Acts and Proceedings*, June 1939, pp. 24-25). To read his glowing accounts of swelling attendance at prayer meetings, Sunday school classes and Bible study groups is to form an impression of considerable wishful thinking on his part; however, in the absence of real statistics (which Zeidman did not provide), it is difficult to gauge the true measure of the mission's success.

18 Following Zeidman's rather abrupt resignation from the Scott Institute on October 31, 1941 because of policy conflicts with the Presbyterian Board of Missions, a less glowing tone crept into the Institute's annual report, together with an implied criticism of the former director's philanthropic approach to evangelism: "Few Gentiles understand how difficult it is for Jews to attend a Christian mission. Before they enter they will look up and down both ways, and when inside will carefully pull down a window blind for fear of being seen here by any of their people.... So we are not surprised when they do not recognize us on the street, do not always answer the door. Even the poorest Jews look upon the Gentiles as Gayim [*sic*]—heathen—and worshippers of a dead carpenter. They despise our Saviour, sneer at His miraculous birth and deny His resurrection. To them He is the cause of all the sorrows of the Jewish race....

"In no mission work is it more dangerous to make use of doles of any kind or give financial support or promise of remunerative employment, the Jews instinctively know where to find their profit and readily avail themselves of it. So they come suddenly and disappear suddenly, just as soon as their profit is exhausted, or they develop into sham Christians without any backbone" ("Presbyterian Mission to Jews," *Acts and Proceedings of the General Assembly*, June 1942, p. 25)

This rather harsh report was unsigned. Since its author, clearly not Zeidman, managed to slip into an antisemitic cliché, the fact is fortunate.

19 See the amusing account by J.B. Salsberg, "The Scott Mission and the Jews in Toronto" and "The Tug-of-War between Rev. Morris Zeidman and Moysche Tarnovsky's

Chenstochover Society" in *The Canadian Jewish News,* December 23, 1982, p. 5, and December 30, 1982, p. 5. Zeidman forwarded relief packages of medicine to Jewish families in Poland, and organized sponsorships in Canada for Jews who wished to immigrate.

20 A. Zeidman, *Good and Faithful Servant,* p. 41.

21 "Scott Institute Report," 1940 (typed manuscript), p. 1.

22 Morris Zeidman, "Gentiles Only—The Slogan of Anti-Semitism," *The Evangelical Christian,* 37, 5 (May 1941): 246.

23 Ibid., p. 247.

24 Ibid., p. 246.

25 From the title of a series of addresses by Dr. Stanley High of Stanford, Connecticut, described in *The Presbyterian Record,* 60, 2 (February 1935): 39.

26 "Oracles," *The Presbyterian Record,* 59, 5 (May 1934): 131.

27 Ibid.

28 "Lest We Forget," *The Presbyterian Record,* 61, 5 (May 1936): 133.

29 "In the Midst of Alarms," *The Presbyterian Record,* 62, 11 (November 1937): 324.

30 T. Christie Innes, "Sound an Alarm," *The Presbyterian Record,* 64, 5 (May 1939): 132.

31 Ibid., p. 134.

32 See "Germany and the Church," *The Presbyterian Record,* 58, 12 (December 1933): 365, and "Religion and the European Mind," *The Presbyterian Record,* 60, 1 (January 1935): 19.

33 The Barmen Declaration (1934) was a ringing statement of Christian faith that explicitly repudiated the *völkisch* ideology of the pro-Nazi "German Christian." It failed, however, to address the persecution of the Jews.

34 E.g., Paul Althaus, Emanuel Hirsch. See Ericksen, *Theologians under Hitler;* see also A. James Reimer, *The Emanuel Hirsch and Paul Tillich Debate: A Study in the Political Ramifications of Theology* (Lewiston, NY: Edwin Mellen Press, 1989).

35 John Calvin, *Institutes of the Christian Religion,* Book I, Chapter XI, section 9.

36 "Germany and the Church," p. 365.

37 "Then Luther, Now Barth," *The Presbyterian Record,* 59, 1 (January 1934): 4.

38 See F. Scott-Mackenzie's favourable review of Adolf Keller's anti-Nazi book *Religion and the European Mind,* in *The Presbyterian Record,* 60, 1 (January 1935): 19; W.H. Leathem's sermon, preached in St. Andrew's Church, Ottawa, "The Church in Revolt," *The Presbyterian Record,* 60, 1 (January 1935): 10-11; the account of a conference on the Third Reich led by James D. Smart at Knox College, Toronto, and attended by the synods of Hamilton and London, "Ministers' Fellowship," *The Presbyterian Record,* 60, 2 (February 1935): 46; and G.D. Henderson, "Karl Barth Is To-day's John Calvin," *The Presbyterian Record,* 63, 6 (June 1937): 169.

39 Leathem, *"The Church in Revolt,"* p. 10.

40 Alfred Rosenberg, author of *Der Mythus des 20. Jahrhunderts* (The myth of the twentieth century), 1930.

41 Unpublished manuscript, September 22, 1935, National Archives of Canada.

42 "Editorial Council," *The Presbyterian Record,* 61, 6 (June 1936): 166.

43 Henderson, "Karl Barth Is To-day's John Calvin."

44 "Here stand I, I can do no other, God help me, Amen." Luther, however, may not have uttered these famous words.

45 "Niemöller," *The Presbyterian Record,* 63, 4 (April 1938): 99.

46 Ross, *So It Was True,* p. 268.

47 Letter to Emil Brunner, in *Against the Stream: Shorter Post-War Writings 1946-52* (London: SCM Press, 1954), p. 115.

48 Cf. Eberhard Bethge, "Troubled Self-Interpretation and Uncertain Responses," in Franklin H. Littell and Hubert G. Locke, eds., *The German Church Struggle and the Holocaust* (Detroit: Wayne State University Press, 1974), p. 167.

49 "Highlights in Jewish Work," *Glad Tidings*, 11, 3 (March 1935): 102.

50 "Germany and the Jews," *The Presbyterian Record*, 61, 5 (May 1936): 132.

51 Presbytery of Chatham, April 23, 1936, *Acts and Proceedings of the General Assembly of the Presbyterian Church in Canada*, Hamilton, Ontario, June 3-10, 1936, p. 140.

52 Ibid., p. 22

53 C.M. Kerr, "The Light of the World," *The Presbyterian Record*, 61, 12 (December 1936): 367.

54 See "Germany and the Jews," *The Presbyterian Record*, 64, 1 (January 1939): 4-5; "Without a Country," *The Presbyterian Record*, 64, 3 (March 1939): 67; "The Jewish Situation," *Glad Tidings*, 15, 3 (March 1939): 91; and D.N. MacMillan, "The Sovereignty of God," *The Presbyterian Record*, 64, 7 (July 1939): 217-219.

55 Abella and Troper, *None Is Too Many*, p. 59.

56 Appendix A.

57 "Central Bureau Relief European Churches," *The Presbyterian Record*, 62, 6 (June 1937): 184.

58 "Germany and the Jews," *The Presbyterian Record*, 64, 1 (January 1939): 5.

59 Ibid.

60 "Without a Country," pp. 67-68.

61 *Acts and Proceedings of the Sixty-Fifth General Assembly of the Presbyterian Church in Canada*, Midland, Ontario, June 7-15, 1939, p. 103.

62 Adolf Keller, "Foreign Affairs Bulletin," *The Presbyterian Record*, 65, 3 (March 1940): 85.

63 "The Need in Europe," *The Presbyterian Record*, 66, 5 (May 1941): 157.

64 Adolf Keller, "Farewell to America," *The Presbyterian Record*, 67, 10 (October 1942): 294-295.

65 *Religion Pleads the Cause of Refugees*, from the personal papers of Harry Joshua Stern.

66 "On Behalf of the Jewish Race," *Acts and Proceedings of the General Assembly of the Presbyterian Church in Canada*, Hamilton, Ontario, June 2-10, 1943, p. 147.

67 Cf. C.P. Stacey, *A Very Double Life: The Private World of Mackenzie King* (Toronto: Macmillan, 1976).

68 W.L. Mackenzie King, Diaries 1893-1931, Thursday, November 16, 1893; Thursday, December 28, 1893; and Monday, January 22, 1894.

69 Ibid., Friday, November 10, 1893; Friday, January 19, 1894; and October 11, 1894 ("I am going to devote my whole life to mission work").

70 Stacey, *A Very Double Life*, p. 68.

71 Joy E. Esberey, *Knight of the Holy Spirit: A Study of William Lyon Mackenzie King* (Toronto: University of Toronto Press, 1980), p. 207.

72 Ibid., p. 109.

73 There is ample evidence for this in the diaries.

74 Stacey, *A Very Double Life*, p. 127.

75 Cf. Abella and Troper, *None Is Too Many*, p. 228, and Tulchinsky, "Goldwin Smith," pp. 67-91.

76 H. Blair Neatby, *William Lyon Mackenzie King 1932-1939: The Prism of Unity* (Toronto: University of Toronto Press, 1976), p. 304.

77 Abella and Troper, *None Is Too Many*, passim. Blair's anti-refugee counterpart in the United States was Breckinridge Long of the State Department, whose views were also coloured by nativist and antisemitic feelings. See Feingold, *The Politics of Rescue*, pp. 131-135.

78 Neatby, *William Lyon Mackenzie King 1932-1939*, p. 304, and Abella and Troper, *None Is Too Many*, p. 39.

79 Sunday, November 13, 1938. See *National Archives of Canada, Ottawa, Canadian Jewish Congress Archives, Montreal*, in Draper and Troper, eds., *Archives of the Holocaust*, Vol. 15, p. 2.

80 King, Diary, March 17, 1938 (cited in Esberey, *Knight of the Holy Spirit*, pp. 212-213).

81 Esberey, *Knight of the Holy Spirit*, p. 212.

82 Abella and Troper, *None Is Too Many*.

83 Cf. John S. Conway, "Canada and the Holocaust," *Remembering for the Future: Jews and Christians During and After the Holocaust*, paper delivered at the International Scholars' Conference, Oxford, July 10-13, 1988, p. 298.

84 "Behind the Nazi Lines," *The Hebrew Evangelist*, 1, 1 (November 1941): 217-219.

85 After Vidkun Quisling. See Chapter VII.

86 "Behind the Nazi Lines," p. 6.

87 Ibid.

88 William T. Elmslie, "Europe in the Furnace," *The Presbyterian Record*, 66, 12 (December 1941): 357, and Sir Robert Vansittart, "Germany's Black Record," *The Presbyterian Record*, 67, 3 (March 1942): 71.

89 For example, Samuel McCrea Cavert, "Churches of Europe—A Wartime Visit," *The Presbyterian Record*, 68, 3 (March 1943): 86-87, and W.M. Rochester, "The Shorter Catechism," *The Presbyterian Record*, 68, 6 (June 1943): 163-164.

90 William Fitch, *Knox Church Toronto: Avant-garde Evangelical Advancing* (Toronto: John Deyell, 1971), pp. 79-80.

91 Morris Zeidman, "Jews in Poland Today" (unpublished manuscript, courtesy of the Zeidman family).

92 One thinks of a long line of Jewish apostates who became persecutors of other Jews, for example, Nicholas Donin and Johannes Pfefferkorn, who instigated attempts to burn the Talmud during the Middle Ages. Unfortunately, Christians often took their information about Judaism from these converts, who were not reliable guides.

Chapter VI

1 "Holy Ground," *The Canadian Baptist*, April 6, 1933, p. 10.

2 T.T. Shields, "Watching Jesus," *The Gospel Witness*, July 6, 1933, pp. 8, 12.

3 "Fascism," *The Canadian Baptist*, April 5, 1934, p. 4.

4 Stanley High, "Religion Beyond the Rhine," *The Canadian Baptist*, November 15, 1934, p. 16.

5 Cf. Ross, *So It Was True*, pp. 48f.

6 "Baptists and Berlin," *The Canadian Baptist*, April 5, 1934, p. 4.

7 "What the Berlin Congress Means for Europe," *The Canadian Baptist*, January 18, 1934, p. 15.

8 John MacNeill, "Echoes from Berlin," *The Canadian Baptist,* August 23, 1934, p. 3.

9 Ross, *So It Was True,* p. 53.

10 "Atlanta Gets Next Alliance," *The Canadian Baptist,* August 16, 1934, p. 2.

11 "Paragraphs," *The Canadian Baptist,* September 28, 1933, p. 2.

12 Hans Luckey, "Freedom of Religion in Germany," *The Canadian Baptist,* September 15, 1938, p. 4.

13 See the report on the clash between M.E. Aubrey, secretary of the British Baptist Union, and Paul Schmidt, general secretary of the German Baptist Union, at the Atlanta Congress, July 1939, in *The Canadian Baptist,* November 1, 1945, p. 3.

14 For a sympathetic biography, see Tarr, *Shields of Canada.* For a less sympathetic account of Shields' attack on modernism, see Grant, *The Church in the Canadian Era,* pp. 123f.

15 See his scornful comments on William Aberhart and Social Credit in *The Gospel Witness,* September 2, 1937, pp. 9-10. Aberhart, of course, was a dispensationalist.

16 "Canada's Problem Religious, Not Racial," *The Gospel Witness and Protestant Advocate,* October 12, 1944, p. 9.

17 "The Nazi Beast and the False Prophet and Their Imminent and Inevitable Doom," *The Gospel Witness,* May 29, 1941, p. 3.

18 "The Pope's Fifth Column—Everywhere," *The Gospel Witness,* August 8, 1940, p. 3.

19 "The Forgiveness of Sins," *The Gospel Witness,* June 13, 1935, p. 3.

20 An ancient Syrian king (1 Kings 20).

21 "Collective Security?," *The Gospel Witness,* March 12, 1936, pp. 2f.

22 "The British Government's Attempt to 'Appease' Hitler and Mussolini," *The Gospel Witness,* March 3, 1938, p. 10. Sennacherib was an Assyrian king who besieged Jerusalem (2 Kings 18).

23 "The Rulers Take Counsel Together," *The Gospel Witness,* March 17, 1938, p. 1.

24 "Did God Answer the Prayer for Peace in Mercy or in Judgment?," *The Gospel Witness,* October 27, 1938, p. 7.

25 "Hitler's Suicide," *The Gospel Witness,* September 14, 1939, p. 3.

26 "Hitler in Old Testament History," *The Gospel Witness,* September 29, 1938, p. 6.

27 "The Menace of Pacifism," *The Gospel Witness,* July 5, 1934, p. 5. For Shields' comments on G. Stanley Russell, a man with, in his words, "no capacity to think," see "Asleep on the Lip of Vesuvius," *The Gospel Witness,* June 12, 1941, p. 3.

28 "The Folly of Pacifism," *The Gospel Witness,* May 21, 1936, p. 5.

29 "Amazing Credulity," *The Gospel Witness,* February 9, 1939, pp. 2f; "Mr. Chamberlain's Hat," *The Gospel Witness,* March 30, 1939, p. 2.

30 "Why Hitler's Oration Must Be Answered with Fire," *The Gospel Witness,* July 25, 1940, p. 1.

31 "God's Call to a Backsliding Church," *The Gospel Witness,* March 2, 1933, p. 4.

32 "The Jarvis Street Pulpit," *The Gospel Witness,* November 17, 1938, pp. 3-6.

33 Cf. J.M.R. Beveridge, "Watson Kirkconnell: A Biographical Sketch," in J.R.C. Perkin, ed., *The Undoing of Babel: Watson Kirkconnell—The Man and His Work* (Toronto: McClelland & Stewart, 1975), pp. 11-15.

34 Watson Kirkconnell, *A Slice of Canada: Memoirs* (Toronto: University of Toronto Press, 1967), p. 191.

35 Ibid., p. 196. Shields, in turn, accused Kirkconnell of being a "secret member of the Jesuit Order."

36 Ibid., p. 316. During the post-war era, Kirkconnell's anti-communism reached gargantuan proportions.

37 Ibid., p. 176.
38 Watson Kirkconnell, *Canada, Europe and Hitler* (Toronto: Oxford University Press, 1939), pp. 5-6.
39 Ibid., p. 21.
40 Ibid., pp. 21-22.
41 Ibid., p. 23.
42 Ibid., p. 122.
43 Betcherman, *The Swastika and the Maple Leaf,* p. 73.
44 Ibid., p. 160.
45 Watson Kirkconnell, *Twilight of Liberty* (London: Oxford University Press, 1941), pp. 91-92.
46 Ibid., pp. 59-60.
47 The predecessor of the Conference of Christians and Jews and the Canadian Council of Christians and Jews.
48 Kirkconnell, *Twilight of Liberty,* p. 62.
49 Kirkconnell, *A Slice of Canada,* p. 273. "The Agony of Israel" was published in the *Canadian Jewish Review,* June 11, 1943, and the *Jewish Standard* (June 1943).
50 "Fabric of Civilization Crackling," *The Maritime Baptist,* March 22, 1933, p. 4.
51 "Race Prejudice," *The Maritime Baptist,* March 29, 1933, p. 4; "Germany," *The Maritime Baptist,* April 5, 1933, p. 16; "Germany," *The Maritime Baptist,* April 12, 1933, p. 16; "Lo! The Poor Jew," *The Maritime Baptist,* August 16, 1933, p. 4 (this editorial contains an extract from Reinhold Niebuhr, recently returned from Germany); "Outrages Protested," *The Maritime Baptist,* October 18, 1933, p. 16; "The Portent of Hitler," *The Maritime Baptist,* October 25, 1933, p. 1; "The Reich Church," *The Maritime Baptist,* November 22, 1933, p. 16; "The German Church," *The Maritime Baptist,* December 6, 1933, p. 4 (on the Aryan laws); "Germany and the Jews," *The Canadian Baptist,* April 6, 1933, p. 3; "Ill Treatment of Jews," *The Canadian Baptist,* April 27, 1933, p. 5; "Barring the Jews," *The Canadian Baptist,* May 4, 1933, p. 3; "Europe Alarming," *The Canadian Baptist,* September 7, 1933, p. 3; and "German-Jew Problem at Novi Sad," *The Canadian Baptist,* October 12, 1933, p. 14.
52 "Germany and the Jews," *The Canadian Baptist,* April 6, 1933, p. 3.
53 "The Trial of Niemöller," *The Canadian Baptist,* March 10, 1938, p. 4.
54 "Ousting Religion," *The Canadian Baptist,* May 2, 1935, p. 2.
55 "Ill Treatment of Jews," p. 5.
56 "German-Jew Problem At Novi Sad," p. 14.
57 "Dismissal of Jews in Nazi Germany," *The Canadian Baptist,* April 12, 1934, p. 14. See also Roberts, "If Jesus Went to Germany," *The Canadian Baptist,* February 1, 1934, p. 4; "Hitler and Jesus," *The Canadian Baptist,* February 15, 1934, p. 3; "Bang Shut the Doors," *The Canadian Baptist,* April 5, 1934, p. 2; "A Savage Business," *The Canadian Baptist,* February 28, 1935, p. 2; "The Saar," *The Canadian Baptist,* March 9, 1935, p. 2; "Dr. Hoffman on Germany," *The Canadian Baptist,* March 14, 1935, p. 11; "Dreyfus Is Dead," *The Canadian Baptist,* July 18, 1935, p. 2; "Reading Dies," *The Canadian Baptist,* January 9, 1936, p. 6; "Germany and the Jews," *The Canadian Baptist,* February 20, 1936, p. 15; "Liberty Lives, in the Middle Road," *The Canadian Baptist,* October 15, 1936, p. 3; "Baptists and Religious Liberty," *The Canadian Baptist,* March 10, 1938, p. 5; "Moose Jaw and the Jews," *The Canadian Baptist,* December 1, 1938, p. 3; "This Could Not Have Happened in Germany," p. 3; "I See

in the Papers," *The Canadian Baptist,* November 17, 1938, p. 2; "Disappointment after the Munich Peace Pact," *The Canadian Baptist,* November 24, 1938, p. 3.; "I See in the Papers," *The Canadian Baptist,* December 1, 1938, p. 2; "Points to Ponder," *The Canadian Baptist,* December 15, 1938, p. 12; "I See in the Papers," *The Canadian Baptist,* January 12, 1939, p. 2; "I See in the Papers," *The Canadian Baptist,* February 2, 1939, p. 2; "In a Jewish Refugee Camp," *The Canadian Baptist,* March 16, 1939, p. 11; Watson Kirkconnell, "Canada and the Refugees," *The Canadian Baptist,* May 25, 1939, p. 14; "The Plight of Jewish Refugees," *The Canadian Baptist,* June 15, 1939, p. 3; and Reginald Kirby, "Christ and Adolph Hitler," *The Canadian Baptist,* March 30, 1939, p. 7.

58 "The Amazing Jew," *The Pentecostal Testimony* (April 1935), p. 5.

59 A.J. Turvey, "The Jew ... God's Barometer," *The Pentecostal Testimony,* July 15, 1939, p. 4.

60 Cf. "The Jew ... A Prophetic Sign," *The Pentecostal Testimony* (July 1933), p. 4; "Heralds of the Kings Return," *The Pentecostal Testimony* (August 1933), p. 6; "Hitlerism Invades America," *The Pentecostal Testimony* (May 1934), p. 5; Ian S. Bain, "Did the Prophets Speak of Germany?," *The Pentecostal Testimony* (June 1938), p. 9; and Vaughn Shoemaker, "Things as They Are in Europe" *The Pentecostal Testimony* (September 1938), p. 17.

61 Oswald F. Smith, "Mein Besuch in Deutschland," *Der Bote,* October 28, 1936, p. 3.

62 Ibid., November 4, 1936, p. 4. Our translation.

63 Joseph Taylor Britan, "An Appeal for Persecuted Israel," *The Evangelical Christian* (January 1939), p. 26.

64 "The Jews in Germany," *The Evangelical Christian* (January 1939), p. 10.

65 "Christ or Ludendorff?," *The War Cry,* March 17, 1937, p. 8.

66 George T.B. Davis, "Seeing Prophecy Fulfilled in Palestine," *The War Cry,* March 19, 1938, p. 7.

67 "How God Provides for Refugees," *The Gospel Witness,* November 24, 1938, pp. 3, 6.

68 "Moose Jaw and the Jews," p. 3. The resolution read in part:

"Whereas there has broken out a fresh and bitter persecution of Jews in Germany, of which all our people are aware through the press,

"Be it resolved, that we express our deep and prayerful sympathy for these suffering people.... That we express our confidence in the right purpose of our Government that Canada may take her place in the solution of the problems of the world.... That in view of many recent statements in the press of the world on moral and spiritual rearmament ... we call upon the people of our churches and community to face honestly the individual and personal implications in this international situation ... that Canada's part in the solution of the problem may call for unusual determination on the part of her leaders and sacrificial co-operation on the part of her people."

69 "In a Jewish Refugee Camp," p. 11.

70 Ibid.

71 "Canada and the Refugees," CJRC, Winnipeg, May 7, 1939, reprinted in *The Canadian Baptist,* May 25, 1939, p. 8. This tale is retold in Kirkconnell, *Twilight of Liberty,* pp. 57-58.

72 Ibid.

73 Unidentified, but various ships with fleeing Jews plied the Danube in 1939 and 1940.

74 Ibid. See also Kirkconnell, *A Slice of Canada,* p. 335, where Kirkconnell specifies the Jewish identity of the three hundred Viennese.

75 "The Plight of Jewish Refugees," p. 3.

76 "European Refugees," *The Baptist Yearbook of Ontario and Quebec* (Toronto), Tuesday, June 13, 1939, p. 78.

77 *The United Baptist Yearbook of the Maritime Provinces of Canada,* Eighth Session, September 2, 1939, p. 19, and *The Baptist Union of Western Canada Yearbook* (1939), p. 78.

78 Cf. "European Refugees," *The Baptist Yearbook of Ontario and Quebec,* June 13, 1940, p. 362, and "European Refugees," *The Baptist Union of Western Canada Yearbook,* June 29, 1940, p. 97.

79 *Religion Pleads the Cause of Refugees,* pp. 12-14, from the personal papers of Harry Joshua Stern.

80 "If the Jews are God's timepiece to tell us where we are in the Divine scheme of things prophetic significance must be attached to what is happening to this ancient people today. That a time of unprecedented trouble for Israel as the age draws to its close is prophesied is generally admitted by students of the Scriptures" ("Jew Haters," *The Evangelical Christian* [November 1937], p. 497).

81 "Jewish Refugees," *The Evangelical Christian* (January 1939), p. 9.

82 J.B Rowell, "Jewish Refugees: Their Present Plight and the Word of God," *The Evangelical Christian* (January 1939), pp. 13f.

83 Ibid., p. 48.

84 "Why Jewish Hate?," *The Evangelical Christian* (July 1939), p. 321.

85 See, for example, Donald Gee, "The Truth about Hitler and Germany," *The Pentecostal Testimony* (February 1935), p. 16; C.M. Ward, "Hitler ... The Nazi Program ... Our Pentecostal Assemblies in Germany," *The Pentecostal Testimony* (September 1936), p. 4; and especially Shoemaker, "Things as They Are in Europe," p. 17.

86 "Why Pray for the Jews," *The Pentecostal Testimony,* January 15, 1940, p. 3. This editorial was republished under the title "The Jew," *The Pentecostal Testimony* (May 1943), p. 2.

87 Just Returned from Europe: A Picture of the Appalling Sufferings of Jews and Jewish Christians, *The Evangelical Christian* (February 1940), p. 79.

88 In a letter to one of the authors, Ronald H. Lewis, current executive secretary of the International Messianic Jewish (Hebrew Christian) Alliance, Ramsgate, England, confirms the fact that, with some financial assistance from the Polish government, the Hebrew Christians did help refugees during the war, especially Christians of Jewish origin, but, because of limited means, not nearly to the extent claimed by Peltz, apparently a man given to overstatement. However, he did succeed in raising a substantial if unspecified sum, which was used for its stated purpose.

89 Ibid.

90 "Churchmen Raise Funds for Jews," *Canadian Jewish Congress Bulletin* (May 1943), p. 2.

91 Cf. Harry Tennant, *The Christadelphians: What They Believe and Preach* (Birmingham: The Christadelphia, 1988), pp. 250-267.

92 Joseph Taylor Britan, "Great Tribulation," *The Evangelical Christian* (January 1941), p. 29.

93 "The Jews in Poland," *The Evangelical Christian* (February 1940), p. 61, and "The Suffering Jew," *The Evangelical Christian* (June 1940), p. 300.

94 Alexander Marks, "Our Debt to Israel," *The Pentecostal Testimony,* September 15, 1940, p. 6.

95 "Haman and Hitler," *The Evangelical Christian* (December 1941), p. 571.

96 "Beware of the Pope's Peace Offensive," *The Gospel Witness,* May 21, 1942, pp. 6f.

97 "The Vilna Massacre," *The Evangelical Christian* (August 1942) p. 307.

98 See especially Morris Zeidman, "Have You Prayed for the Jews Today?," *The Pentecostal Testimony,* May 1, 1942, p. 15; "Can Hitler Exterminate the Jews of Europe?," *The Pentecostal Testimony* (September 1942), p. 4; "Nazi Attempt to Exterminate Jews," *The Pentecostal Testimony,* October 15, 1942, p. 15; and "Tribulation Comes to Mlicka," *The Pentecostal Testimony,* May 15, 1943, p. 7.

99 "The Sufferings of the Jewish People," *The Canadian Baptist,* January 15, 1943, p. 10.

100 "They Were Not Just Foreigners," *The Canadian Baptist,* February 1, 1943, p. 9.

101 "Men and Affairs," *The Canadian Baptist,* July 1, 1943, p. 2.

102 "Canada and the Refugee Problem," *The Canadian Baptist,* January 1, 1944, p. 2.

103 "Care for Refugees," *The War Cry,* January 14, 1939, p. 8.

104 See Appendix A.

105 Kirkconnell, *A Slice of Canada,* p. 213.

Chapter VII

1 Cf. Bernard M.G. Reardon, *Religious Thought in the Reformation* (London: Longman, 1981), p. 48.

2 Little, "Unwarranted Strictures on Luther," *The Canada Lutheran,* 14, 1 (January 1934): 3, 15. It is interesting that the author of the offending article neglected Luther's antisemitism as an example of his evil influence.

3 "Luther under Attack," *The Canada Lutheran,* 32, 11 (November 1944): 4.

4 Specifically, Luther's 1543 tracts, *Von den Juden und ihren Lügen, Vom Shem Hamphoras, Von den letzen Wurten Davids.*

It should be mentioned that the Lutheran churches today have acknowledged and dissociated themselves publicly from Luther's antisemitism: "We Lutherans take our name and much of our understanding of Christianity from Martin Luther. But we cannot accept or condone the violent verbal attacks that the Reformer made against the Jews.... We recognize with deep regret ... that Luther has been used to justify such anti-Semitism in the period of national socialism [*sic*] and that his writings lent themselves to such abuse" (from "Luther, Lutheranism and the Jews," Lutheran World Fellowship Dialogue with International Jewish Committee on Interreligious Consultations, Stockholm, 1983.

On July 14, 1995, the Evangelical Lutheran Church in Canada endorsed a resolution at its national convention in Winnipeg also dissociating the church from Luther's anti-Jewish writings and those who seek to exploit them today for their own racist ends: "We reject this violent invective as did many of [Luther's] companions in the sixteenth century, and we are moved to deep and abiding sorrow at its tragic effects on later generations of Jews" (*Globe and Mail,* July 14, 1995).

5 Mission to the Jews.

6 Franz Delitzsch, an important biblical scholar of the late nineteenth century, was both an ardent pietist and a consistent foe of the German antisemites of the Second Reich, especially the notorious August Rohling, author of *Der Talmudjude.*

7 *Yearbook,* The United Danish Evangelical Lutheran Church, 40th Annual Convention, June 2-7, 1936, p. 14.

8 Cf. Theodore G. Tappert, "The Doctrine of the Two Kingdoms after Luther in Europe and America," in Paul D. Opsahl and Marc H. Tanenbaum, eds., *Speaking of God Today: Jews and Lutherans in Conversation* (Philadelphia: Fortress Press, 1974), p. 85.

9 Tal, "Lutheran Theology and the Third Reich," p. 94.

10 "Germany is above all Luther's country"; ("Präsident Dr. F.H. Knubels Ansprache vor dem lutherischen Rat in Berlin," *Der Synodalbote*, 9, 3 [November 1937]: 2).

11 Moellering, "Lutheran-Jewish Relations and the Holocaust," p. 30.

12 "Dr. Reble's Visit," *The Canada Lutheran*, 16, 8 (October 1935): 5.

13 "Dr. and Mrs. Reble in Germany," *The Canada Lutheran*, 16, 8 (October 1935): 8-9.

14 Ibid.

15 Moellering, "Lutheran-Jewish Relations and the Holocaust."

16 "New Horizons," *The Canada Lutheran*, 28, 1 (November 1939): 1.

17 *Minutes of the 72nd Annual Convention of the Evangelical Lutheran Synod of Canada,* June 5-10, 1934, p. 15. On Reble's recommendation, the synod forwarded its greeting and message of sympathy to the Lutheran churches of Germany.

18 After Paul de Lagarde, a German academic and political tractarian of the Second Reich whose fierce Germanic nationalism and hatred of Christianity as well as Judaism (and Jews) earned him the dubious distinction of being hailed as a prophet of the Third Reich. In his *Deutsche Schriften* (German writings), he called for the creation of a new Germanic Religion.

19 William Kraft, *Christ Versus Hitler* (New York: The Lutheran Press, 1937).

20 *The Canada Lutheran*, 18, 1 (July 1937): 13.

21 "Präsident Dr. F.H. Knubels Ansprache vor dem lutherischen Rat in Berlin," p. 8.

22 "Germany has no greater, no better friend in the entire world than the Lutheran Church" ("Das Alte Testament," *Der Synodalbote*, 11, 8 [April 1940]: 2).

23 "Churchmen Protest Niemoeller Imprisonment," *The Canada Lutheran*, 26, 6 (April 1938): 16.

24 "Was ist Deutschland?... Das deutsche Land ist vor allem Luthers Land.... Deutschland ist das Land des Heilandes Jesus Christi, der auch Luthers Herr und Heiland war, das Land, in dem Luthers innere Gewissheit von einer göttlichen Gnade, des göttlichen Evangeliums Fuss gefasst hat. Deutschland ist ferner das Land der Wahrheit" ("Präsident Dr. F.H. Knubels Ansprache vor dem lutherischen Rat in Berlin," pp. 2-3).

25 *44th Annual Convention of the United Danish Evangelical Church,* June 4-9, 1940, p. 19.

26 "For even if the government does injustice, yet God would have it obeyed, without treachery and deception" (Martin Luther, *Treatise on Good Works*).

27 Vidkun Quisling, a Norwegian politician, was installed as "minister-president" of Norway by the German occupation on February 1, 1942, displacing the exiled King Haakon VII. Tried and executed following the war by the Norwegians, his name has become a synonym for high treason.

28 "Conquered?" *The Hyrden-Shepherd*, 18, 17 (September 1942): 1.

29 "Jewish Persecution Spreading," *Hyrden/The Good Shepherd* (February 1934), p. 4.

30 *Yearbook,* The United Danish Evangelical Lutheran Church, 42nd Annual Convention, June 14-19, 1938, p. 15.

31 *Yearbook,* The United Danish Evangelical Lutheran Church, 43rd Annual Convention, June 12-18, 1939, p. 12.

32 Cf. the following resolution approved by the 78th Annual Convention of the Evangelical Lutheran Synod of Canada in June, 1940: "Resolved that the Canada Synod

urge upon the Canadian Lutheran Commission to advise those caring for refugees who may be brought to our shores, that we shall do everything in our power to secure places for them within the bounds of our Canada Synod" (*Minutes*, p. 81).

If the kind of refugee intended by the framers of this resolution is not entirely clear, the question is easily settled. After a commission visit to the refugee camp at Sherlock, Quebec, to interview German Lutheran internees, the 1942 synod recommended that "the Canada Synod Committee on Social Missions be charged to act as sponsors or to secure sponsors for one or more of the Lutheran refugees" (*Minutes*, 80th Annual Convention, p. 79).

33 See the account of Richard Rubenstein's well-publicized interview with Grüber in Rubenstein and Roth, *Approaches to Auschwitz*, p. 309.

34 K.F. Hoever, "The Christian and the Signs of the Times," *Eleventh Annual Convention*, Canada District, American Lutheran Church, July 3-8, 1941, p. 18.

35 Cf. "Jewish Mission," *Annual Report*, Norwegian Lutheran Church of America (1940), p. 28.

36 "Friends of Israel," *The Shepherd-Hyrden* (May 1943), p. 4.

37 Ibid.

38 Ibid.

39 Cf. "Germany Is Facing Church Problem," *The Canada Lutheran*, 18, 3 (January 1938): 5, and "Das Alte Testament," p. 2.

40 "Anti-Semitism in Canada," *The Shepherd-Hyrden*, 19, 10 (May 1943): 4.

41 Ibid.

42 Notably Epp, *Mennonites in Canada, 1920-1940;* Frank H. Epp, "An Analysis of Germanism and National Socialism in the Immigrant Newspaper of a Canadian Minority Group, the Mennonites in the 1930s" (unpublished thesis, University of Manitoba, 1965); Benjamin W. Redekop, "Germanism among Mennonite Brethren Immigrants in Canada, 1930-1960: A Struggle for Ethno-Religious Integrity," *Canadian Ethnic Studies*, 24, 1 (1992): 20-31, 35-42; and Redekop, "The German Identity of Mennonite Brethren Immigrants in Canada."

43 Magdalene Redekop, "Escape from the Bloody Theatre: The Making of Mennonite Stories," *Journal of Mennonite Studies*, 2 (1993): 19.

44 Cf. Wagner, *Brothers Beyond the Sea*, p. 21.

45 This seems to have been a recurrent argument in the Mennonite press, especially *Der Bote*.

46 Wagner, *Brothers Beyond the Sea*, p. 21.

47 J. John Friesen, "Streiflichter auf die deutsche Sprache," *Die Mennonitische Rundschau*, April 30, 1930, p. 2, cited in Redekop, "Germanism among Mennonite Brethren Immigrants in Canada," p. 28.

48 Walter Quiring, "Kennst Du Deine Mutter nicht," *Der Bote*, July 25, 1934, p. 1. Our translation.

49 "Pilatus' Bericht über dies Gefangennahme, das Gericht und die Kreuzigung Jesu," *Der Bote*, April 17, 1935, p. 1. Our translation.

50 Epp, *Mennonites in Canada, 1920-1940*, p. 548.

51 "Das neue Deutschland," *Der Bote*, November 15, 1933, p. 3.

52 "Ein Bekenntnis," *Der Bote*, November 7, 1934, p. 2.

53 "Aus dem neuen Deutschland," *Der Bote*, March 27, 1935, p. 5. Our translation.

54 "Fascism—Friend or Foe—Which?," *Christian Monitor* (October 1933), p. 318.

55 "Mussolini: A Protector from Vaticanism and Communism," *Christian Monitor* (March 1934), pp. 93-94.

56 "Hitler Starts Life as German Caesar," *Christian Monitor* (October 1934), p. 318.

57 "Kirche und Staat," *Der Bote*, June 6, 1934, p. 1.

58 "Schwierigkeiten," *Der Bote*, November 20, 1935, p. 2.

59 Cf. Redekop, "German Identity of Mennonite Brethren Immigrants in Canada," p. 65. The article by B.B. Janz, "Kommt Menno Simons unter die Nationalsozialisten?," was published in *Der Bote*, December 26, 1934, p. 1, and in *Die Mennonitische Rundschau*, December 26, 1934, pp. 2-3.

60 "Bin ich Nationalsozialist? Bewahre!," *Der Bote*, January 11, 1939, p. 1; also *Die Mennonitische Rundschau*, January 11, 1939, p. 4.

61 "König Georges Botschaft," *Der Bote*, September 13, 1939, p. 3.

62 Epp, *Mennonites in Canada, 1920-1940*, p. 577.

63 Ibid., pp. 48-93.

64 "'... Das Heil kommt von den Juden' Joh.4,22," *Der Bote*, October 11, 1939, p. 1.

65 "A Glimpse at the Worldwide Growth of Anti-Semitism," *Christian Monitor* (July 1934), p. 222.

66 "'... Das Heil kommt von den Juden' Joh.4,22," p. 1.

67 For example, the following resolution, passed at a Mennonite conference in Ontario: "In view of the great need of Jewish Evangelism, be it resolved that, 1. We express our heartfelt appreciation for the rich heritage of faith we have received through Jewish instrumentality, and 2. We express our willingness to co-operate and sponsor a concerted effort to evangelize the Jew, and 3. We instruct our Executive Committee to study the needs and opportunities of evangelizing the Jew...." *(Calendar of Appointments of the Mennonite Church of Ontario* [45th English], June 30, 1934, July 1, 1935, p. 20).

68 "Die Entrückung," *Der Bote*, March 10, 1937, p. 1.

69 "The Invincible Jew," *Christian Monitor* (August 1935), p. 236.

70 Chapter VI.

71 "Impressions of the Nazi Regime and Its Effect on the Churches," *Christian Monitor* (January 1934), p. 31.

72 "Anti-Semitism a Dangerous Boomerang," *Christian Monitor* (May 1935), p. 158.

73 "The Invincible Jew," p. 236.

74 "Ein jüdisches Problem," *Der Bote*, May 1, 1940, p. 2.

75 Benjamin H. Unruh, "Grundsätzliche Fragen," *Der Bote*, July 17, 1935, p. 1. Our translation.

76 "Who does not know Ford's book?" The allusion, of course, is to Henry Ford's best-selling *The International Jew*. See Chapter I.

77 Cf. Redekop, "German Identity of Mennonite Brethren Immigrants in Canada," p. 58.

78 "Wie ich Deutschland wiedersah," *Der Bote*, March 6, 1935, p. 2.

79 "Kampf dem Kommunismus," *Der Bote*, April 28, 1937, p. 4. Fritsch, Langbehn, Chamberlain, Lagarde and Luther were all the authors of antisemitic classics.

80 "Kommunismus ohne Maske," *Der Bote*, November 6, 1935, p. 4, and November 13, 1935, p. 4.

81 "Daemonismus—eine Weltgefahr!," *Die Mennonitische Rundschau*, September 19, 1934, p. 4.

82 "Information," *Der Bote*, April 25, 1934, p. 5.

83 "Vorläufige Antwort zur 'Judenfrage,'" *Die Mennonitische Rundschau,* June 5, 1935, p. 5.

84 "Auch ein 'Wahrheitssucher!,'" *Der Bote,* September 14, 1938, p. 2. Our translation.

85 Dederich Ravall, "Gegen die geistlose Judenhetze," *Der Bote,* April 12, 1933, p. 3 (our translation). Not surprisingly, Ravall's letter produced some furious replies, e.g., "Gegen die geistlose Judenhetze," *Der Bote,* April 19, 1933, p. 2, and "Eine Anwort auf den Artikel: 'Gegen die geistlose Judenhetze,'" *Der Bote,* April 26, 1933, pp. 2-3.

86 "Um hohen Preis," *Der Bote,* June 27, 1934, pp. 2-3.

87 Cf. Betcherman, *The Swastika and the Maple Leaf,* p. 66. Whittaker and Neufeld were sued successfully for libel in 1935 by a Jewish war veteran, Captain W.V. Tobias (ibid., p. 74).

88 Although Derstine, the world news editor of the *Monitor,* was an American, he lived in Kitchener, becoming a bishop of the Ontario church and an important voice of Mennonite opinion in Canada. Many Canadian Mennonites read his paper. Kitchener, formerly known as Berlin, was in effect the capital of the German population in Canada.

89 In his personal reminiscences of a Manitoba boyhood, William Klassen notes the total absence of antisemitism in his family home despite its presence elsewhere in the Mennonite community. William Klassen, "Antisemitism among Mennonites in Southern Manitoba: One Family's Perspective" (unpublished manuscript), p. 8.

90 "Aus der Stille," *Der Bote,* March 31, 1937, p. 3. Our translation.

91 "Die Juden," *Der Bote,* August 2, 1939, p. 2. Our translation.

92 "Ein Leser," *Der Bote,* January 29, 1936, p. 3.

93 Literally, "defencelessness."

94 Cf. Epp, *Mennonites in Canada, 1920-1940,* p. 553.

95 "Greuelpropaganda im Ausland," *Der Bote,* April 26, 1933, p. 3.

96 "Noch einmal, gegen die geistlose Judenhetze," *Die Mennonitische Rundschau,* May 3, 1933, pp. 3-2, and May 17, 1933, p. 11.

97 Cf. Redekop, "The German Identity of Mennonite Brethren Immigrants in Canada," p. 56; also Wagner, *Brothers Beyond the Sea,* p. 106.

98 According to Wagner (ibid.), of the seven German papers in Canada, five were openly pro-Nazi, including the three Mennonite papers, *Der Bote, Die Mennonitische Rundschau* and *Die Steinbach Post.*

99 Cited in "Ein offenes Wort zur Judenfrage," *Der Bote,* September 13, 1933, p. 3. Our translation.

100 "Neue Verordnungen für Eheschliessungen im Deutschen Reiche," *Der Bote,* December 25, 1935, pp. 4-5.

101 "Einige Reiseeindruecke," *Der Bote,* September 30, 1936, p. 2. Our translation.

102 "Hitler with His Hands on the Jew," *Christian Monitor* (May 1933), p. 159.

103 "Fascism—Friend or Foe—Which?," p. 318.

104 "Impressions of the Nazi Regime and Its Effects on the Churches," p. 30.

105 "A Glimpse at the Worldwide Growth of Anti-Semitism," pp. 222-223.

106 "World Jewry Today—and the Protocols," *Christian Monitor* (February 1935), p. 62.

107 "European Jewry in Dire Distress," *Christian Monitor* (July 1938), pp. 226-227, and "The Only Hope of the Jew in Our Present Mad World," *Christian Monitor* (December 1938), pp. 384-385.

108 "Zu 'Unsere Pflicht,'" *Der Bote,* May 26, 1937, p. 3.

109 It was mentioned briefly in *Der Bote* ("Aus Welt und Zeit," November 10, 1938, p. 4).

110 "Deutsche Pressekritik an Amerikas 'hysterischer Popaganda' [*sic*]," *Der Bote*, November 30, 1938, p. 4.

111 Ibid.

112 "Jehovah's Judgments on Jew Jingo Nations," *Christian Monitor* (January 1939), p. 30.

113 "Aus Welt und Zeit," *Der Bote*, August 3, 1938, p. 4. Our translation.

114 Ibid. Our translation.

115 Ibid.

116 "Eine gewissenlose Hetze," *Der Bote*, April 5, 1939, p. 4.

117 Ibid. Our translation.

118 "The Christian Attitude in the Rising Tide of Anti-Semitism," *Christian Monitor* (September 1939), p. 286.

119 "The Rising Head of Religious Persecution," *Christian Monitor* (November 1939), p. 350.

120 "Prayer of a Jewish Refugee," *The Mennonite*, June 27, 1939, p. 7:

"Oh, Master of the World, all roads are closed against us. All strength has been taken away from us upon this earth. Our life has been ruined and our security has been undermined. We no longer dare to contemplate the future of our people. In this hour of need, of persecution, of unrest and despondency, in this hour of humiliation and hopelessness we turn to Thee, O Lord, with our prayer.

"Nowhere do we see a guiding light; nowhere a ray of hope. With the last of our strength we cling to every straw to keep our heads above the water. Shall we defend ourselves? Shall we justify ourselves? Shall we raise our voices? Loudly we call upon Thee, O Lord. Father of all mankind, of all creation, strengthen us in our prayer. Take us into Thine arms. Press us to Thy breast. Bless us with the consolation of Thy voice. Let our tears speak for us. Place healing fingers upon our beating heart."

121 Socknat, *Witness against War*, p. 229.

122 Ibid., p. 266. For a detailed account, see T.D. Regehr, *Mennonites in Canada 1939-1970: A People Transformed* (Toronto: University of Toronto Press, 1996), pp. 35-67.

123 Cf. A. Roy Eckardt, *Jews and Christians: The Contemporary Meeting* (Bloomington, IN: Indiana University Press, 1986), pp. 108-110. Eckardt accuses the (American) Quakers of embodying both "Christian hypocrisy and Christian antisemitism" because of their criticisms of the present-day state of Israel and its policies towards the Palestinians. To Eckardt, the Quaker is "a speaker of peace but a supporter of terror." It is difficult to accept this judgment.

124 Cf. Haim Genizi, *American Apathy: The Plight of Christian Refugees from Nazism* (Jerusalem: Bar-Ilan University Press, 1983), p. 188.

125 *The Canadian Friend* (June 1930), p. 4.

126 "And Look at This," *The Canadian Friend* (March 1933), p. 4.

127 "Disarmament—Another Stalemate?" *The Canadian Friend* (December 1933), pp. 9-10.

128 "A Brighter World Outlook," *The Canadian Friend* (July 1933), p. 9.

129 "An Appeal to Germany," *The Canadian Friend* (September 1935), p. 2.

130 Cf. Nawyn, *American Protestantism's Response*, p. 109.

131 "German Refugees, American Christians," *The Canadian Friend* (December 1935), p. 14.

132 "The Refugee Problem," *The Canadian Friend* (February 1936), p. 7.

133 Ibid, p. 16.

134 Chapter III.

135 Chapter III.

136 Nawyn, *American Protestantism's Response*, p. 115.

137 Ibid., p. 110-111.

138 "Our Brothers—The Jews of Germany," *The Canadian Friend* (December 1938), p. 6.

139 Nawyn, *American Protestantism's Response*.

140 Cf. Haim Genizi, "The Attitude of the American Friends Service Committee to Refugees from Nazism, 1933-1950," *Remembering for the Future: Jews and Christians During and After the Holocaust,* paper delivered at the International Scholars Conference, Oxford, July 10-13, 1988, pp. 339-340.

141 *Minutes of Toronto Monthly Meeting of Friends,* November 16, 1938, p. 2.

142 Cited in Elizabeth Gray Vining, *Friend of Life: The Biography of Rufus M. Jones* (Philadelphia: J.B. Lippincott, 1958), p. 286.

143 "The Visit to Germany," *The Canadian Friend* (February 1939), pp. 5-6.

144 "The Case of Jewish Refugees," *The Canadian Friend* (April 1939), p. 4.

145 *Minutes of the Toronto Meeting of Friends* (March 15, 1939), p. 2.

146 Fred Haslam, *A Record of Experience with Canadian Friends (Quakers) and the Canadian Ecumenical Movement 1921-1967* (N.p.: n.p., 1968), p. 10.

147 "Seventh Annual Report," *The Canadian Friend* (March 1935), p. 7.

148 Cf. Socknat, *Witness against War.*

149 G. Raymond Booth, *What They Say* (reprinted from *The American Friend,* n.d., p. 5).

150 "A Political Refugee," *The Canadian Friend* (April 1939), p. 5.

151 See, for example, the report in *The United Church Observer* (December 1939), p. 30, of an evening address by Booth before the Muskoka Presbytery of the United Church on the refugee problem. He was obviously active on the speaking circuit.

152 Booth, *What They Say,* pp. 2-7.

153 "Working in Canada for European Refugees," *The Canadian Friend* (August 1939), p. 13.

154 "Refugee Children," *The Canadian Friend* (January 1940), p. 10, and "News of Our Meetings," *The Canadian Friend* (June 1940), p. 14.

155 "News of Our Meetings," *The Canadian Friend* (June 1941), p. 13.

156 A subcommittee of the Canadian Friends Service Committee under the convenorship of Burton L. Hill.

157 "Canadian Friends Service Committee," *The Canadian Friend* (March 1941), pp. 6-8.

158 Abella and Troper, *None Is Too Many,* p. 203, fn.

159 Several future eminent Canadian artists and academics were among their number, including the Jewish philosopher Emil Fackenheim, the Catholic theologian Gregory Baum, the literary scholar David Hoeniger and the pianist Helmut Blume. For a description of the extraordinary array of talent among the internees and cultural richness in the camps, see Paula Jean Draper, "Muses behind Barbed Wire: Canada and the Interned Refugees," in *The Muses Flee Hitler* (Washington: Smithsonian Institution Press, 1983), pp. 271-281.

160 Cf. Conway, "Canada and the Holocaust," pp. 300-301.

161 C.E. Silcox, "Young Refugees Interned in Canada," *The Canadian Friend* (January 1942), pp. 8-10.

162 *The Canadian Friend* (June 1943), p. 3.

163 Nawyn, *American Protestantism's Response,* p. 121.

164 Cf. "Starvation in Europe," *The Canadian Friend* (November 1943), p. 8, and "The World's Most Terrible Story," *The Canadian Friend* (December 1943), pp. 8-9.

165 "War Victims' Relief," *The Canadian Friend* (January 1944), p. 7.

166 "They Are All Our Children," *The Canadian Friend* (February 1944), p. 6.

167 Genizi, "The Attitude of the American Friends Service Committee to Refugees from Nazism, 1933-1950," p. 343.

168 Ibid.

169 Nawyn, *American Protestantism's Response,* p. 132.

170 Ibid., p. 135.

171 Chapter III.

Chapter VIII (Conclusion)

1 Abella and Troper, *None Is Too Many,* p. 284.

2 Wright, *A World Mission,* pp. 218, 220.

3 Cf. the article by Silcox, "Canadian Universities and the Jews," pp. 94-99.

4 Matthew 27:25. This verse, contrary to its Matthaean meaning, is still cited by anti-semites as a proof-text for the ongoing suffering of Jews.

5 Late sixteenth to eighteenth century.

6 Hence the often-criticized insipid character of the founding document of the new domination, *The Basis of Union.*

7 Cf. Darrell J. Fasching, *Narrative Theology after Auschwitz: From Alienation to Ethics* (Minneapolis: Fortress Press, 1992), p. 105.

8 Johan M. Snoek, *The Grey Book: A Collection of Protests against Anti-Semitism and the Persecution of Jews issued by Non-Roman Catholic Churches and Church Leaders during Hitler's Rule* (New York: Humanities Press, 1970), p. 289.

9 The extraordinary rescue of the Danish Jews in October 1943—a rescue operation masterminded by the Danes themselves—perhaps was one such occasion.

10 Reinhold Niebuhr, *Moral Man and Immoral Society* (New York: Charles Scribner's Sons, 1932).

11 Feingold, *The Politics of Rescue,* p. 304.

12 For example, Rubenstein and Roth, *Approaches to Auschwitz,* p. 207. Rubenstein and Roth level this charge against the pro-Nazi German Christians, but, as antisemitic as the latter certainly were, even they cannot be accused of placing the Jews outside the Christian universe of moral obligation, although they can be accused of not protesting against persecution and murder when persecution and murder occurred. A. James Reimer writes the following about the great and tragic Lutheran theologian Emanuel Hirsch: "He does not shrink from ...declaring ... that Jews and Germans are racially distinct and ought to be kept separate from each other. While spiritually united in Christ, historically they are alien to each other and Jews ought to be given 'guest status' in Germany. In contrast to many, he speaks warmly of individual Jews; encourages Christians to continue their personal fellowship with individual Jews without thereby withholding their support for the restructuring of German society; and makes a point of rejecting terms of inferiority when talking about the Jew [*sic*] as a people" (Reimer, *The Emanuel Hirsch and Paul Tillich Debate,* p. 339.)

13 Cf. Steven T. Katz, *The Holocaust in Historical Context,* Vol. 1 (New York: Oxford University Press, 1994), chap. 7.

14 See, for example, the various books of the eminent contemporary Protestant theologian Jürgen Moltmann, especially *The Way of Jesus Christ: Christology in Messianic Dimensions,* translated by Margaret Kohl (London: SCM Press, 1990).

15 See, for example, the study program on Jewish-Anglican relations produced by the Anglican Church of Canada, *From Darkness to Dawn: Rethinking Christian Attitudes toward Jews and Judaism in the Light of the Holocaust* (1989). See also the recently approved (by the General Council, 1997) United Church study document *Bearing Faithful Witness: United Church – Jewish Relations Today.*

16 For a short description, see Alan Davies, "The Holocaust and Christian Thought," in Marvin Perry and Frederick M. Schweitzer, eds., *Jewish-Christian Encounters over the Centuries: Symbiosis, Prejudice, Holocaust, Dialogue* (New York: Peter Lang, 1994), pp. 341-367.

Appendix A

1 For a fuller account, see Rome, *Clouds in the Thirties,* Section 12, pp. 652-654.

Appendix B

1 The following organizations were affiliated with the Christian Social Council of Canada:
The Baptist Churches in Canada
The Church of England in Canada
The Evangelical Church
The Salvation Army
The Presbyterian Church in Canada
The Society of Friends
The United Church of Canada
The National Council Y.M.C.A.
The National Council Y.W.C.A.

Index